MW01120719

Children's Rights

Children's Rights

From Philosophy to Public Policy

Mhairi Cowden

HUMBER LIBRARIES LAKESHORE CAMPUS
3199 Lakeshore Blvd West
TORONTO, ON.   M8V 1K8

palgrave
macmillan

CHILDREN'S RIGHTS
Copyright © Mhairi Cowden 2016

All rights reserved. No reproduction, copy or transmission of this publication may be made without written permission. No portion of this publication may be reproduced, copied or transmitted save with written permission. In accordance with the provisions of the Copyright, Designs and Patents Act 1988, or under the terms of any licence permitting limited copying issued by the Copyright Licensing Agency, Saffron House, 6-10 Kirby Street, London EC1N 8TS.

Any person who does any unauthorized act in relation to this publication may be liable to criminal prosecution and civil claims for damages.

First published 2016 by
PALGRAVE MACMILLAN

The author has asserted her right to be identified as the author of this work in accordance with the Copyright, Designs and Patents Act 1988.

Palgrave Macmillan in the UK is an imprint of Macmillan Publishers Limited, registered in England, company number 785998, of Houndmills, Basingstoke, Hampshire, RG21 6XS.

Palgrave Macmillan in the US is a division of Nature America, Inc., One New York Plaza, Suite 4500, New York, NY 10004-1562.

Palgrave Macmillan is the global academic imprint of the above companies and has companies and representatives throughout the world.

Hardback ISBN: 978–1–137–49227–2
E-PUB ISBN: 978–1–137–49228–9
E-PDF ISBN: 978–1–137–49229–6
DOI: 10.1057/9781137492296

Distribution in the UK, Europe and the rest of the world is by Palgrave Macmillan®, a division of Macmillan Publishers Limited, registered in England, company number 785998, of Houndmills, Basingstoke, Hampshire RG21 6XS.

Library of Congress Cataloging-in-Publication Data
Cowden, Mhairi, 1986–
    Children's rights : from philosophy to public policy / Mhairi Cowden.
      pages cm
    Includes bibliographical references and index.
    Summary: "Despite the existence of the UN Convention on the Rights of the Child there is still a debate about whether children can really hold rights. This book presents a clear theory of children's rights by examining controversial case studies. Understanding why children have rights presents a pathway to translating rights into practical social and political instruments for change"—Provided by publisher.
    ISBN 978–1–137–49227–2 (hardcover)
    1. Children's rights.   2. Children—Government policy.   I. Title.
HQ789.C69 2015
323.3′52—dc23   2015020079

A catalogue record for the book is available from the British Library.

For Alistair and Rosemary Cowden for always protecting
my rights as a child

Contents

Figures

Preface

The problem of why children have rights first arose for me many years ago when I was asked to write a brief article for the UNICEF newsletter entitled, "What are rights and why children have them." Being interested in moral and political philosophy, I thought the question would be an easy one to answer, for as the concept of children's rights is so pervasive in our society, there would surely be a clear understanding of it. However, after doing some preliminary reading, I found that surprisingly there was a lack of consensus on either question. It struck me that without such foundational theory, the rhetoric to advocate and protect children's rights seemed fairly empty—a country built on shaky foundations.

This question started a ten-year journey. Throughout this time, I have completed a PhD on the subject and spoken to many philosophers and practitioners on why they believe children have rights. It has never ceased to amaze me how children are often used as a "test-case" for a theory or moral quandary but rarely considered as moral subjects in their own right. Since leaving academia, I have been lucky enough to be involved in the flip side of the coin and witness how governments make policy about children in practice. Here too, I have observed that despite the best intentions (and the brightest minds), children are often treated as secondary citizens. This is despite our understanding that many of the fundamental social challenges that face modern societies are rooted in the experiences and lives of children.

Furthermore, it is rare to see those that deal with the theory of children and rights talking to those that are concerned with the policy (and vice versa). I passionately believe that there needs to be a link between our theoretical understanding of important concepts and the way in which they are put into practice. It is for this reason that I have endeavored throughout this book to discuss contemporary and controversial questions of children's rights to demonstrate how philosophy can help us navigate their challenges and pitfalls.

Bringing this project to fruition, however, was a lot harder than identifying the problem. I could not have done it without the help of many people. First thanks must go to my PhD supervisor, Keith Dowding. Without his help and guidance, I would never have read Hohfeld and been equipped with the right language to articulate the question that I wanted to ask. I am also indebted to J. C. Lau for many useful discussions and collaborations. Thanks to the School of Politics and International Relations at the Australian National University for providing the institutional support for my work.

Outside ANU, sincere thanks to David Archard for welcoming me to Lancaster University and for his insightful work in this area. Thanks to *Contemporary Political Theory*, *Critical Review of International Social and Political Philosophy*, and the *International Journal of Law, Policy and the Family* for allowing me to reproduce amended versions of my previously published work here.

Thanks to my parents for providing me with the education and support to be able to accomplish this task, for treating me like a person and not a "child," and for arguing with me over the dinner table. However, most of all, thanks to Nicholas Duff for his tireless support and his constantly intelligent mind that pushed my ideas further, questioned the weaknesses in my argument, and made this book a better piece of work.

Part I

Children's Rights in Theory

1

Introduction

In 1973, Hillary Rodham Clinton wrote that children's rights were a "slogan in search of a definition."[1] Over 40 years have passed since Clinton wrote these words and much has changed. At the time, Clinton was an unknown lawyer who was ridiculed for suggesting that children held rights. Now she is an esteemed international stateswoman, and rights for children are no longer just a slogan, but a reality. The United Nations (UN) Convention on the Rights of the Child (CROC) was adopted in 1989 and now stands as the most ratified UN Convention. Following the recent signing of the ratification instrument by the new Somali Government, all member States, with the exception of the United States, have ratified the Convention. There are now national and regional charters on children's rights, and individual States have made significant steps to integrate CROC into national law.[2] The work of organizations such as UNICEF, Save the Children, and Defence for Children International (DCI) continues to provide a high profile for the rights of the child.

However, all is not well in the world of children's rights. Clinton's standing may no longer be doubted but children's rights are still ridiculed. Despite significant progress, the rights of children remain under-theorized and the fundamental question "do children have rights?" remains contested. Although, on the surface, policy makers and politicians seem to be in furious agreement in support of children's rights, philosophers and political theorists are not always sure rights work for those who are not quite adults. One reply to this may simply be—so what? Philosophers and theorists often spend their time examining issues that do not affect people's lives.[3] If the world has a Convention protecting the rights of the child that is internationally binding, does it really matter if theorists disagree on the details? I believe that in this case the answer is yes. It does matter because the lack of theory underpinning rights for children hinders their implementation.

Near universal ratification of CROC, and the rhetoric of policy makers, does not guarantee that children's rights exist as a logically coherent concept in theory or that they are adequately protected and implemented in practice. It is not clear that simply by drafting an article, treaty, or legislation that a right can be effectively justified and implemented outside of the black letter of the law. For example, the Australian Parliament could pass a law tomorrow that protected the rights of domestic pets such as cats and dogs to vote in federal elections. Despite the existence of this right in law, there would still be doubts over whether it had moral justification or whether it could ever be implemented in practice. There is also disagreement about whether rights in international law are in fact individual rights at all. Some claim that the rights outlined in international treaties are nothing more than social ideas or goals, albeit justified ones.[4] Others worry that this means that the rights outlined in CROC will never be translated into meaningful legal rights.[5]

In practice, CROC has been poorly implemented and as Caroline Moorhead observed in her study of the treaty, it has for many become "something of a sham," being violated "systematically and contemptuously."[6] A more recent study by Alston and Tobin on the implementation of the Convention reaches similar conclusions.[7] Although advances have been made, these are hard to reconcile with the massive violations that continue across the world. In 1995, Hillary Clinton (then First Lady) announced that the United States would be signing CROC. Following the announcement several news articles appeared satirizing her work from the 1970s. These articles portrayed the concept of rights for children as inappropriate and potentially dangerous as they could break down the family unit.[8] An article by humorist Art Buchwald titled "Make bed then sue" depicted the "worst case scenario," a child asking a judge to be divorced from her parents and little sister due to irreconcilable differences and asking for part custody of the family dog. Comic portraits like this do little to help engender understanding of children's rights. It will come as no surprise that the announcement did not lead to ratification of the Convention by the United States.

Why, despite the existence of international law and many organizations dedicated to children's rights, do they continue to be undermined and poorly implemented? What can explain this mismatch between aspirational statements from our politicians and insubstantial action and a lack of engagement on the ground? I argue throughout this book that part of the explanation may lie in the lack of a strong theoretical explanation for *why* children have rights in the first place. Much work has been done on the concept of human rights and we now have a solid grounding of theory to draw on when making the case for these rights.[9] The controversies surrounding human rights have been visited and revisited so that we are comfortable in our use of them (or at least comfortable in our disagreement over them). Discussion of children's rights has generally lacked such analytical rigor. This means that when children's rights are translated from paper into practice they lack the strong theory that underpins human rights in general. This can have real consequences for their implementation.

It may come as a surprise to some people that given the popularity of children's rights, they lack the same rigorous literature as the general category of human rights. Before beginning to examine these broader questions, this introductory chapter provides a short history of the concept of children's rights to date and an argument for why we need a better theory than what is currently out there.

Traditional Political Theory

Children are notably absent from the western liberal philosophical tradition as a genuine subject of philosophical inquiry. John Locke's *Thoughts on Education* along with Rousseau's *Emile* are exceptions to this rule. Although *Emile* is a seminal text, Rousseau was not the great defender of children in practice. He famously left his own illegitimate children at an orphanage. However, his words in the preface to *Emile* still ring true today about children's place in society. He stated,

> Childhood is unknown. Starting from the false idea one has of it, the farther one goes, the more one loses one's way. The wisest men concentrate on what it is important for men to know without considering what children are in a condition to learn. They are always seeking the man in the child without thinking of what he is before being a man.[10]

It is not that other philosophers ignored childhood altogether. Remarks concerning the moral and political status of children are often scattered throughout the work of traditional liberal philosophers.[11] However, the remarks are often cursory and not very rigorous. Frequently they make illiberal assumptions about children's moral status, as Rousseau commented, "seeking the man in the child" rather than considering the child in their own right. One explanation for why children receive so little attention throughout this literature may be that claims regarding children's moral status were considered obvious, trivially true, and not susceptible to rational doubt. For example, Hobbes considered children to be "in most absolute subjection" to the parent.[12] Hobbes assumes that children are not part of the social contract—he states, in *De Cive*,

> So let us return to the state of nature once again and consider men as though they were suddenly sprung from the earth (like mushrooms) as adults right now.[13]

Hobbes simply assumes we do not need to consider the child's place in the social contract. Children are, therefore, potential problems to Hobbes' theory of the state of nature, for people clearly do not spring from the earth like mushrooms, fully formed. Children, for Hobbes, are not just an exception to the rational liberal agent, they are not considered at all. In a similar vein, Locke's contractarian theory simply presumes that children lack what adult human beings possess. According to Locke, children lack knowledge, moral sense, and reason.[14] Children are given a little more attention in the work of John Stuart Mill. However, Mill's concern with explaining the status of children arises from his desire to ensure that the argument for the female suffrage, which he sets out in *The Subjection of Women,* would not be reduced to "absurdity" by being applied to the enfranchisement of children.[15] In short, the treatment of children in traditional liberal political philosophy has been to view them as obviously and significantly different from adults and therefore excluded from political theory. Consequently, it was not considered necessary to explain *why* children did not hold rights.

Child Liberation

Throughout the 1970s, there was a growing movement of thought that it was no longer sufficient to consider the status of children as "obvious." The simple assumptions regarding the status of children were critiqued and deemed inadequate. This new movement argued that the position of children in social and political life should be challenged and subject to inquiry. These radical statements were headlined by a group of scholars who called themselves child liberationists.

Child liberationists argued that society considerably underestimates the capacities of children. Foster and Freed, for example, argued that adults exploited their power over children and that children's inferior status should be radically reassessed.[16] Other liberationists built upon the work of Philippe Ariès, who argued that childhood was a modern invention. If we recognize children as socially constructed, there should be no reason to exclude them from the adult world. To do so would be a form of oppression and unjustified discrimination much like the discrimination leveled against women or African Americans at the time in the 1970s. Child liberationists therefore argued that there was no justified reason that children should be denied the same rights as adults.[17] For example, Foster and Freed stated that a child should have the right to "earn and keep his own earnings," "to emancipation from the parent-child relationship when that relationship has broken down," and "to be free of legal disabilities or incapacities save where such are convincingly shown to be necessary and protective of the actual best interest of the child."[18] Holt and Farson advocated a similar set of rights, but went further to suggest that children also had the right to vote, to work, to choose their own education, to use drugs, and to control their own sexual lives.[19] The fact that children do not, and indeed do not have the ability to, exercise some of these rights is not problematic for child liberationists. They argue that this is simply the part of the child's choice regarding the exercise of their rights.

There are, understandably, major criticisms of the child liberation movement. Hafen argues that there are considerable risks associated with the uncritical transfer of egalitarian concepts to the unique context of the family,[20] and Wald argues that liberationists misunderstand the type of rights children hold which he claims are primarily rights to protection.[21] It has been suggested that liberationists appear to ignore the evidence on developmental growth throughout childhood. Children are not just simply small adults; they have different capacities, competencies, and interests. As Fortin argues,

> It seems clear, however, that the relatively slow development of children's cognitive processes makes the *majority* of children unfit to take complete responsibility for their own lives by being granted adult freedoms before they reach mid-adolescence.[22]

Unlike the women's rights movement or the civil rights movement that sought to demonstrate that those who are subject to different treatment do not hold different (or at least significantly different) capacities, children *are* different in many real and relevant ways. I will discuss these differences in more detail in Chapter 2. It is arguable that child liberationists did the children's rights movement a disservice by creating the impression that it is all about giving children adult freedoms and rights.[23] Hafen's critique demonstrates that the immediate reaction to child liberation was to reject the idea of children's rights altogether. Hafen argues that children's rights could, in the long term, harm children's interests and destroy the family unit. Children should not be "abandoned to their rights."[24] Caught up in this is a misunderstanding that the children's rights movement is solely concerned with guaranteeing and achieving children's autonomy rights. This mischaracterizes the debate. Where autonomy rights *are* sought they are usually of a very different kind from those held by adults. I will endeavor throughout this book to demonstrate how this holds true.

Although the liberationists might go further than most regarding which particular rights they afford to children, the presence of their work within the scholastic tradition of children's rights represents a shift toward recognizing the developing capacities of children. As the UN CROC outlines, children's rights are not only about recognizing children's capacity to contribute to their own lives but also to protect children from the exploitation of adults. It is not just children who hold rights to "both care for one purpose and autonomy or self-determination for another."[25] This is also true for all human rights.

Convention on the Rights of the Child

The development of this theoretical literature is punctuated by perhaps the biggest real step forward in the children's rights movement: the adoption of the UN CROC by the UN General Assembly in 1989. CROC is an ambitious document that begins with the assumption that children, as human beings, are entitled to rights.

The special status of children as a group had been recognized previously on the international stage. The *Declaration of the Rights of the Child* or the "Declaration of Geneva" was adopted by the fifth assembly of the League of Nations in 1924. It contained five basic principles that were seen to work as guiding principles in the work of child welfare. The more comprehensive *Declaration of the Rights of the Child* (1959) was adopted by the General Assembly of the UN and contained an expanded ten principles. However, the rights listed in the Declaration did not constitute legal obligations and were therefore not binding on member States. The Declaration was also dominated with outdated stereotypical ideas, such as the proper roles played by mothers and fathers in the family. The principles were overly general and contained no recognition that children could hold first-generation political or civil rights.[26] However, it does represent the first real attempt to describe, in an organized way, a child's overriding claims.

By the 1970s there was a global push for a document that would guarantee legal obligations. It was believed that governments would continue to ignore their obligations to children unless a document was binding in a way that was sufficiently specific and realistic. Following a period of consultation and drafting, the CROC was submitted to the Commission on Human Rights for approval in 1989, subsequently adopted by the General Assembly, and entered into force in 1990. CROC contains 54 articles and departs from earlier documents that primarily focused on a child's need for care. As such, it reflects the growing recognition that children are not just in need of protection but active participants in social and political life. However, CROC contains what has been called "a strange mix of idealism and practical realism."[27] Some articles contain detailed policy provisions while others contain broad aspirational philosophical statements. There is concern regarding whether some of these articles can ever be translated into meaningful legal rights.

The Committee on the Rights of the Child has elevated article two—the freedom from discrimination; article three—the child's best interests; article six—the right to life; and article twelve—respect for the child's view and right to participate to the status of general principles. None are more important than the others but it is often pointed out that article three (concerning the child's best interests) underpins all of the other articles. Much of the literature following the adoption of CROC has been concerned with the interpretation of this key principle of the best interests of the child.[28] Understandably, the focus post CROC has been on the interpretation and implementation of the Convention.[29] CROC does not provide a detailed analysis on *why* children have rights. Indeed, it is not its job to do so. However, this has the effect of neutralizing the question of why children have rights. Most scholars can now simply point to the existence of the Convention to answer the prior question of "do children have rights." The role of political theory and philosophy is to continue to critique this, to counter the assumption that if children do have rights then it must be those particular rights set out in the Convention.

Legal scholarship on children's rights is therefore primarily concerned with the jurisprudence of the Convention. This approach takes CROC as the starting point and seeks to justify the rights it outlines. I believe this is the wrong way around. The adoption of CROC by the international community has not resolved the disagreement that exists regarding children as right-holders. The concerns raised in the literature still stand (I discuss this in detail in Chapter 3). In fact, if anything, CROC adds an added layer of complexity to the debate. Language in CROC is often promising, such as reference to the "evolving capacities" of the child, yet there is no clear definition in the treaty document on what these are, how they should be treated, and how they influence the implementation of other rights.

The approach I take throughout this book is "bottom up" rather than "top down." I start by piecing together the theory of why children hold rights and then applying this to cases to determine how we should shape the corresponding duties. This does not mean that CROC is not valuable. CROC serves as a reference point, a point of critical examination to be revised and improved upon, a basis on which to deepen our understanding and from which to launch normative and philosophical discussions.

The Challenge of Children's Rights

What has been discussed so far is the considerable work of a number of intelligent scholars and tireless advocates. Yet there is a notable lack of attention being paid to the philosophy of children's rights since the start of the new millennium. This lack of philosophical scholarship is doing us harm. The challenge is to provide children's rights with the same rich debate and attention that other areas of human rights scholarship garner.

A good example of where a more solid framework for children's rights would be useful is the discussion of child soldiers. For most people, politicians and public alike, the issue of child soldiers is an easy on. Children have a right not to fight in conflicts; and their involvement is without a doubt wrong. However, this statement of simplicity hides complexities associated with how to ensure such a right is protected.

Across the world, we are commemorating 100 years since World War I. For Australians, this means 100 years since the Gallipoli campaign. On April 25, 1915, only a few months after departing for war, the Australian and New Zealand Army Corps (ANZAC) troops made their ill-fated landing at Gallipoli in what we now know was for many their first and last taste of conflict. During this campaign, Private James Martin died of typhoid fever. He was the youngest Australian to die in World War I. James was only 14 years and 9 months.

James Martin was only able to enlist so young because he provided a false birth date to the recruiting officer as at the time in Australia only those over the age of 18 could enlist. Though they may have had their misgivings, James enlisted in the Australian Defence Force (ADF) with his parents' consent. At first James' parents refused but they relented after he said he would enlist under a false name if they did not give their permission.

James' story stands in stark contrast to the way we think about children in conflict today. Take, for example, the discussion of children in conflict that arose during the campaign Kony 2012 that sought to achieve the arrest of indicted Ugandan war criminal Joseph Kony. Kony is notorious for the use of child soldiers in his Lord's Resistance Army (LRA). The film that accompanied the campaign shocked many and increased awareness of child soldiers. There was general moral outrage regarding the participation of children in the LRA in a way that was not felt in 1915 when James Martin enlisted for War.

Why do we commemorate James Martin's sacrifice but not those children who fought in Uganda? In the case of Kony's child soldiers, the answer may lie in their forced coercion into the LRA. While being forced to fight against one's will is clearly against the interests of children, it is also against the interest of adults. Here, we seem to be identifying the lack of *choice* as the wrong, not the fact that these individuals are children. What is it about being a child that makes participation in conflict so abhorrent?

Many child soldiers in modern conflicts are not coerced into participating but, like young James Martin, they join autonomously. Joining a military group is often an ideological choice for children, a way to gain social standing or demonstrate solidarity with family, clan, or nation.

In Uganda, in 1986, many children joined the National Resistance Army and LRA as a refuge from the violence in the rest of the country. Joining an army can offer protection, shelter, and food. Like adults, children often want to fight for reasons such as social justice, religious belief, and cultural identity or to seek revenge for the deaths of their family.

The international legal definition of a child soldier, however, does not recognize this. Instead, it states that no child under the age of 18 is capable of consenting to fight.[30] Does this mean that we should ignore the choices that children such as James Martin made? Should we ignore the clearly passionate argument that he made to his parents about why he wanted to enlist? Children are killed in conflict every year, sometimes by other children. It is a hard fact to come to terms with that not only do some child soldiers join voluntarily but they can often be the most vicious combatants.

It is clear that the case of child soldier is more complex than it first seems. We can understand these complexities by asking the right questions. Simply stating that children have a right not to be soldiers is not enough. We need to understand *why* they have this right in order to properly shape our corresponding duties, to make strong arguments to others in favor of these duties, and to see the way these rights interlock and relate to the rights of others.

The vague language of CROC ungrounded in any strong theory lets governments "off the hook" as it allows them to couch their language in formalistic terms while avoiding any substantive improvements in children's lives.[31] Acting to prevent children from becoming soldiers may address one particular problem, yet do nothing to enfranchise children's agency or address their true needs and interests in conflict zones. Despite the Convention's recognition that children have "evolving capacities," most measures to protect children's rights work from the starting point that children are static in their incompetence. Underestimating children's capacities, and their development of competencies, ignores a child's participation and contribution to their environment. The assumption of static incompetence may deny rights where they are due and miss the complexity of implementing children's rights according to their development. A sound, nuanced, and expressly articulated theoretical basis is necessary to identify when rights-oriented action is meeting its moral objectives and when it is not.

It is this methodological approach that I will use in this book. I will explain the theory behind why children have rights and then utilize this theory to examine a number of policy cases. In this way, I hope to demonstrate how strong theory can assist in public policy decision making. A healthy well-developed theory of why children have rights is not just about words but also about action.

The Structure of This Book

The Canadian philosopher Samantha Brennan has argued that anyone responding to the challenge of children's rights must do two things.[32] First, they must address the theoretical issues and show that we can overcome the logical problems within theories of rights as applied to children. Second, once it has been demonstrated that it is conceptually possible for children to have rights, we must also show what it means for children to actually have particular rights. This can only be done through the application of rights theory to real cases.

This book will follow Brennan's logic and as a result is split into two parts. Part I builds the theoretical argument for why children have rights. Chapter 2 will address the question, what is special about children? Although this may seem an obvious question for anyone who has children, it becomes clear that the consideration of why children have rights necessitates a more thorough examination of the particularities of childhood itself. Chapter 3 will outline the existing arguments about why children do not have rights, arguments that often draw from the special status of children and, in particular, their incompetence. This chapter identifies the conceptual challenges we must meet in order to build a substantial theory of children's rights. Chapter 4 examines in more detail the distinction between capacity and competence. I argue that it is often by using these terms interchangeably that we introduce confusion when discussing children and their rights. Finally, Chapter 5 will draw the prior discussion together and outline why children have rights. Children have rights because they have interests that are sufficiently important to impose duties on others. However, this chapter also identifies some important limits on these rights by returning to the concepts of capacity and competence.

Part II then discusses the theory of children's rights in the context of a number of contemporary case studies. Chapter 6 examines whether children have a right to develop. In particular, I examine whether Deaf parents with a congenitally deaf child can choose not to give their child cochlear implants. The case of cochlear implants brings out questions of whether there are certain capacities or competencies that children have a right to develop. Chapter 7 examines whether children have a right to know information about their identity. I ask whether children who are born from donated gametes (sperm and egg) have a right to first of all be told that they are donor conceived, and second whether they should have a right to know the identity of their donor. Chapter 8 asks whether children have a right to make decisions about their medical treatment. In order to draw out the complexities of how the competence to make decisions interacts with the best interests of the child, I examine whether children with gender dysphoria should be given puberty-inhibiting drugs. Finally, Chapter 9 asks whether children have a right to be loved. I argue that while children may have a right to certain desirable treatment, they do not have a right to be loved, as love is not the sort of action that can be required as a duty.

I have chosen to examine contemporary and controversial cases as I believe these are the cases that demonstrate the limits and the edges of children's rights. It may be easier to address core rights that children hold, such as a right to shelter or food. These rights are clearly in a child's interests and will be more relevant for most children than the cases I have chosen here, many of which are only applicable to small numbers of children. However, by examining more controversial and complex cases we can begin to draw out how concepts like claims, interests, duties, and competence interact to bring about rights for children. The lessons therefore draw out important general lessons that are relevant to understanding how children's rights work for less controversial rights.

The final chapter in this book sets the scene for the future of children's rights. I draw together the main conclusions of this book and discuss how public policy plays a role in protecting children's rights. This book aims to present a theoretical argument for why children have rights; examine and unpack the role of "capacity" and "competence" in rights theory and their application to children's rights; and demonstrate the power of a strong theory in bringing children's rights from the realm of "slogan" into reality. I believe, and argue so throughout this book, that by developing this theory we can begin to bridge the divide between the philosophy and policy of children's rights.

2

What Is Special about Children?

For those who remember what it was like to be a child, answering the question, "What is special about children?" might seem easy. Childhood is a period of time in one's life that seems particularly distinct from others. It is a period of discovery, growth, adventure, novelty, challenges, and often fear. We often describe what happens during childhood as "growing up" and the implication is that it is during this time that we become the people we are supposed to be as adults. Yet, even this relatively innocuous statement is laden with disagreement. For, if childhood is the period of time that we become ourselves, what are we when we are children? Are children persons proper or not yet formed adult humans? What are children?

It should be easy to identify what we mean by children for they are everywhere throughout our lives. We have children, we see them going to school, we teach them, we play with them, and we were all once children ourselves (indeed some of us may feel like we still are children). The simple answer is that children are young human beings. However, this definition hides complexities associated with the fact that the nature of childhood varies greatly. Young human beings change dramatically in a short period of time. A six-month-old child and a nine-year-old are very different creatures. One is nearly entirely dependent on others for their existence, while the other has opinions, feelings, and life goals with the capacity to pursue (and certainly express) them. This leads us to ask, is age the best way to classify children, or should we use some other criteria?

It is worth investigating in further detail the debates surrounding children and childhood in order to understand the types of assumptions that often underpin statements regarding their rights. In this chapter, I argue that children are defined in two ways, first by age and second by normative significance. The two often, but not always, align and overlap. In addition, the definition of children differs between cultural traditions and has changed throughout history. I argue that for the purposes of considering whether children have rights, it is not necessary to have a strict definition of children. However, for the purposes of policy in regulating rights, it is necessary to have a clear requirement for who qualifies as a right-holder.

Age

The most common way to answer the question, "What are children?" is by age. According to the United Nations Convention on the Rights of the Child (CROC), children are those individuals under the age of 18. Article One of CROC defines children as, "every human being below the age of eighteen unless under the law applicable to the child, majority is attained earlier."

In most countries, 18 is the age of majority.[1] However, the Convention does allow for individuals younger than 18 to be no longer considered a child by the domestic law of the State. For many countries, this means that children can be considered to have full legal capacity with regard to various matters at differing ages. For example, in Australia an individual can apply to join the Australian Defence Force (ADF) at 16 and six months,[2] drive a car at 17, and vote in elections at 18. Defining children by age is simple and useful, as it provides a clear and unequivocal point by which all individuals of a given age are treated equally. In this sense, the age of 18 as stipulated in the Convention represents an upper limit to childhood, a threshold above which individuals must be treated as full citizens and cannot be denied certain rights.

Despite its ubiquity much has been made of the arbitrary nature of an age-based definition of childhood.[3] The age of 18 is itself a relatively new threshold. Previously, it was common to set the age at 21 for no other reason than this was the age in Medieval England that a man was deemed strong enough to wear full armor.[4] Any age, whether 18 or 21, is necessarily arbitrary. What is special about 18 that is not captured in 17? Yet, arbitrariness itself cannot be the sole concern. Many standards in life are arbitrary. For example, there is no significant difference in the probability of an accident if one drives 51 km per hour rather than 49 km per hour. Yet, in suburban Australia, driving at 51 km per hour is "speeding" and, therefore, illegal.[5] The limit of 50 km per hour is arbitrary in that it is no more significant than 49 or 51; however, it is clear that to have a law against speeding there must be *some* threshold by which driving at a certain speed is illegal. There is no great harm in choosing 50 km per hour and, therefore, the arbitrary nature of the law is acceptable, indeed necessary. Childhood, for the law, is the same. No one seriously claims that there is a significant difference between an individual who is 17 and 364 days old and someone who is 18 years old, but in order to maintain a distinction between child and adult there needs to be an agreed stipulated age. The problem is not that the cut-off is arbitrarily chosen, but that age is used as a proxy for assessing an individual's competence.

Using age as a proxy for competence is usually unproblematic. For example, the harm that arises from excluding a competent and intelligent 17-year-old from casting their vote, or including an 18-year-old who does not yet know how the political system works, is in most situations very small, especially since the 17-year-old will usually be able to vote in the next election. The problem for age-based definitions arises when we are dealing with individuals for whom the consequences of the competence assessment are much higher.

Consider a girl under the age of 16 who wishes to obtain contraception from her GP, her parents refuse to give their permission and she cannot obtain it alone as being under 16 she is deemed incompetent to consent to such treatment. Despite this, she clearly understands the nature of contraception, the consequences of unprotected sex, and wishes to enter a consensual sexual relationship with her boyfriend. For her, the assumption of incompetence that excludes her from autonomous action has grave consequences. It was this exact case that was considered in the 1986 House of Lords case, *Gillick v West Norfolk and Wisbech Area Health Authority.* The case established the standard of "Gillick competence" that measures a child's capacity to consent to medical treatment on their individual understanding of the treatment involved. *Gillick* established that it is no longer appropriate to tie age unmovably to an assessment of competence. *Gillick* recognizes that one can be legally a child but competent in making decisions about one's life. I discuss *Gillick* and the application of children's rights in medical decision-making in more detail in Part II of this book. The arbitrary nature of the legal definition of the child is still valuable and valid; however, it cannot be strictly used as a proxy assessment of the competence of a child. This observation about competence brings us to a broader issue regarding children. "Child" carries not just implicit assumptions about competence but also other normative judgments.

Normative Significance of Children

If we wished to resolve some of the problems related to an age-based definition of children we could choose to adopt a strictly biological definition. That is, children are those human beings who have not yet developed a certain body size, physical features, or cognitive abilities. We could even develop more complex methods for measuring the development of the brain and the body to decide exactly when one ceases to be a child and becomes an adult. Yet, to do so would fail to recognize the deeper meaning society attaches to childhood. We do not use the word "child" just to mean those people of a certain biological state but also those who act or represent a certain normative state. For example, we call adults "children" when they act irrationally, white Americans historically called African Americans "boy," and frequently other civilizations were deemed "children of the Empire" during periods of colonialism. The clear implication in this type of use of the word "child" is that children, whether real or symbolic, are inferior to adults. As Schapiro points out, this indicates the existence of a deeper meaning attached to children—one of moral status.[6] It is these types of observations that have prompted scholars to conclude that childhood is socially constructed.

In 1962, French historian Philippe Ariès' text *Centuries of Childhood* was translated into English. The text is influential as it was the first general historical study of childhood.[7] Ariès' central argument was that within medieval society the idea of childhood did not exist. Although children were recognized to be vulnerable, they were treated much the same as adults and did not have the special status in society that they currently enjoy. Therefore, childhood, according to Ariès, is a modern invention.[8] There is now considerable criticism of the evidence used to support his thesis.[9] Ariès drew these conclusions from observations such as the depiction of children as scaled down adults in paintings, the clothing children wore at the time, the games they played, and finally from evidence in the diary of Heroard, Henri IV's doctor. Historians now argue that he ignored other sources such as legal documents from the time and important evidence of artistic conventions that would lead to differing interpretations.[10] It is not just that there are flaws with Ariès' evidence but also that his conclusions and discussion are value laden.[11] Ariès judged that the past lacked *any* idea of childhood, but in fact what it lacked was our *present* understanding of childhood. So, although Ariès was trying to argue that any idea of childhood is a modern invention, he unwittingly laid the foundation for the fuller and deeper understanding of childhood that now exists in the literature—that the modern understanding of childhood is not solid and unchanging but is fluid and contextual. This observation has been important in informing the growing scholarship of sociocultural theorists.

Throughout the 1980s, many scholars grew increasingly dissatisfied with the superficial treatment and understanding of childhood within disciplines such as sociology, psychology, and philosophy.[12] As a result, the new school of "childhood studies" emerged. The movement critiqued the previous emphasis on the inevitable unfolding of child development.

Psychologists such as Jean Piaget claimed that children move through a series of developmental stages that represent a universal path from immaturity toward rationality and autonomy.[13] Sociocultural theorists argue that there is no one route to development dependent on innate biological structures such as the developmental stages set out by Piaget, but rather development is dependent on cultural goals.[14] The way we understand children as incompetent and developing is not grounded in biological facts but rather socially constructed.

The socially constructed nature of childhood means that it is natural that different understandings of children and childhood will exist within different social contexts. The definition of who is a child, and what children are expected to do, will differ widely and fundamentally both between and within countries.[15] For example, children within Australia are expected to attend school until they are 16, reflecting the idea that childhood is a period of learning, development, and play. Childhood in Australia is a period free from work and separate from adult decision-making. Yet, for children of other countries, such as the newly created state of South Sudan, childhood necessarily includes work such as looking after cattle, assisting in collecting water, and participating in family decision-making.

Sociocultural theory also tells us something important about *how* children and childhood is constructed. The normative significance we afford children is produced and reproduced through government policy, media representation, historical and philosophical influences, and individual experiences of childhood and family.[16] Often, the depiction of children can be contradictory. The trial of Jon Venables and Bobby Thompson for the murder of James Bulger in the United Kingdom in 1993 saw children represented in the media as both "victims" and "villains." Bulger was depicted as the classic innocent child, free from the corruption of the world, a *tabula rasa*. The two boys Venables and Thompson were depicted as inherently evil and dangerous, a confirmation of the suspicion that all children are bad and need to be cured, socialized, and controlled by society.[17] Archard suggests that children simply reflect what adults want or need them to be.[18] Indeed, the status that children are accorded by adults can shape the way the children see themselves.[19]

Children as a Concept and a Conception

It is important not to overstate the conclusions of sociocultural theory. Recognizing that childhood can be socially constructed does not mean that the biological differences between children and adults are irrelevant. Childhood cannot be a "purely social" phenomenon.[20] There are real and identifiable biological differences between a 25-year-old and a five-year-old. However, the *meaning* we give to these biological facts is informed by normative assumptions of society. Children are both young human beings and beings that are interpreted and understood differently across time and culture. Given this, it is useful to adopt a distinction suggested by David Archard between the concept and the conception of childhood. Building on the distinction between a concept and a conception of justice set out by Rawls in *A Theory of Justice*, Archard suggests that childhood can be understood in a similar way. The *concept* of childhood requires that children be distinguishable from adults in respect of some unspecified set of attributes, whereby a *conception* of childhood is a specification of those attributes.[21] The concept of childhood simply recognizes that children differ from adults. A conception of childhood is to specify how children differ and why it is significant.[22]

Distinguishing between a concept and a conception of childhood allows us to address again the suggestions by the child liberationists Holt and Farson that recognizing children as a construct means that we have no reason to exclude them from the adult world. Holt and Farson had rightly noticed that much of how children were understood in the 1970s was socially constructed. The saying "children are to be seen and not heard" was a specific product of hundreds of years of assessing the opinions and engagement of children in day-to-day life as unnecessary and distracting. Now, we recognize that allowing children to express their opinions (and teaching them how to do so appropriately) is essential to their mental health. Our conception of children has changed. However, recognizing that part of our understanding of childhood is socially constructed does not mean that there is no distinction between children and adults. We can maintain the concept of children while debating what the content of that conception should be. Indeed, as I will argue, there is something distinct and special about children and childhood that may mean we need to think about it differently when considering the idea of rights.

The Development of Childhood

Humans, in our evolutionary journey, came to a point where they were simultaneously beginning to walk upright and evolving larger and larger brains. As our early ancestors began to walk upright, significant changes occurred in their skeletons to accommodate this new way of moving. Most significantly their pelvises tilted and narrowed in order to allow them to walk forward smoothly rather than swaying side to side as you sometimes see chimpanzees do. At the same time, as they began to stand and walk upright the brains of our ancestors were becoming bigger and bigger. These two developments, upright walking and larger brains, are often credited as the beginning of the distinctive aspects that made humans such a successful animal capable of adapting to environments all over the world. But it was also these two physiological changes that led to the development of the unique period of human childhood.

The combination of tilted and narrow pelvises and larger and larger brains meant that it became increasingly difficult to give birth. The larger head of the child now had to fit through a narrow pelvic opening. It was clear that something needed to give in, and as a result our human ancestors started to give birth earlier in the gestational development when the brain was smaller and less developed and, therefore, able to fit through the birth canal. It is thought that it was the early gracile humans that began to bring children into the world early.[23] The result is that unlike other mammals that give birth to their young at a stage where they are relatively advanced in their development, humans give birth to babies that are in some sense 'half baked'. Unlike calves that are able to walk on their own within hours of being born, newborn humans cannot lift their heads unassisted, crawl or walk. If human children were to be born as physically mature as a baby gorilla, they would not be born at nine months but at 20 months.[24]

This move toward having children earlier in their development creates a period of life for a child that for many mammals is still spent in the womb. As a result, humans have a comparatively longer childhood than most other animals. This period of time also has the strange effect of meaning that humans are more readily influenced by their outside environment than other mammals. Children do more developing outside of the safe environment of the womb. For example, a monkey is born with 70 percent of its brain growth complete and the remaining 30 percent is completed in the following six months after birth. Human babies are born with 23 percent of an adult brain. Our brains then triple in size within three years, grows for three more years, and continue to be rewired (significantly throughout our adolescence) and does not finish until we are in our early twenties.

Our neurons are not just growing, they are feverishly linking up. A 36-month child's brain is twice as active as a normal adult's, with trillions of dendrites and axons making contact.[25] The contact being made between the neurons in the brain is conducting the wiring that is necessary to build a healthy human brain. At this stage of development our brains are particularly susceptible to external influences from the outside environment.

The field of epigenetics tells us that although our DNA dictates much of how we develop, the epigenome dictates how it is expressed. It is this expression that is influenced by our environments and our experiences. Our epigenome is not just our DNA but also the proteins around it called histones. In simple terms, our DNA may tell our brain to develop in a certain way, but the influence of experiences and environment can change how the epigenome expresses this. The classic case to demonstrate the role of epigenome is studies of twins who are genetically identical. As anyone who knows twins will know, they are two separate individuals with distinct personalities and often different physical features. Research shows that although monozygotic (identical) twins are genetically identical, it is not uncommon for one twin to have a condition such as schizophrenia or autism and the other not to.[26] Longitudinal studies such as the *Minnesota Study of Twins Reared Apart* have detailed the physical and psychological differences of 100 pairs of twins who had been reared apart since childhood.[27] The differences observed, and the degree of difference compared to twins reared together, indicate that the epigenome plays an important role when interacting with the environment, to produce different expressions of the same genetic code.[28]

This means we are incredibly sensitive to environmental influences. Key capacities such as learning to understand and speak language develop during what is called "sensitive periods." Once this time is over the circuits in our brain are usually not so easily changed. Much of the modern research in epigenetics has started to pinpoint what has already been known anecdotally, the effect of stress and trauma on children during the critical formative years can have lifelong consequences.[29] Researchers now know that exposure to stress hormones has an impact on brain structures involved in cognition and mental health.[30] As humans spend more time out of the womb and, therefore, exposed to a wider variety of environmental stressors, the vulnerability of human children is greater. As Walter explains,

> Because we are born early and since we have extended our brain development well beyond the womb, neuronal networks that in other animals would never have been susceptible to change remain open and flexible, like the branches of a sapling. Although other primates enjoy these "sensitive periods", too, they pass rapidly, and their circuits become "hardwired" by age one, leaving them far less touched by the experiences of their youth. This epigenetic difference helps explain how chimpanzees, remarkable as they are, can have 99 percent of our DNA, but nothing like the same level of intellect, creativity, or complexity.[31]

This points to the unusual vulnerability of human children. Our extended childhood is the very thing that not only gives us part of our uniqueness but also exposes us to increased vulnerability. Childhood is, therefore, special as it is a period of time in our lives when key parts of ourselves are developing.

Does It Matter?

This conception of childhood as a fluid period of development and vulnerability would seem to cause problems for an assessment of their rights. For, how will we pinpoint if children have the type of capacities necessary to hold rights? I argue throughout this book that the truth is quite the opposite. The complex nature of childhood and children does not pose a significant problem for a theory of children's rights. For the theory of rights that I will present here, it does not strictly matter whether an individual falls within the bounds of "child" or "adult." This is because I will argue that rights are determined by particular interests. Interests differ not only between children and adults but also between individual children and between individual adults.

What does matter is being *aware* of the various conceptions of children that exist and how they inform the types of decisions we take regarding their rights. As Fortin points out,

> Ideas about children's rights undoubtedly reflect the nature of the society in which they are being brought up and the type of childhood they will experience.[32]

Differing conceptions of children will affect which rights we recognize for children. Some conceptions of children hinder the implementation of rights. For example, if a particular society sees children as passive beings that are primarily in need of protection, rights such as Article 12 of CROC, which states that children have a right to participate in decisions that affect their lives, may be more difficult to implement into policy and practice. Yet, conceptions of children can be useful too. The very same understanding of children as helpless and vulnerable may aid in controlling and shaping society's actions toward them. It may foster strong expectations that children are not neglected or abused and guarantee this outcome in a far more effective way than any government legislation. Tamar Schapiro in her article, "What is a child," concludes that

> The enlightenment did away with arbitrary distinctions in status, distinctions based upon lineage and wealth. The danger is in concluding that all distinctions in status are therefore arbitrary. Some differences ought to count, such as the difference between adults and children.[33]

From the discussion of rights and children that will follow, it becomes clear that the appropriate question to ask is *why* the difference ought to count. I believe that the difference should count because it tells us something distinct about children, first that they have fewer capacities and competencies than adults, that they are in a period of rapidly acquiring new capacities and competencies, and that this rapid period development also corresponds with increased vulnerability. This matters because this shapes the types of claims children can make and the type of duties that adults hold them to. In short, it shapes the determination of their rights.

Conclusion

For the purposes of the fundamental question of this book—do children have rights?—I take children to broadly be young human beings who are in a period of rapid development of their capacities and competencies and are vulnerable in their development. In the next chapter, we will see how the developing capacities of children are used to justify the denial of their rights.

Why Children Do Not Have Rights

Having spent so long examining the developmental nature of childhood, it will probably not come as a surprise that the central argument for why children do not hold rights focuses on their reduced capacities. I call this argument here the argument from incompetence. This chapter will outline the argument from incompetence and then show how it manifests in rights theory through the will theory of rights. I will introduce the Hohfeldian framework of rights in order to establish a set of analytical tools that will assist in identifying exactly how capacity and competence interact with rights and what this means for children.

The most common argument employed when denying children of any age the rights afforded to adults is that they have reduced physical and cognitive capacities. The argument from incompetence generally can be described as below:

> To hold a right one must have certain capacities, such as the capacity to feel pain, make choices, or to think rationally. Children are in a state of developing those capacities and acquiring competency and therefore cannot hold rights, unlike adults whose physical and cognitive competencies are fully developed.

The argument from incompetence is so pervasive in society that we probably do not even notice when we invoke it, let alone critically analyze it. For example, we deem it appropriate to exclude children from those who are allowed the right to vote primarily due to their lack of capacity to make informed political decisions. We do not allow very young children to make medical decisions about their own body, and instead require parents to make this decision for them, based on the argument that children lack the cognitive capacity to choose appropriately. We decide what children should eat, how and when they should go to school, when they should go to bed, and what TV shows and movies they should be able to watch because we accept the argument that adults know better than children. The incompetence, lack of cognitive capacity, and irrationality of children are routinely used as reasons as to why children do not hold the same types of rights that adults do.

The argument from incompetence is not a new phenomenon. As I noted in the introductory chapter, traditional liberal theorists such as Hobbes, Locke, and Mill employed variations on the argument from incompetence to exclude children from the realm of right-holders. Hobbes regarded children as lacking the capacity to enter into the social contract because of their inability to reason; Locke argued that children were in a temporary state of inequality because of their irrationality; and John Stuart Mill stated with regard to his political theory that it was "hardly necessary to say why we are not speaking of children."[1] Recent literature on the rights of children has focused on "autonomy" rights—those rights that involve the uncoerced choices and actions of the right-holder according to their conception of the good life.[2] Brighouse argues that it is not sensible to ascribe agency rights to children.[3] Griffin, too, in an extension of his definition of human rights, has argued that infants do not have rights by virtue of their lack of the capacity for agency.[4]

A version of the argument from incompetence pervades one of the leading theories of rights, the will (or choice) theory, hereafter referred to as will theory.[5] Will theory claims that children cannot be right bearers because they lack the capacity to make rational choices. If such significance is placed on a child's lack of capacity, with implications for their moral and political status, then it seems necessary to locate the exact way in which capacity, or the lack of it, is important to rights theory. To do so, we need to know exactly what it means when we speak of rights.

What Are Rights?

The question, "what are rights?" is one that has concerned philosophers for centuries and is still an area of political and moral philosophy riddled with intractable disagreements. This is true, despite the ubiquity of "rights" throughout modern political and public discourse. There is disagreement on who can hold rights, children or adults, groups or individuals, humans or animals; whether rights protect choices or interests, are universal or culturally relative; whether rights are primarily legal instruments or moral creatures. There is even debate on the validity of a rights-based approach at all.[6]

The most conventional way to begin any discussion of the concept of rights is to separate out discussion of their *structure* from their *justification*—that is—distinguishing the logical description of how a right is constructed from the normative significance it is given by various theorists. In this way, rights could be seen to be a bit like cars; it is possible to separate the discussion of the mechanics of how a car physically fits together and is constructed, from discussion of *why*, or for what *purpose*, it is constructed in this way. While two interlocutors may both agree that cars are machines with four wheels that propel passengers forward, they may disagree as to whether a car's real purpose is to safely carry its passengers or if it is a machine whose sole purpose is to maximize speed. This "justification" for cars may then influence which parts of the car's construction are deemed the most important. Our safety-conscious driver may argue that a solid structure able to travel in a stable manner is the most important, whereas our speed fiend may think that these aspects of construction can be compromised in order to make the car as aerodynamic and fast as possible. They might also add that these characteristics are the "true" features of the car. For the safety-conscious driver, a Volvo is the epitome of "carness," but for our speedster, a Ferrari represents the true "car." The debate over rights often proceeds in much the same way. Most rights theorists can identify the core structure of a right but many disagree on its justification or its key function. Disagreement on the function then influences what parts of the right's structure are considered the most important.

The internal structure of rights was elucidated in an analytical framework conceived by American legal theorist Wesley Hohfeld. Hohfeld argued that we often conflate various meanings of the term "right," sometimes switching senses of the word several times in a single sentence.[7] He sought to clarify the structure of rights in order to facilitate reasoning. As Steiner points out, the consequences of non-univocality entail unacceptable costs, as rights are concepts that constrain and guide our actions. False assessments due to any confusion over language are harmful and unnecessary.[8] Therefore, the examination of the structure of rights is an analytical project, separate from the debates regarding moral weight, function, and content of rights.[9]

Hohfeld identified eight incidents that are referred to when we speak of rights. These eight are divided into first- and second-order incidents and are relational. The first-order incidents consist of *claim, duty, liberty* and *no claim*.[10] These form two correlative pairs. Therefore, when there is a claim there is always a duty, when there is a liberty there is always no claim.[11]

First-Order Correlatives Pairs

Claim—Duty
Liberty—No Claim

A claim is defined by the type of action or inaction of people who bear the correlative duty. A claim is held by an individual and creates a duty in others to either (1) abstain from interference or (2) render assistance or remuneration. As a claim and a duty form a correlative pair, a claim always has a duty. For example, I have a claim to my life and, therefore, you have a duty not to kill me. However, some scholars dispute this correlativity axiom. For example, MacCormick argues that the axiom reduces any talk of rights to logically prior duties and, therefore, rights become a simple reflex on duties.[12] This is to misunderstand the axiom. Neither Hohfeldian duties nor claims are logically or existentially prior to the other, just as one side of a coin is not logically prior to its other side. The existence of each is a necessary and sufficient condition for the existence of the other.[13]

Others argue that duties exist without correlative claims and, therefore, the correlativity axiom cannot hold.[14] For example, we may have duties to animals and children, yet they, so this argument goes, do not hold claims against us. For a moment, we must put aside the question of whether children or animals can hold claims and consider the observation that there are certainly *some* types of duties and obligations we hold that do not seem to be connected with a claim held by another. If this is true, this is not to deny the correlativity axiom, it is simply to state that the Hohfeldian duty is one type of obligation, it is an obligation that is always associated with a correlative claim.[15] Other obligations may arise out of relationships or promises.[16] For example, I may hold special obligations to my students because of my *role* as a teacher, or I may hold an obligation to lend a book to a colleague because I promised to do so. If we really think that there is no claim associated with these obligations, then they cannot be understood as Hohfeldian duties.

Importantly for our purposes, a claim is always defined by the actions of the duty bearer, that is, the duty to abstain from interference or render assistance or remuneration. As a claim is not defined by the actions of the claim-holder, neither capacity nor competency on the part of the claim-holder is relevant to their status within Hohfeld's framework. In this sense, a child's incapacity or lack of competence will not prevent them from being a claim-holder.

Unlike a claim, a liberty is specified by reference to the actions of the people who hold the liberties, not the correlative no claim. Liberty is defined by the absence of both duty and claim. For example, I have a liberty to cook myself a risotto for dinner because there exists no claim, held by another person, producing a duty not to do so. It may seem, therefore, that liberties, as the absence of claim or duty, are completely unprotected from other people's actions. Then, why speak of them at all? Despite the absence of both claim and duty, acts and omissions based on a liberty can be effectively protected through a combination of other claims and duties.[17] For example, consider that instead of cooking myself a risotto I am impatient and choose to eat at a fast food outlet. I have a liberty to eat fast food every day of the week if I choose. As this is a liberty and not a claim, my health-conscious friend is under no duty to allow me to eat fast food every day, free from interference. My friend can, therefore, try and dissuade me with logical argument, take me out for dinner, or even lie to me and tell me that all fast food outlets have been shut down, in order to prevent me from eating there.[18] However, my friend's actions in this respect are constrained by his other duties toward me. He cannot tie me up to a chair, as he has a duty not to deny me freedom of movement, nor can he tamper with my car to prevent me driving to buy fast food as I have a claim over my property. Liberties are, therefore, an important aspect of our moral relations.

This demonstrates that X has a liberty to do A if and only if X has no duty not to do A. A liberty is, therefore, specified by reference to the actions of, A, the liberty-holder. For example, my liberty to ride my bike is my freedom from any duty to refrain from riding my bike. However, although a liberty is specified by the action of the liberty-holder, liberties are not dependent on the liberty-holder's actual competence or capacity to exercise the liberty.[19] For example, if I break my leg and am bound to bedrest, I am still at liberty to walk down the street, even though I am currently unable to exercise this liberty. In this way, a liberty is not concerned with the liberty-holder's competence or capacity. If this holds true, then a child's developing capacities and competencies do not preclude them from holding a liberty. A baby holds a liberty to walk down the street before it has developed the actual competence to do so.

Hohfeld's second-order incidents consist of *power, liability, immunity,* and *disability*. Again these incidents form two correlative pairs.

Second-Order Correlative Pairs

Power—Liability
Immunity—Disability

Second-order incidents specify how agents can change their own or other people's first-order and second-order incidents. A power consists in one's ability to effect changes in other's or one's own claim, duty, immunity, and power.[20] For example, if I wish to no longer continue to eat fast food, I have the power to waive my friend's duty not to physically restrain me, in order to prevent me from succumbing in a moment of weakness. One has a liability when one is unshielded from the bringing about of changes by the exertion of a power. My friend, therefore, has a liability as the existence of his duty is subject to my power to waive or enforce it.

Powers, like liberties, are specified in reference to the actions of the holder. However, unlike a liberty, in order to hold a power, one must be factually competent.[21] There is an important difference between factual and legal competence (often called authorization) as one can be factually competent in an act but not be legally authorized.[22] For example, one may be legally authorized to drive a car, but be temporarily factually incompetent to do so due to a broken arm. Therefore, for a child to hold a power we must consider their factual competence to exercise that power. We are not concerned with one's counterfactual capacity to alter one's own or another's Hohfeldian incidents but with one's actual competence. For example, if I am in a coma I may have the capacity to speak and make decisions regarding my life and property but currently lack the competence to do so. This incompetence means I lack the power to waive my rights.

The necessity of factual competency poses a problem for children because they are, at any given time, at different stages of gaining both physical and cognitive competency. Therefore, at varying points of their development they may not have the factual competency required to hold a power.

One has immunity when one is shielded from another's power. A landowner's immunity prevents the government from compulsorily acquiring their land without just compensation. Therefore, X has an immunity if and only if Y lacks the ability to alter A's Hohfeldian incidents. As an immunity relates to one's protection from the exercise of another's power, not to the immunity holder's capacity or competence, a child would seem to be equally capable of holding an immunity as an adult.

The Hohfeldian framework demonstrates that when we consider the essential building blocks of rights, it is the incident of power that is of most concern for children as right-holders. For the majority of Hohfeldian incidents—claim, liberty, and immunity—a child's developing capacities and competencies pose no problem. We can also observe that it is competence, one's actual ability to do the act, which is necessary for a child to hold a power.

These first- and second-order relations can be seen in isolation as "atomic" incidents. However, Wenar argues that most rights, legal or

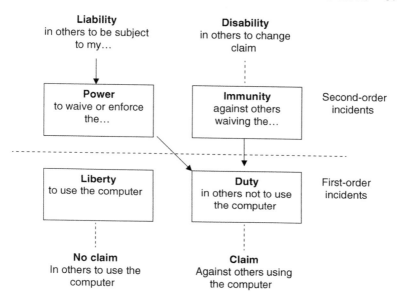

Figure 3.1   Molecular nature of the property right over my computer[24]

moral, are atomic Hohfeldian incidents bonded together in ways to create a *molecular* right.[23] Figure 3.1 represents an adaptation of Wenar's complex molecular right as applied to my claim right over my computer.

This molecular right can be further qualified by other people's first-order claims and second-order powers in much the same way as the fast food case discussed above. For example, I have a liberty to use my computer but not to strike someone over the head with it *or* my immunity may not block the state's power to obtain my computer in a criminal case. These qualifications determine the details of the contours of my property right but do not affect its basic shape. In this sense, Wellman describes each right as having a "defining core" surrounded by "associated incidents."[25]

Over this framework of Hohfeldian incidents and pairs, a number of classifications such as active or passive and negative or positive can be transposed. These classifications are also important in beginning to understand the different fundamentals of rights. Liberties and powers can be seen as *active* incidents as they are defined by the actions of liberty or power-holder. *X* has a liberty or power to *A*. Claims and immunities, however, are *passive* incidents as they are defined by the actions of the duty or disability-holder. *X* has a claim or an immunity that *Y* do *A*.[26] Another way to think of the distinction may be that liberties and powers are *exercised* while immunities and claims are *enjoyed*.[27]

Negative or positive incidents are both forms of passive incidents and, therefore, the negative or positive distinction cannot be used to classify all Hohfeldian incidents. A claim is *negative* when the right-holder is entitled to noninterference, the claim is *positive* when the claim-holder is entitled to some good or service. However, when it comes to *enforcing* negative or positive claims the distinction becomes far less clear. It may take as much time and resources to run a competent legal system to protect negative claims as it would to provide social services to protect positive claims. It could, therefore, be said that in the context of citizens' claims to state enforcement all rights are positive.[28]

Before moving on to the justification of rights, it is useful to draw one further distinction between moral and legal rights. Without a distinction, one may assume that legal rights are the archetypal rights and this could lead to equating the law with morality. As Raz argues,

> It is true that one ought to keep one's promises but false that it is the law that one ought do so. It is (in many legal systems) true that it is the law that one may kill one's pets at will but it is false that one may do so.[29]

Legal rights are rights that exist in law. Legal rights can have normative justification or no normative justification. For example, as previously discussed, it is conceptually possible for the Australian Parliament to pass legislation tomorrow conferring on domestic pets a legal right to vote in federal elections. Such a legal right could be seen to lack normative justification. That is to say that it is possible to construct all types of legal rights. Most legal rights do have normative justification and many legal rights are justified as they codify rights we believe exist outside the law. These rights that exist whether they have been translated into law or not can be called moral rights, or nonlegal rights. In this sense, moral rights are normatively justified claims.

Not all justified legal rights have a corresponding moral right. For example, within the law corporations have certain rights as legal persons; these rights are usually justified through pragmatic reasons for effective functioning of the law. The rights of corporations as legal persons are a "legal fiction" to judge the legality of business proceedings and relationships.[30] However, outside of such a legal system we would be unwilling to argue that the corporation holds some sort of normatively justified claim right in the same way that real persons do.

Similarly, not all moral rights should be translated into legal rights, often for reasons to do with the boundaries of appropriate state intervention. For example, one may have a claim to be told the truth based on a right to respect.[31] However, for most instances it is not appropriate to translate this into a legal right, enforceable through the judicial system, every time someone tells a lie. This particular problem is explored in Part II of this book where I argue that children conceived using donated sperm and eggs have a right to be told the nature of their conception based on their right to be treated with respect.

When I talk about rights, I am, therefore, talking about normatively justified claims, some of which should for their effective functioning be translated into law, some which are more appropriately seen as rights and duties between two individuals that can exist and function outside of the legal system. In this sense, I take a similar position to Raz that the best approach is to think about rights in general first and then to consider which of these rights should be translated into law.[32] Although Hohfeld's jural relations were originally conceived to analyze legal rights, they can also be effectively used to analyze nonlegal rights. The Hohfeldian framework demonstrates the different incidents we consider to be associated with the term "right" and the ways that these can interact. What combination of Hohfeldian incidents we consider to be a "right" will depend on the function we wish rights to fulfill.

Justification of rights

Although a combination of Hohfeldian incidents make a right, not every combination represents what we would think of as a "true" right. Hohfeld's analysis provides us with the useful tools of analytical jurisprudence but rights themselves also hold moral and political weight. Rights serve a function and we have them for justified reasons. Broadly speaking, there are two philosophical approaches to explaining why rights should be protected, a deontological or status approach and a consequentialist approach. A deontological approach argues that there is something specific to the right-holder's status that means that their rights should be respected. Early theories of rights, such as those of natural rights theorists, often relied on a deontological justification. A consequentialist approach argues that rights should be respected because they bring about good outcomes, to protect the welfare or interests of the right-holder.

Contemporary debate over the function of rights plays out these two philosophical approaches; indeed, it has been suggested that the debate over rights is a proxy for a debate over normative commitments.[33] The heated debate is between two theories and famously described as a "standoff."[34] These are will theory and interest theory.[35] The intractable nature of this standoff is no better exemplified in the exchange between Matthew Kramer, Nigel Simmonds, and Hillel Steiner in *A Debate Over Rights*.

Will theory

Will theory understands rights as normative allocations of freedom as they demarcate domains or spheres of practical choice where individuals are not subject to interference.[36] Thus, a right makes the right-holder a "small scale sovereign."[37] Those that adhere to will theory, such as H. L. A. Hart, Carl Wellman, and Hillel Steiner, argue that the core function of a right is to protect or enable an individual's will or choice. In order to protect this choice the right-holder must have a claim that invokes not only a duty but also the power to enforce or waive it. This is because the power to enforce or waive allows claim-holders control over the corresponding duty and, therefore, full control over their right. This power can be broken down into three distinct steps:

1. I can waive the duty or leave it in existence before any breach of my claim.
2. I can seek or not seek remedy after a breach of my claim.
3. I can waive or enforce the obligation to implement remedy for the breach of my claim.

Each step includes two choices, thus I as the claim-holder have six distinct Hohfeldian powers.[38] As a result, enforcing or waiving a claim is not a single event but happens in stages. Different versions of will theory disagree on whether one needs to have power over all or just some of these steps but the common element is that the claim-holder must enjoy decisive control over the effectuation of their claim.

Therefore, a will theory right = a Hohfeldian claim + Hohfeldian power. The Hohfeldian rights framework tells us that one must have factual competence in order to hold a power. The particular factual competence at play is the competence to make a rational decision to waive or enforce the right as outlined above. This emphasis on choice and control has a number of consequences. Many have observed that this often means that will theory will not recognize the more serious claims as rights, such as the claim not to be enslaved or the claim not to be tortured, as these claims do not have a corresponding power to waive their correlative duties.[39] MacCormick argues powerfully for the existence of unwaivable rights such as these.[40] MacCormick argues that these types of rights are so important that we cannot choose to waive them and enslave ourselves. Just because we cannot waive these types of rights should not mean that they are not rights at all. To exclude them is to place undue significance on the power to choose.

Furthermore, beings that are not competent in rational decision-making cannot hold rights. This will exclude animals, mentally incapacitated individuals, and, as we will see below, children from holding rights.

However, it also excludes adults that are temporarily incompetent. Consider, for example, an adult who is in a coma and is no longer able to make decisions regarding the enforcement of waiver of their rights. Our intuitive response would be that someone in a coma no longer holds a right over their body just because they are no longer capable of waiving or enforcing this right. Again, MacCormick provides a compelling argument that we would easily agree that those in a coma held a right not to be tortured.[41]

It is this emphasis on factual competency and the necessity of the inclusion of power within a will theorist's definition of a right that is fatal for children's rights. For a child to be able to hold a will theory right, they must be factually competent of the rational choice to enforce or waive one's right.[42] As much as we have recognized that children's capacities are rapidly developing, very young children are still developing the competence to distinguish between self and others. It is clear that without such a competence, a very young child would be incapable of making the decisions relating to the enforcement or waiver of their claims, because to make such a decision would necessarily involve the ability to conceive of interpersonal concepts such as "claim."

Will theorists have famously had little problem boldly grasping this political nettle. Under their theory, as children, particularly infants and young children, are incompetent to engage in enforcement and waiver decisions, they cannot hold the enforcement/waiver powers and, therefore, cannot hold rights.[43] The distinctive feature of children's rights in will theory seems to be that they do not exist.[44]

Legal theorist H. L. A. Hart originally embraced the position that will theory did not recognize children as right-holders. In 1955, he claimed that the use of "right" to describe the existence of a duty to behave well to children is "idle use" and confuses it with other moral expressions.[45] In the 1980s Hart refined his position and attempted to reconcile the notion of children as right-holders within will theory. He argued that when infants or younger children do not hold the enforcement or waiver powers, they can be exercised on their behalf by an appointed representative. Even though this representative is exercising these powers,

(a) the representative is bound by the consideration that their exercise of power is determined by what the right-holder could have done if sui juris[46]; and

(b) when the right-holder becomes sui juris they can exercise the powers without any transfer or fresh assignment.

Therefore, it can be said that the powers remain with the right-holder throughout.[47] Those that support Hart's revised position on children's rights believe that he offers a compelling argument for how legal rights can be ascribed to children even when the relevant powers of waiver/enforcement are exercised by adults.[48] However, it is apparent that this revised argument represents a departure from traditional will theory, for how can a power reside with a child if (a) they do not have the factual competence necessary to hold the power and (b) the power is exercised by another? The Hohfeldian analytical logic seems to break down at this point.

In addition, Hart's revision suffers from epistemic weaknesses due to considerable problems with the first constraint—that the appointed representative must act as the right-holder would have done if *sui juris*. Actual knowledge of what the child would have done if they were factually competent is clearly epistemologically inaccessible; we cannot know what they would have chosen or what they would have judged to be beneficial to them except retrospectively. Therefore, despite the constraints laid on the representative, practically the power would seem to lie with them and not the child.

Will theory's emphasis on choice has a "confining effect" on the articulation of children's rights that cannot be avoided. Children's state of evolving capacities means that according to will theory they fall into the same category as all other non-right-holders, such as the mentally incapacitated, animals, or inanimate objects. Will theory, therefore, is unable to distinguish between children and other incapacitated groups; it fails to recognize that although children may not currently have the requisite factual competency, they do hold the capacity to one day become competent. It is owing to these difficulties that many reject will theory as an appropriate theory to properly define how we wish to use rights.

Interest Theory

Hart's concessions are not enough for most scholars, and other theorists have mounted sustained attacks against will theory on the question of children's rights in order to demonstrate the superiority of interest theory. MacCormick's 1975 article employed rights for children as a "test case" to assess each theory. Campbell argued that the will theory was inadequate as an expression of the "moral significance of persons" as it cannot account for children. Those that adhere to interest theory, such as Joseph Raz, Neil MacCormick, and Matthew Kramer, argue that the function of a right is not to protect choice but to further a right-holder's interests. Instead of constraining the function of rights to the protection of an agent's choice or free will, interest theory seeks to encompass a wider domain.

Interest theorists argue that rights also have an important function in protecting those things, goods, and services that are in our "interest." Those people who may lack the power to obtain these goods for themselves, who lack capacities, or who are powerless and vulnerable to oppression are often those that need the protective force of rights the most. In this broad definition, an interest that grounds a right is an interest that is deemed worthy of protection as it is of sufficient importance to impose a duty on another person. An interest is generally deemed to be worth protecting and of sufficient importance when it will intrinsically benefit the claim-holder.[49] Interest theory and will theory, therefore, fundamentally disagree on the function and justification of a right.

Interest theorists argue that by shifting the focus of rights theory away from choice, with its requirement of factual competency of rational decision-making, they have successfully provided a theory of rights that can explain rights for children. Children, even extremely young children, have an interest in the most basic aspects of life such as shelter and food. These interests, so the argument goes, ground rights. However, it may be the case that interest theory too has not adequately examined how capacity and competence operate with the various Hohfeldian building blocks of rights. The following chapters will unpack the distinction between capacity and competency and will then show how these concepts are still important to a full and functional theory of children's rights.

Conclusion

The argument from incompetence, which claims that children's incapacities exclude them from the realm of right-holders, has traditionally provided a powerful argument for denying children rights. This is exemplified in the will theory of rights, which claims that children must be competent in rational decision-making in order to hold the power to waive or enforce their claim. Interest theory, however, argues that by shifting the emphasis to interests instead of choice, children can be afforded rights. In the next few chapters, I will further examine the distinction between capacity and competence and argue that children's incapacity may still play an important role in determining and constraining their rights.

4

Capacity and Competence

The previous chapter identified that a child's reduced cognitive capacities, specifically their lack of factual competency in rational decision-making, is key to the argument of why they do not hold rights under the will theory. Interest theory, on the other hand, has argued that by shifting the focus or rationale for rights from choice to interest, it becomes theoretically possible to afford children the status of right-holder. Before moving on to my argument for why children hold rights, it is necessary to further interrogate the concepts of capacity and competence, as it is these concepts that hold such a critical role in this debate on rights. I argue here that there is an important distinction between capacity and competency that helps us to draw out the special nature of children's rights.

The Use of Capacity and Competence

The terms "capacity" and "competence" are often used interchangeably.[1] The Oxford English Dictionary defines capacity as "the ability or power to do or understand something" and competence as "the ability to do something successfully or efficiently."[2] At first pass, these definitions seem to be sufficiently similar in order to justify their interchangeable use. It has even been observed that the only difference between the concepts is professional discourse; medical practitioners will give an assessment of an individual's *capacity*, while the legal system will determine whether they are *competent* or not.[3] Since this distinction is only one of convention, it is argued that the terms can and indeed *should* be used interchangeably.[4]

Using terms interchangeably is common and usually does not present a problem for everyday use. However, this does not hold true when the terms are used throughout the literature of rights and, in particular, in relation to the rights of the child. Capacity and competence are central to the decision over whether an individual holds a right or not, and children often inhabit the boundary between competence and incompetence, capacity and incapacity. As discussed in the previous chapter, the terms "capacity" and "competence" are, therefore, important as they can determine what rights (if any) a child holds.

The problematic use of capacity and competence has led to problems within the children's rights literature, including lack of clarity and talking past each other. For example, in *Deciding for Others*, Buchanan and Brock consider the threshold an individual must meet in order to have a right to medical decision-making. They state that in order to be *competent* in decision-making one must have

1. the *capacity* for understanding and communication and
2. the *capacity* for reasoning and deliberation.[5]

This may seem an adequate description, but upon closer examination, it only serves to produce further questions. It cannot be that competence in decision-making is merely the same as having the capacity for understanding, communication, reasoning, and deliberation. There seems to be a great difference between a 14-year-old girl who has the *capacities* for understanding and communication, and for reasoning and deliberation, but who has never been able to exercise these capacities, and someone who is clearly a competent negotiator, such as Henry Kissinger. The 14-year-old may have the capacity to understand and communicate but has never learnt how, nor had the opportunity to express these capacities. Can she properly be considered competent? This seems to be a very different type of competence from a person who has extreme experience in understanding and communicating with others, reasoning and deliberating, such as Kissinger.

Therefore, having the capacities to do an act may not be enough to do the act that one wishes to be competent in. However, if the conclusion is that Kissinger is competent in decision-making and our 14-year-old girl is not, on what ground is that determination made? Does it follow that she would not be allowed to choose for herself? Even if she is not competent in the same way as Kissinger, she has capacities that a 6-month-old baby does not. Surely, we still want to say that there is something different about the girl that sets her apart from other incompetents. But do we treat these as differences in capacity or competence, or both? This is not simply an issue of semantics. It leaves us without the adequate tools to properly conceive of the relation between capacity and competence and, therefore, understand how the concepts should operate regarding rights for children.

The problems arising from a lack of definition are not limited to philosophical debates. One of the key principles of the United Nations

Convention on the Rights of the Child (CROC) is that of "evolving capacities." Article Five of the Convention states that children have a right to begin involvement in the exercise of their rights in a manner "consistent with the evolving capacities of the child." Article Five makes no mention of age as the determining factor for the child to exercise rights on their own behalf, but rather recognizes the "demonstration of the requisite skills, knowledge and understanding is crucial to the exercise of rights."[6] The importance of the principle of evolving capacities is, therefore, central to realizing a child's right to participation. Despite this, the principle continues to be one of the most widely violated—why? One answer may lie in the lack of clarity on exactly what a child's capacities *are*, how they acquire them, and what threshold must be met in order to qualify. In order for people to fulfill their duties and assist children in the realization of their rights, we must be clear exactly what these evolving capacities are.

A clear definition of capacity and competence will, therefore, provide a more precise set of concepts in order to help to prevent talking past each other in political discourse, and clarify how a right applies in practical contexts such as the UN CROC guiding principle of "evolving capacities."

A Case of Capacity and Competence: The Student and the Turtle

Consider, first, a case of a student and a turtle.[7] Both the (human) student and the turtle are unable to speak Russian—neither of them can articulate the correct tones and accents required to be a Russian speaker. However, given the right training and enough practice, the student can eventually speak Russian. That is, he has what it takes to become a competent Russian speaker. However, the turtle, no matter how much training it receives, will never be able to speak Russian. The crucial difference is that the student already has the right physiological and neurological equipment to process and understand the language, whereas the turtle does not, and will not. From this, we can say that the student has the capacity to speak Russian but not the competence, but the turtle lacks not only the competence but also the capacity to speak Russian.

There is a clear difference between a student's inability to speak Russian and the turtle's. That difference lies in the student's *potential* mastery of Russian. This can be captured through the use of conditional analysis (CA). The simplest form of CA would be as follows:[8]

(CA) Someone S is able to Action A if S would likely A if S tried to A.[9]

The qualifier that S *would likely* A is used to allow for unforeseen and extraordinary instances of failure. We might think that the student would be able to speak Russian if he tried to, but perhaps a muscle spasm causes him to mispronounce a word or two. We would not, on this account, say that the student is unable to speak Russian because of such factors. As such, we might think that, under ordinary conditions, if an agent would be likely to succeed in an action, then that is sufficient to say that he is able to perform that action.

How can we use a CA to understand capacity? Roughly speaking, we distinguish the student from the turtle by features *internal* to each. At first pass, the capacity to do X, for our purposes, refers to the *potential* to do X. That is, the agent has the *capacity* to do X when the agent has the requisite set of skills internal to him for X-ing, but perhaps has not exercised those skills yet. To have a skill set required for a capacity is to possess the requisite skills necessary to be able to exercise that capacity. The capacity to speak Russian, therefore, attaches to the existence of the physiological abilities within the student to speak Russian. As the student has the appropriate language center in his brain, can move his mouth in the correct way to intone Russian words, and is able to hear and interpret sounds from others, we would say that he has the capacity for speaking Russian. The turtle, however, does not have the mental or physical apparatus for language, and so lacks the capacity to speak Russian.

From the above example, internal features are those that are innate to the agent and are also necessary for the agent to do the task in question. We take these to be physiological features, such as the wiring of the student's brain, his auditory system, and the ability of his mouth muscles to move appropriately to intone Russian words. These features, however, are not present in the turtle. So, the turtle lacks the requisite internal features and, therefore, the capacity to speak Russian. Nevertheless, as we will discuss shortly, some features *external* to the agent may also be relevant, such that the student might have the capacity to speak Russian (in terms of having the relevant internal features or skill set), but still be unable to speak Russian on account of not having anyone to teach him, or because he is currently asleep, or because he has temporarily lost his voice. So, the student's cognitive and physiological properties count as internal features, because they necessarily facilitate the student speaking Russian and are innate or ordinarily present in the student.

With this understanding of the term, we can now construct the CA for "capacity." First, by optimizing all external conditions. External conditions include training, experience, resources and opportunity, and mental states, such as the knowledge arising from this training, and also the intention to act. Second, we hold fixed everything else and see whether the agent would be able to perform the action. In this way, we are isolating that which is internal to the agent. Therefore, a CA for capacity can be stated as

(Cap—CA) S has the capacity to A if, optimizing all external conditions and mental states, S would likely A if S tried to A.

Despite the optimization of external conditions such as training, experience, resources and opportunity, and mental states such as "know how" and intention, the turtle would still be unable to speak Russian, while the student would be able to. In this analysis, then, the student has the capacity to speak Russian, while the turtle does not. To see this, we have isolated those features internal to the subjects. Therefore, one has the capacity to A if, optimizing all external conditions and mental states, one would A if one tried to A.

A Conditional Analysis of Competence

In our story, neither the student nor the turtle can *actually* speak Russian. Competence to do A, on our account, attaches to the combination of internal capacity and mental states, bringing about the actual demonstrable ability to do A. Once the student has had enough lessons, he will be deemed a competent speaker. We say that the student is competent if he can fluently speak Russian on command. In this way, competence usually requires that the agent has (or gains) the experience of doing A, and can successfully A when he wants to. That is, the student has to have the requisite mental states necessary to understand the Russian language, knowledge about how to speak Russian, and the intention to speak Russian when he wants to speak Russian.[10] Effectively conversing in Russian requires the student to have not only the right physiological apparatus, but also the requisite mental states to do so. Notice that we say that the student is not competent until he can *effectively converse* in Russian. That is, the agent must be generally successful at A-ing in order to be deemed competent. Knowing how to A, then, might be necessary for competence in A, but it is not sufficient.

We can perform the same CA for competence by holding fixed that internal to the agent and also his mental states and optimizing external conditions of resources and opportunity. A CA for competence can be stated as

(Comp—CA) S has the competence to A if, optimizing resources and opportunity, S would likely A if S tried to A.

Notice that we do not specifically refer to success. However, that S could A if S tried to A *implies* that S has successfully done A. The student would not be deemed a competent speaker of Russian unless he could successfully speak Russian if he wanted to. That is, to be competent is not to be acting out of accident.

The CA demonstrates an important point regarding competence—it is task specific. In order to assess if the agent is actually competent, not just that he has the requisite internal condition to have the capacity, we must examine the CA in relation to each task. If an agent is competent at driving a car, this does not mean that he is competent at driving a truck. Competence is always competence *for some task*, or competence *to do something*.[11] Whether or not an agent is competent at a particular task will depend on how we describe the task in question.[12]

It may also be the case that the competence to do one task may be related to the competence to do another task under a different description. If I am competent at running a four-minute mile, then I am also competent at running a four-minute mile on Sundays, and I am presumably also competent at running a five-minute mile. Interesting cases arise, however, where the competence to do X may be related to the capacity to do Y. Suppose that I have had piano lessons for a while and I can play "Twinkle, Twinkle, Little Star" perfectly. I have the capacity to play it: I have the coordination and skills to read music, and I know where the keys are on a piano. And because I can *actually* play it, I am competent in playing "Twinkle, Twinkle, Little Star." In some sense, then, I can be said to be a competent pianist. But this only applies at quite a general sense. I might be able to play "Twinkle, Twinkle, Little Star" perfectly, but perhaps I have not learnt how to play something more complicated, such as Beethoven's "Moonlight Sonata." Perhaps learning how to play "Twinkle, Twinkle, Little Star" is something that one needs to learn to play before "Moonlight Sonata." In this way, being competent at "Twinkle, Twinkle, Little Star" helps me develop the capacity to become competent at something else, like "Moonlight Sonata."

What becomes important is the level of description and analysis in which we discuss what we have the capacity and the competence to do. In other words, what we are interested in here is the relevant *task*—if we are interested in competence *simpliciter*, it might be sufficient if I can play "Twinkle, Twinkle, Little Star." But if I am interested in competence *qua* concert pianist, then obviously "Twinkle, Twinkle, Little Star" will not cut it, and we may have to look at other tasks to determine competence.[13]

External Conditions and Ableness

The discussion so far has examined what we mean by "capacity" and "competence." An agent has the capacity to A when he has the requisite skill set internal to him to be able to A. Competence to A, on the other hand, relates to an agent's ability to exercise that skill set to successfully A. Having shown that there is a simple intuitive distinction between competence and capacity, we now further fine-tune the meaning of "competence" by examining the distinction between competence and ableness.

Pete Morriss offers a distinction between power as ability and power as ableness. Ableness, on his account, roughly relates to the presence of external features necessary for an agent to successfully do a particular action. So, for example, a piano player who has the requisite coordination and training to play the piano has the capacity to play the piano. We would also say that the pianist is competent if he is successful at piano playing more often than not, and that he was able to do so, on cue, if a piano were available. However, in the absence of a piano, the pianist is unable to play. But, this is not because he is defective in his piano playing skills, but rather because he lacks the opportunity or resources necessary to play the piano. This shows that the difference between the capacity to do A and the ableness to do A is contingent on whether the relevant factors are internal or external to the agent.[14]

Following the structure of the previous section, we could do a CA on ableness as follows:

(Ableness—CA) S has the ableness to A if S would likely A if S tried to A.

Notice that the CA for ableness is the same as the original form of CA outlined at the beginning of the previous section. This is because an agent is able to perform an action when he has both the capacity and competence to do it, and also is not impeded by any external factors. That is, ableness to A necessarily requires an agent to be competent to A, and in order to be competent to A, the agent necessarily has to have the capacity to A. Consequently, the relationship between the three concepts can be seen in Figure 4.1.

This establishes a symmetrical relationship between capacity, competence, and ableness. Capacity requires an agent's internal physiological abilities or skill set, while competence involves the agent's internal physical and mental states. Ableness, then, is the aggregation of the agent's internal physical states, mental states, and the presence of the right external conditions.

There are some circumstances, however, where ableness seems to be not so distinct from competence and capacity. A man who has lost both of his arms, for example, has not only lost the competence to pick up heavy objects, but also the capacity to do so, as he no longer has the skills internal to him to develop the competence in lifting heavy objects (viz., the requisite motor skills, muscles, and ligaments). However, if the man is given bionic arms, he can once again lift heavy objects.[15] At first, being able to lift heavy objects with bionic arms might seem to be an instance of ableness.

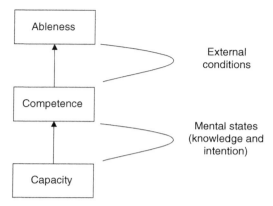

Figure 4.1   Relationship between capacity, competence, and ableness

However, he is being given the underlying capacity to be competent in acts such as heavy lifting. Having arms is usually considered a capacity, as they are physiological features of the agent. The bionic arms merely replace the agent's own arms in allowing him to be competent in lifting heavy objects, if he so desired. Given the relationship between capacity and competence, in that capacity is necessary for competence, we would argue that if the bionic arms are necessary for the agent to be a competent object-lifter, then they would be an instance of capacity.

Instances of ableness, on the other hand, are those that would truly be *external* to the agent such as opportunities or resources such as money. In order for the man to lift heavy objects, he must already have the capacity to lift heavy objects and, as we have claimed, that capacity exists in his having arms. If there were no heavy objects around, we would say that the man is unable to lift heavy objects, even if he had bionic arms. The bionic arm example seems to be an unusual case as arms (and the capacity to lift objects) are ordinary features of agents.[16] However, on our account, the distinction stands. Therefore, on our account, an agent has the capacity to A when he has all the requisite features and skills *internal* to him to A and the potential to do A. Competence is one's actual ability to A.[17] By "actual ability," we mean the successful, intentional exercise of that capacity to A. Finally, ableness is one's competence to do A in the presence of external resources and opportunity to do so.

The Series Problem

So far, we have defined capacity, competence, and ableness. On our account, capacities are necessary for an agent to be competent. However, it is obvious that not everyone has all capacities at all times. An objection to this understanding of capacity, then, is that it could continue *ad infinitum*, in that one needs the capacity to have a capacity, and so on.

Consider driving a car. In our analysis, the ableness required to drive a car is to have the requisite skills and coordination to drive a car, as well as any relevant external factors, such as being licensed and having the freedom and opportunity to take a car out whenever one chooses. To be a competent driver is to have the actual ability (i.e., successful exercise of a capacity) to drive a car, as evidenced by taking driving lessons and acquiring the skills to do so. To have the capacity to drive a car is to have the skill set necessary to learn to drive (such as the relevant hand–eye coordination or cognitive potential to understand road rules), whether or not one has actually driven yet. For example, an unlicensed 16-year-old has the capacity to drive a car, but has yet to take lessons to gain the competence.

Yet, what do we say of a toddler who is learning how to stand? A toddler certainly does not yet have the relevant motor skills to drive a car, but he will develop these motor skills over the course of a normal life. Does this mean that we should say that he has the capacity to drive a car, if he will develop into a 16-year-old with the relevant coordination and motor skills to learn to drive a car? If so, why stop there? If we say that the toddler has the capacity to drive a car (on the basis that he has the capacity to develop the capacity to be a competent car driver), we could continue along this path and say that since a zygote has the capacity to develop limbs, it has the capacity to drive a car. Or, even a group of four cells without a form has the capacity to drive a car, because it will one day turn into a zygote, which becomes a child, which becomes the 16-year-old that can learn how to drive. But it is absurd to claim that a group of cells has the capacity to drive, on the basis that it has a causal connection to some (distant) future agent with the competence to do so.

So, here are the six potential agents for our case:

1. Licensed driver who has a car
2. Licensed driver who does not have a car
3. 16-year-old who has not yet had driving lessons
4. Toddler who is learning how to stand
5. Embryo, in utero
6. Group of four cells, in utero

How do we distinguish between them? Morriss identifies this problem in his analysis of ability but simply dismisses it as irrelevant for most discussion. He states that

> there is, at least in principle, the possibility of an infinite chain of abilities: one can have the ability to acquire the ability to acquire the ability to . . . I doubt, though, whether we usually want to look beyond second order abilities.[18]

We could, in theory, simply follow his argument and stop at the second level of series, but this seems to be unsatisfactory and ad hoc. However, it is also possible to consider again the CAs we gave above for capacity, competence, and ableness. Despite the optimization, the only potential agents who would be able to drive the car would be the two licensed drivers and the 16-year-old. We consequently isolate those features internal to the subjects, their *capacity*. The toddler, embryo, and group of four cells cannot drive the car as they lack the requisite capacity.

Likewise, our understanding of competence also yields the right results. If we optimize external conditions of resources and opportunity, the agents that are competent are only the two licensed drivers. The other potential agents are not. Further, the same sort of analysis can also be done for ableness: when we no longer optimize external resources and opportunity, the only agent who could do the act of driving a car would be the licensed driver who has a car at hand.

This CA neatly aligns with our earlier working definitions of capacity and competence and it also draws a distinction between the capacity held by the 16-year-old and that of the embryo. It indicates that the 16-year-old holds what we may call "capacity proper," but the embryo does not. If we return to our example of the turtle and the student, the crucial difference there was that the student would one day be able to speak Russian. It still remains true that the toddler, embryo, and group of four cells will one day become something that can drive a car, but, as we have just demonstrated through the CA, they do not have capacity proper. Instead, we can call the capacity of the toddler, embryo, and group of cells a "latent capacity"—the capacity to acquire a capacity.

What makes a capacity latent is that it is a preexisting capacity that requires development or enhancement *in the agent* to become a capacity proper. The embryo has a latent capacity to drive a car because, under optimal circumstances, it will develop into the kind of thing that can drive a car. Latent capacities can also themselves be tiered, such that the group of cells has the latent capacity to become a toddler, even if it cannot become a toddler yet. The relevant feature, then, for latent capacities is temporal: the agent will likely develop into something that holds the relevant capacity we are interested in. Consequently, a CA for latent capacities would be as follows:

> (Latent Cap—CA) S has the latent capacity to A if, optimizing all external conditions and mental states, S would likely develop into something that could A if, at that time, S tried to A.

However, it may be countered that the series problem still exists, as the capacity to have a capacity could continue *ad infinitum*. Even so, we may acknowledge that although the series exists, it is not problematic for our purposes. What we are interested in is the capacity to drive a car, not the capacity to have a capacity to drive a car. That, strictly speaking, is a different capacity. To have a capacity to A is not the same as A. This is evidenced by the fact that not all latent capacities manifest into actual capacities. We can envisage that, as a toddler, an agent may have the capacity to become many things: an Olympic athlete, an astronaut, or an academic. But, over time, some of those possibilities become closed to the agent.[19] Perhaps he is severely injured and will no longer be able to achieve a high level of sporting prowess, or perhaps future preferences, external factors, and interests will steer him in a particular direction away from sports. In some sense, it might be true that the toddler has the capacity to become an Olympic athlete, but what is really being expressed in "the toddler has the capacity to become an athlete" is shorthand for "the toddler has the latent capacity to have the skill set required to become an athlete," where, as we have stipulated, to have a capacity is to have a particular set of skills to be able to perform a particular task. As such, while we can concede that capacity-speak gives rise to a series it is still possible to differentiate between capacities proper and latent capacities and, insofar as latent capacities give rise to series, we can also argue that it is not a vicious series.

Recognizing the nature of latent capacities and their relationship with capacities proper, we may amend our earlier diagram. See Figure 4.2.

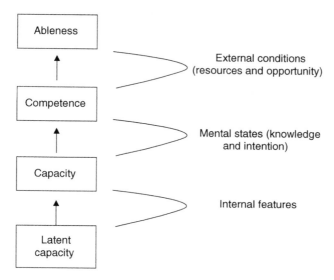

Figure 4.2 Relationship between ableness, competence, capacity, and latent capacity

Children's Rights

Having outlined the distinction between latent capacities, capacities, competence, and ableness, we can now return to examine what these distinctions can offer for our understanding of children's rights.

Let us briefly return to the examples set out at the beginning of the chapter. Brock and Buchanan outlined the threshold an individual must meet in order to have a right to decision making. With the distinction between "capacity" and "competence" now in mind, we can begin to differentiate between the type of decision-making abilities held by someone like Henry Kissinger and a 14-year-old girl. We can now say that Kissinger is a competent decision maker as he has not only those internal elements necessary for decision-making, but also the mental states such as knowledge, intention, and experience. However, the 14-year-old girl may be said to hold the capacities for good decision-making but may not yet have acquired the competence. She has those elements internal to her for good decision-making but may lack the experience. Furthermore, the distinctions allow us to distinguish between the 14-year-old girl and a six-month-old baby who does not yet have the capacity for good decision-making. However, the six-month-old has the *latent* capacity for good decision-making. These sorts of distinctions show us that we must be clear on which threshold we award rights. For example, if a right to consent to medical treatment necessitates rational decision-making, is it necessary that the right-holder have the competence, the capacity, or merely the latent capacity for decision-making? The stipulative distinctions between these terms offered provide us with the tools necessary to engage in this type of debate. They help us to avoid the lack of clarity that often plagues the allocation of rights.

The recognition of the development of latent capacities into capacities proper and then into competencies aligns with the language used in the UN CROC. Article Five of CROC discusses the *"evolving* capacities" of the child. Recognition of the child's capacities as evolving allows us to make a crucial distinction between a child and other incapacitated groups. Other incompetent groups, such as the mentally disabled and animals, lack latent capacities because their capacities are static. Identifying latent capacities allows children to inhabit a separate and distinct moral sphere, which clearly has implications for their rights.

Conclusion

This chapter has unpacked the distinction between capacity and competence. A capacity is the counterfactual ability to do A. One has the capacity to A when one has all the relevant skills internal to that person to A. Competence is one's actual ability to A. By actual ability, we mean the capacity to A plus the relevant mental states (such as knowledge and intention) necessary for successfully doing A. We then fine-tuned this framework by introducing the additional concepts of ableness and latent capacities. Ableness is one's actual ability (viz., competence) to do A plus the availability of external resources and opportunity to do so. Latent capacities refer to the capacity to develop a capacity.

The project of distinguishing between these terms is not an isolated case of semantics; it has implications on how we understand children's rights. The distinction provides a useful tool to engage in debates regarding the requisite threshold children may have to meet in order to be awarded rights. The precise use of language is relevant not only in philosophical debates but also in policy making. The current literature on children's rights is plagued by inconsistent and, often, imprecise use of these terms which can lead to talking past each other. Finally, as the next chapter will more fully explain, the articulation of latent capacities has significance to why children are a special set of right-holders. Because children are neither wholly incompetent nor fully competent, they inhabit a separate moral sphere defined by their latent capacities.

5

Why Children Have Rights

So far we have examined what is special about children[1] and the arguments why they do not hold rights and have further unpacked the
distinction between the concepts of capacity and competence. In this
chapter, I pull these arguments together to outline why children have rights
and the potential limits to those rights.

As discussed earlier, we often assume that it is correct to deny children
rights by reference to their lack of competence. We find it acceptable that
there is a fixed age in law below which one is incapable of consenting to sex
or driving a car or incompetent to stand trial. However, while we are willing
to acknowledge this lack of competence, it is not true that society is willing
to let go of the concept of rights for children in its entirety. The moral
and legal personhood of children is reflected in our most fundamental
institutions.[2] The challenge, then, is to elucidate a theory that adequately
grounds rights for children while recognizing what is special about them,
that is, their reduced and developing capacities and competencies. Answering this challenge involves building upon interest theory as it currently
stands.

I argue that while competence may not be necessary for the enforcement
or waiver of a right, it is necessary for the realization of a right. Competence plays an integral role in interest theory, one that is fundamental to
understanding the structure of children's rights. Rights, including those
for children, are constrained by the competence of the claim-holder and
the importance of their interest to impose upon others' Hohfeldian liberties. Conceiving of rights in this way will provide us with the building
blocks with which to begin more complicated theoretical conversations
concerning the position of children within moral and political theory.

Interest Theory

In will theory, children are denied the status of right-holder owing to a
focus on their lack of competence for rational decision-making. However,

interest theory places no such emphasis on capacity, power, and self-determination. The separation between claim and power logically allows for the fact that a child lacking the competency to hold a power is not excluded from holding an interest theory right. As observed previously, there is no competence-related impediment involved with a child holding a Hohfeldian claim, as claims are defined by reference to the actions of the duty bearer. Therefore, interest theory argues that children are capable of holding rights if we understand rights as Hohfeldian claims held by an individual that pertain to a duty to either do or refrain from doing a particular action. The power to enforce this claim can be held by the right-holder or another designated entity. The claim-holder does not need to also hold this specific power.

By removing the requirement for both claim and power to be held by the right-holder, interest theory overcomes the problem faced by will theory of not being able to afford rights to incompetents (such as those that are in a coma or permanently disabled). In the example of a person who has been injured in a car crash and placed in a coma, this person will still retain rights over their property and their body; however, decisions to waive these rights (or indeed enforce them) may be made by a surrogate decision maker such as a family member holding an enduring power of attorney.

The idea that Hohfeldian incidents may be able to be exercised by a third party on behalf of a child has been an appealing one throughout the discourse on children's rights. Howard Cohen built upon the work of child liberationists during the 1970s to develop a theory of "borrowed capacities." Cohen differed from other liberationists by acknowledging and conceding that children have lesser capacities than adults; however, he argued that it is not true that these incapacities disqualified children from holding rights, as capacities can be "borrowed." Cohen argued that most adults do not have all capacities they need in order to exercise their own rights. For example, I have a right to a fair trial, but I do not have the legal knowledge or skills to ensure this myself; instead, I can engage a lawyer and "borrow" their legal capacities.[3]

Cohen, therefore, employs a different version of the arbitrariness argument. He argues that because all adults use and borrow capacities, any line which uses age to afford people rights from can be shown to be arbitrary.[4] On this argument, there is no real threshold at which one gains a sufficient set of capacities or competencies, and children should be able to "borrow" the capacities they need through a system of child "agents." Child agents could advise children with a view to ensuring that the child's right is properly exercised on the child's behalf. Yet, there are clear questions regarding Cohen's idea of "borrowing" capacities. Who are these advisors? What principles should guide the advisors—the opinions of the child or their best interest? Is the child free to not follow the advice the advisor gives? Archard provides a sustained critique of Cohen's theory. Cohen's position may pose problems, but it successfully challenges the idea of how capacity relates to rights.[5]

As I will examine in more detail below, there is a difference between the competence needed to realize the benefit of a claim and the competence to enforce or waive that claim. This distinction might mean that while we may be comfortable with adults holding the power to waive or enforce a claim, we may not be willing to go as far as Cohen suggests in entrusting and empowering third parties' control over children's rights.

Even without going as far as Cohen proposes, there are definite difficulties that arise when we recognize that the power to waive or enforce a child's right can be held by an adult on their behalf. Will theory rightly recognizes that having control over one's claim in this way is a powerful position to be in and, therefore, we must ensure that adults are entrusted with this act appropriately. However, these problems are not fatal to the conceptual ability for children to hold rights. They are questions of how the rights are implemented in practice. They call for consideration and proper thought both in private cases and in public policy making. I will consider some of these questions in the later part of this book.

As none of these objections are fatal to the conceptual premise of interest theory, it has been largely successful in overcoming the issues presented by will theory. In addition, interest theory can recognize rights that cannot be waived, such as the right not to be tortured. It is also clear that having choices can be in one's interests. From here, the conclusion drawn by interest theorists is that by shifting the focus of rights to interests, the argument from incompetence is overcome. Children can now hold rights unconstrained by concerns regarding competence or capacity.[6] Campbell concludes that a child's lack of development does not pose a problem for children holding rights. He argues that lack of development is really just a "superficial point of theory"; the incapacities of the child and the implications these have for protecting a right are really a political question.[7] Federle, too, despite her belief in its inadequacies, claims that "in this regard, the interest theory appears most promising to children's rights theorists because it proposes to resolve the problem of having a right without the present ability to exercise it."[8]

I argue, however, that interest theory has not accomplished this. A proper understanding of the relationship between competence and interest theory demonstrates that a child cannot hold a right without the present ability to exercise it. A child's developing capacities and competencies are not just a superficial point of theory. Interest theory may have shown that competence is unnecessary to qualify as the type of thing that could hold a right; it may still be necessary to realize a particular right.

Interests

In order to properly unpack this, it is useful to ask what exactly constitutes an interest. One has a claim or right not because one is capable of choice but because the claims make the claim-holder better off. Rights under interest theory are Hohfeldian incidents that are good for you.

I take an interest simply to mean something that is presumptively beneficial to the claim-holder.[9] The thin evaluative stance of interest theory assumes the basic distinction between beneficial and detrimental.[10] This is not to say that the boundaries of what constitutes presumptively beneficial are not controversial; there will always be (and rightly so) debate regarding the edges of what is beneficial. However, a controversial fringe does not logically preclude that such beneficial interests do exist.

Many have pointed out that one can have an interest in x without having a claim to x. In this category are third-party beneficiaries.[11,12] For example, I may have an interest in my husband getting a promotion at work as it will mean extra money coming into the household and may allow me to take time off to write. At first pass, it would seem that this situation has met the thin evaluative stance of interest theory; however, we are unlikely to argue that these types of interests would ground any claim on my part that would produce a duty held by my husband's boss to give him the promotion.[13]

The other objection raised against interest theory is the opposite statement that, in addition to not all interests being rights, not all rights are in the interest of the claim-holder. For example, I may have certain rights that result from a relationship or role that do not necessarily benefit me in any way. Wenar explains that to engage in this objection is to misunderstand the nature of interest theory. Interest theory is not in the business of stating that all rights are always in the interest of each individual right-holder; "rather, the interest theory holds that the function of rights is to promote rightholders' interests in the general sense."[14]

In response to these types of objections, Joseph Raz has further refined the understanding of interests when it comes to rights. For Raz, an interest alone is not sufficient to ground a claim; instead, the interest must be sufficient to justify its normative impact, that is, the corresponding duty imposed on the duty-holder. On this understanding, it is unlikely that my interest in having more money coming into the household would be sufficiently important to justify the normative imposition on my husband's boss, that is, the duty on him to give my husband the promotion.[15]

Even if one accepts these objections, it seems relatively uncontroversial that children do hold some interests that are of benefit to them that do not fall prey to the objection of third-party beneficiaries or claims that one does not have an interest in. Such uncontroversial interest may be a baby's interest in receiving adequate nutrition or a young child's interest in not being tortured. If we accept that children are beings that have interests, then a child (so far) can hold an interest theory right.

Realizing Interests

From this first step, the clearest way to identify the role competence plays in interest theory is by examining the different ways in which a right comes not to be fulfilled. Disregarding the intentional choice of the duty-holder to breach their duty or the choice of the right-holder to waive a duty, why would a right not be fulfilled? I identify four situations where this may be the case.

1. *External conditions affecting the duty-holder*: There may be times where a right cannot be fulfilled when the external environment precludes the duty-bearer from fulfilling their duty. For example, a government may wish to fulfill its duty to provide young children with adequate food and nutrition; however, the country suffers a debilitating drought. Although the government wishes to fulfill its duty, it is prevented from doing so.
2. *External conditions affecting the claim-holder*: Under this scenario, external factors may prevent a claim-holder from exercising their right. For example, I may have a right to drive my car that produces a duty in others not to interfere or prevent me from doing so. However, there may be external factors such as a shortage of petrol that prevents me from realizing this right even though no duty has been abrogated.
3. *Internal factors affecting the duty-holder*: A right cannot be fulfilled when the duty-holder does not have the competence to fulfill the duty. For example, we may state that children have a right to be loved by their parents; yet, a mother who suffers from severe postnatal depression may be incapable of loving her child.
4. *Internal factors affecting the claim-holder*: Under this scenario, a right cannot be fulfilled when the right-holder does not have the competence to realize it. For example, the claim that one has a right to work may produce a duty in the state to assist those who are unemployed to find employment. This would not hold for a newborn baby who lacks the competence to work at a job.

Do any or all of these extinguish the existence of the right, or do they simply point to its abrogation? The first two situations can be understood through reintroducing consideration of the concept of ableness set out earlier in this book. Ableness encompasses two parts: competence plus external resources. In the first situation, the government of the country may have the competence to deliver food to its child citizenry, as it has a bureaucracy for effective distribution. However, the existence of a drought deprives the government of the external resources and the opportunity to do so. Similarly, in situation two, I have the actual competence to drive my car but lack the external resources (i.e., petrol) and, therefore, the ableness to do so.

These types of situations present complicated and important questions for those concerned with the implementation of rights. However, as it is about external circumstances and does not address the issue currently at hand, that of the claim-holder's competence, I will not consider it further here. I do consider these types of cases relating to the need for external resources to support rights later in this book.

As we saw above, the claim-holder is able to realize the content of their claim when they have both the competence, as in the actual ability, and the ableness, as in the external resources and opportunity, to do so. By putting aside the necessity of external resources, we have singled out the requirement of competence. This reflects the conditional analysis set out in Chapter 4. The conditional analysis for competence states what when we hold fixed internal factors, S has the competence to A if, optimizing resources and opportunity, S would likely A is S tried to A.

The issue of competence becomes interesting again when we exclude the situations concerning external resources (as we would optimize external conditions in a conditional analysis) and further examine the third and fourth situations. The third and fourth situations demonstrate that the competence required to realize a claim is distinct from the previously discussed competence required to hold the power to waive or enforce that claim.

For example, I realize my claim to vote when I fill out the ballot paper. I enforce my claim to vote, however, when someone breaches their duty to allow me to vote and I take them to court. I waive my right to vote when I decide not to attend the polling booth. If the state legislates against me voting, I have lost my power to enforce or waive my claim, but not my competence to realize it. Therefore, the competence relating to the power to enforce or waive one's claims can be unrelated to the competence required to realize one's claim. As we have seen, interest theory allows the power to enforce a claim to reside outside the claim-holder; therefore, the competence to enforce or to waive is no longer necessary to hold a right. What interest theorists have not done is to demonstrate that the competence to realize the claim is also unnecessary for children.

The fourth situation identifies the type of cases when a right cannot be realized because of factors internal to the claim-holder themselves. In these types of situations, we may ask whether a claim actually exists at all. This is because to have a claim right under interest theory, one must have an interest that is presumptively beneficial to the claim-holder. If the prospective claim-holder does not have the competence to realize the benefit to which the claim pertains, the interest may not qualify as of sufficient importance to be protected. This draws upon Raz's argument that an interest must be sufficient to justify the normative imposition on others.[16]

To illustrate this, we can consider whether a blind man has a right to illumination. A blind man can have no interest in the lights being on so he can read the newspaper, whereas an able-sighted person may do. If we consider the thin evaluative stance of presumptively beneficial, the presence or absence of light can have neither benefit nor detriment to someone who cannot detect it. As the blind man cannot see, he cannot realize the benefit of the light and, therefore, can have no interest on which to ground a claim. Without the relevant competence of seeing, he has no right to illumination.

At this point, in order to avoid confusion, it is necessary to address the question of whether temporary incompetence indicates that a claim does not exist. For example, if I am temporarily incompetent and cannot walk down the street because I have broken my leg, I am still at liberty to do so, but it may be argued that my lack of competence means it is of insufficient importance to impose a duty on others, as I will not be able to realize the benefit to which the claim pertains.

However, one does not simply drop in and out of competence if one is not exercising this competence. On our conception of competence, to be competent at A is to have the capacity to A, as well as the successful exercise of using those capacities to A. Clearly, an agent is competent if they are A-ing successfully. However, competence does not have to necessarily be demonstrated to be present. But, if an agent can be deemed competent in A without actually doing A, what motivates us to say that they are competent? It seems that it would be difficult to distinguish between cases where an agent is competent at A and merely not A-ing, and cases where they cannot A at all. Yet, consider the Aristotelian distinction between the actuality of capacities.[17] Schellenberg describes it as follows:

> We can distinguish between an English speaker's innate capacity to speak a language, her capacity to speak English when she is sleeping (first actuality), and her capacity to speak English when she is talking English (second actuality). The distinction between first and second actuality is the distinction

between the developed capacity to do something and the execution of this doing... First actuality is not itself an activity, but only a capacity to act. Therefore, Aristotle understands it as a kind of potentiality.[18]

Translating Aristotle's actualities into our terminology, the agent is a competent English speaker on both accounts. This is demonstrated when the speaker actually speaks English (the second actuality). Regarding the first actuality, our account would say that as long as the speaker still has the right capacities and *could* speak English (successfully) if he were awake, he would remain competent. One's competence is not extinguished simply because one is not exercising it. We attribute competence to agents once they have demonstrated that they can consistently do the action in question, regardless of whether they are *currently* performing that action. Our piano player, for instance, was still competent at playing the piano even when there is no piano available to him.

In this sense, there is a distinction between a "material existence" and a "formal existence" of a right.[19] For example, if I have broken my leg and am temporarily unable to walk, my claim to walk down the street free from interference may still have formal existence in that it is still formally recognized in theory, but it does not have material existence, as it cannot currently be exercised. Therefore, temporary incompetence in exercising a right does not always preclude its existence.[20]

Let us return to consider an alternative example: assume I have a deep and intense interest in flying without the assistance of external mechanisms; it is of constant concern to me, and it occupies my thoughts day and night. The fulfillment of this would greatly enhance my intrinsic well-being. Flying without assistance seems, at first glance, to be presumptively beneficial to me and, therefore, in my interest. I also assert that this claim produces a positive duty in others to help me to realize it. However, we know that it is impossible for me to fly without assistance, because I lack not only the competence to currently achieve it but also the underlying capacities to ever be able to do so in the future. Furthermore, unlike the example of the blind man, to impose a duty on others to help me achieve my interest in flying is to impose a duty on others that they can never fulfill, a situation I will return to below. It, therefore, seems that the competence of the claim-holder to realize the benefit to which the claim pertains is extremely relevant to whether or not it constitutes a right. To return to our original example in situation four, a newborn cannot hold a right to gainful employment, because they lack the competence to work at a job and, therefore, cannot realize the benefit to which their claim pertains.

The impossibility of fulfilling one's duty leads us to the second important feature of an interest theory right. As we have seen according to Raz's version of interest theory, rights ground requirements for action in other people.[21] An interest, therefore, must be of sufficient importance to impose a duty on someone else. If we are protecting the right-holder's interests by imposing normative constraints on other people's Hohfeldian liberties, then these actions of constraint must be justified.[22] Furthermore, the constraints must be reasonable and achievable. It is not just the competence of the claim-holder that is relevant, but also the *cost* of fulfilling the duty imposed on the duty-holder.

Let us consider again the blind man's prospective right to illumination. Although the blind man lacks the competence to realize the benefit of the right, the correlative duty would still be possible to comply with. In other words, the potential duty is still achievable—for example, if we considered that the blind man did have an interest in illumination, perhaps based on considerations of treating blind people equally with seeing people, we could dictate that we must turn the light on for him and enforce this duty. Now, consider two people in a room, an able-sighted person who wishes to go to sleep and the blind man who wishes to keep the light on. The sleeper's liberty to sleep in the dark would be constrained by their duty to keep the light on for the blind man. The cost of the duty, in depriving the able-sighted person of their liberty to sleep in the dark, seems to outweigh the negligible benefits the blind man could derive from illumination. Therefore, the assessment that the blind man's interest in illumination is not of sufficient importance to impose a duty rests not only on the blind man's lack of competence to realize the interest, but also on the disproportionate costs imposed on the potential duty-holder's liberties.

Determining whether one holds a right under interest theory is, therefore, a balance between (a) determining whether the claim-holder has the competence to realize the benefit to which the claim pertains and (b) the cost to others of bearing the duty.

Figure 5.1 depicts the relationship between claims and interests. Circle 1 shows the interests one may hold. For an interest to fall into Circle 1, it must be presumptively beneficial and, therefore, the interest-holder must have the relevant competence to realize the benefit to which the claim pertains. There may be some of these interests that are presumptively beneficial, but, due to the cost imposed on others, it does not justify the normative imposition on the liberties of the potential duty-holder. My interest in flying without assistance falls into this category.

Circle 2 depicts claims that one may hold. There may be some claims, such as a property right claim to a useless broken computer that does not have a clear interest underpinning it. These claims may be grounded in other ways and, therefore, enforceable; we may choose not to call these

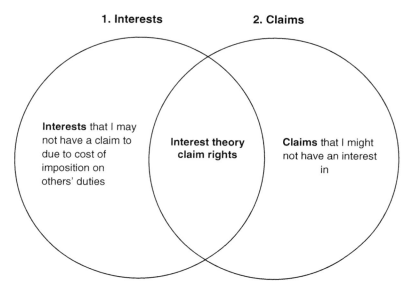

1. Interests   **2. Claims**

Interests that I may not have a claim to due to cost of imposition on others' duties

Interest theory claim rights

Claims that I might not have an interest in

Figure 5.1   The intersection of interests and claims

types of claims rights in the same way we refer to interest theory rights. The overlap of the two circles depicts what we think of as interest theory claim rights.

Depicting the rights in this way demonstrates how lacking some competences can put certain interests out of scope. However, it is not the case that there needs to be a clearly identifiable competence connected to an interest for it to be valid. Some interests held by people, including children, are clearly presumptively beneficial but do not have a clear competence that must reside in the interest-holder. For example, I might have an interest in bodily integrity and noninterference by other people with my body, but there is no clear competence that is related to this interest. The discussion regarding the relationship between competence, interests, and rights is not designed to be the defining feature of rights for children; it is simply an important part of the picture of how we understand rights to function.

Interest theory may have shown us that there is no conceptual need for competence in order to qualify as a right-holder. However, the theory necessitates that the right-holder have the competence to realize the right in order for the interest to be of sufficient importance to impose duties and restrict the liberties of others. This assessment is of particular relevance when considering whether children hold rights. In particular, it tells us two things:

1. The limited and evolving capacities and competencies of children of all ages do not preclude them from being recognized as a person capable of holding rights; however,
2. the evolving competencies of individual children are relevant to the question of which specific rights they hold.

Interest theory, thus understood, demonstrates that a child's capacities and competencies are an essential part of their rights claims. Therefore, a child only holds a right when they have the competence to realize the benefit to which the claim pertains.

Conceiving of the relationship between capacity, competency, and rights in this way lessens the importance of the distinction between child and adult in rights theory. In order to decide whether one can hold rights and which rights they have, it is not crucial to know whether one falls directly into the category of child or adult, but rather what interests, constrained by the competencies, that individual holds. This aligns to recent work on the enfranchisement of the child, as Lopez-Guerra has argued:

> A person ought to have the right to vote if she has this capacity in the minimum degree required for voting – that is, to the extent where she can understand what an election is about and complain for not being allowed to participate.[23]

Similarly, persons that do not have the required competency to vote "cannot suffer the harms of disfranchisement."[24] This point allows us to draw out the subtleties of rights for children. Let us return to the child liberationists and the argument about what types of rights children should hold. The argument of the child liberationists was that if we think of children as holding rights (which we must do if we accept that according to them age is an arbitrary and invalid marker), then they must hold the same types of rights as adults. Children under this understanding would hold the right to vote, a right to make decisions about their medical treatment, and rights to live independently out of home and to choose not to attend school. Understanding the role of competence allows us to refute these types of arguments. Although lacking competence in rational decision-making may not preclude a child from being the type of being that can hold rights, it may preclude them from holding some specific rights. Living independently out of home is a clear example of this. Children, especially very young children, are dependent on others to deliver the goods they need to live, such as shelter and food. A young baby is unable to produce food for its own survival; therefore, to talk about this baby having a right to live independently is nonsensical.

Latent Capacities

If this argument is correct, the type of rights one holds may change throughout one's lives as our competences change and develop. Not only are the types of rights children hold different from those adults hold, but rights differ between children at different ages, in different environments, with different needs, and with different interests. A six-year-old Aboriginal girl child living in remote Western Australia will have many of the same interests and, therefore, rights, as a 15-year-old boy living in the suburbs of Melbourne. However, it is also likely that, in addition to the overlapping interests and rights (such as a right to education, clean water, and health care), there will be a number of interests and claims that are distinct to these two individuals and their circumstances. For example, the 15-year-old boy's competence regarding rational decision-making may mean that he has a clear interest in taking a role in medical decisions regarding his health, while the six-year-old girl may have interests and claims grounded in her cultural heritage that produce duties in other people to protect her cultural rights.

The accrual of rights and competencies may not be a clear linear progression throughout one's life. An individual's competencies and interests may fluctuate throughout their life. This may, in turn, challenge the idea that there exists a static full set of rights for adults. Just as rights change for children as they gain or lose competencies, the same may be true for adults. On this account, the interest and rights held by older people may rightly be different from someone in their thirties.

However, children still present a distinct case from others with reduced competencies (such as the elderly and the mentally incapacitated) for two reasons. First, children are in a unique period of development. They acquire competencies at a rate unparalleled in other stages of life. Because of this rapid change, if we are not clear on exactly how competence interacts with rights, we are in very real danger of disenfranchising those who should be enfranchised. Second, as children are not in a static state of incompetence, unlike the mentally disabled, they may hold rights to develop competencies in the future, which will produce new and different duties. To put children in the same basket as animals, the mentally disabled, or the elderly, as many traditional liberal philosophers have done, is to overlook the differences in their state of being, a grave mistake that may be of detriment to members of all groups.

Once we recognize this, we can also begin to see the importance of latent capacities for the concept of children's rights. As outlined previously, latent capacities are those capacities one is yet to develop. The conditional analysis for latent capacities can be stated as

(Latent Cap—CA) S has the latent capacity to A if, optimizing all external conditions and mental states, S would likely develop into something that could A if, at that time, S tried to A.

An important question in considering this is, therefore, how latent capacities relate to rights. A child's latent capacities may mean that others have duties to assist in developing these capacities. Any comprehensive theory of rights for children needs to able to account for and protect not only the present interests of the child but also the future interests. For example, a child may not currently hold an interest in working as they lack the requisite capacity to have a job. This does not mean we do not hold duties to assist children develop their future capacity and interest in being employed. In Part II of this book, I consider the question of latent capacities and future interests in more detail when examining a number of case studies.

Conclusion

A clear understanding of these concepts—capacity, competence, and rights—and the relationship between them provides us with a solid framework, the necessary tools if you like, in order to properly tackle the contemporary challenges to children's rights, for example, how to translate these rights into a legislative regime, or to protect the future interests of the current child. The framework of rights presented above allows us to recognize children as right-holders, but still constrain the particular types of rights they hold according to their competencies.

I have argued that children are capable of holding rights, if we understand rights as Hohfeldian claims that pertain to a duty to either do or to refrain from doing a particular action. The power to enforce this action can be held by the right-holder or by another designated entity. Interest theory has successfully removed the conceptual impediments to children being right-holders by determining that it is not necessary to have the capacity to enforce a claim in order to hold a right. However, it has not shown that it is unnecessary to have the capacity to realize a claim. I have argued that one's competency to realize the interest to which the claim pertains is necessary for that claim to constitute a right and to justify the cost of the duty imposed on the liberties of others.

Understanding the relationship between competence and rights is necessary for the specific challenges the rights of children present us, such as their rights to develop future competencies. Part II of this book will apply this theory in a number of in-depth case studies to demonstrate how a solid understanding of *why* children have rights is important to formulating our response not only in our private relationship with children, but also in our actions as policy makers in government making decisions about children's lives.

Part II

Children's Rights in Practice

6

A Right to Develop

In thinking about how parents and society act toward children, we are more often than not concerned with protecting their future. This includes equipping children with the right skills and knowledge to live a fulfilled and happy life when they are adults. It also includes protecting children from actions that will "close off" or harm this future. For example, ensuring adequate child nutrition is not simply about the child's current state of hunger and health, but also about their future physical development. Laws about child labor are as much concerned with ensuring a child's opportunity to receive education for their future life as it is about their present experience of labor. These interrelated twin goals of developing capacities and protecting futures appear consistently throughout government policy and legislation regarding children.

However, within the tradition of rights theory, protecting the future of an individual in terms of rights has presented certain challenges. I have argued so far that children have rights because they have interests that are sufficiently important to justify imposing a duty on others. Interest theory works best when protecting clearly identifiable present interests. Children, however, are in a process of developing their interests. This may lead to situations where actions taken toward children may not necessarily harm their *present* interests but can certainly impact the interests they are likely to develop in the *future*. This is particularly a problem when we are discussing rights that depend upon a certain capacity or competence in the right-holder, in order for the right, and, therefore, interest, to be enjoyed.

In this chapter, I will first outline in more detail what I will call the "future interest" problem. The future interest problem is the question of how interest theory should characterize actions taken toward a child that can impact on the future interests, capacities, or rights of the adult that child will become. I argue that past discussion of the future interest problem is lacking in two ways. First, it mischaracterizes the temporal nature of the right by placing rights with the future adult and not the present child. Second, it frequently under-conceptualizes the nature of these rights, failing to answer *why* they deserve to be thought of as rights.

I argue, instead, that these types of future interest rights are held by children now, not by their future adult selves, and that this produces a present duty of noninterference in the child's development of capacities. This is because the interests to be protected are not *future* interests but *present* interests in the development of *future* capacities. I then consider whether this right can also ground a positive duty to assist in the development of these capacities and, in doing so, I examine the well-known case of cochlear implants for congenitally deaf children.

Although this chapter cannot provide a complete analysis of how *all* rights of this type may operate, the consideration of the cochlear implant case presents a useful framework and brings into focus some of the challenges in protecting the development of children's capacities and competencies through rights theory.

The Future Interest Problem

As I have argued in Part I of this book, interest theory holds that the function of a right is to further a right-holder's interests. These interests ground claims that produce duties in others to act or refrain from acting, if the interest is sufficiently important to justify the imposition on the liberties of others. Interest theory argues that it is not logically necessary for the power to enforce or waive a claim to reside within the right-holder themselves. Children, therefore, hold rights even if, in cognitive terms, they lack certain decision-making abilities, because they have interests sufficiently important to be worthy of protection. At the most basic level, children have an interest in living that produces duties in others not to kill them. Despite the fact that a young child may not be able to enforce these claims personally, they can be enforced by others on their behalf.

Yet, I have also argued that interest theory does not allow children to hold all rights that adults might possess. For many rights, an interest is only of sufficient importance to produce duties in others when the right-holder has the competence to realize the benefit to which that interest pertains. This is particularly true when the realization of that right involves autonomous action. For example, when the realization of a right involves rational decision-making, one may not be able to hold that right until one possesses the relevant competence. In this way, we constrain the rights of children so as to exclude decision-making activities such as voting. This manner of differential allocation of rights is grounded in the proposition that we cannot have a claim-right to things we have no competence to realize. That proposition is not just a feature of children's rights but of rights generally: as Singer points out, it seems unreasonable to argue that a man has a right to an abortion, as he lacks the capacity to ever become pregnant.[1]

The importance of capacity and competence in interest theory is, therefore, a problem for children as right-holders. Interest theory functions best when there is an identifiable present interest, and this entails that the interest is directly and presently applicable to the right-holder. Children, however, are not static in their capacities like most adults, but are in a constant process of developing them. As the growing literature on child development demonstrates, capacities such as literacy, intellect, and counterfactual reasoning are developing rapidly throughout childhood.[2] The United Nations Convention on the Rights of the Child also recognizes this feature: Article Five outlines that the exercise of a child's rights should be in close relation to their "evolving capacities" (CROC). Children, therefore, are constantly developing and evolving new capacities—their capacities are not static but fluid. This adds a temporal problem to this understanding of the interest theory of rights, which, so far, often relies on the present capacities and competencies an individual holds.

If children will have capacities in the future that they do not have now, it follows that they may have rights in the future that they do not have now. This may result in problems. For example, consider the case of a young prepubescent girl who has not yet developed the capacity to have children nor developed the secondary sex characteristics that lead to the enjoyment of sex.[3] According to the logic set out above, because she lacks the competence for bearing children and sexual enjoyment, she can have no legitimate interest in those activities and, therefore, lacking this interest, she can have no claim against interference by others that deprives her of them. At first, this may seem unproblematic. Why should she presently have a right to protect her nonexistent competence to have children? However, in the extreme case, does this mean that a young prepubescent girl has no right against genital cutting? Practices of female circumcision can certainly prevent women from ever developing the competence to enjoy sex, and the complications or infections that may arise from such practices can sometimes render women unable to conceive.[4] Of course, there may be other interests that the young girl presently holds that would generate a right not to be subjected to genital cutting, for example, the right to bodily integrity or the right to be free from pain and harm. However, it is not just these rights that we intuitively believe are being violated; it is also the deprivation of some *future* interest—that of having children or enjoying sex—that we believe is at play.

If rights are to be useful for children, we must be able to demonstrate how they protect the development of interests a child will have in the future. This is not isolated to what may be taken as extreme cases such as female genital cutting. Choices and actions are made toward children every day that impact on their future interests. Therefore, we are left with the question of how to account for future interests in the world of rights theory. Neatly stated: if an interest an individual may have in the future can be harmed by actions in the present, does that individual have a right to protect their future interests now?

Potential Solutions

This issue has not been completely ignored throughout rights theory. However, it may be the case that the problem of developing capacities and interests throughout the life of an individual has received little attention as it is less of an issue for the traditional liberal agent—the fully developed rational adult.[5]

The most influential account of the future interest problem has been Feinberg's article "The Child's Right to an Open Future."[6] Feinberg suggests that children hold "rights in trust" for their future interests. These rights in trust look like claim-rights to autonomous action but cannot be currently exercised by children as they lack the present capacity. According to the theoretical rights framework I have outlined, this would mean they were not actually rights at all. However, Feinberg says that these autonomy rights refer to rights that are to be *saved* for children until they are capable of exercising them and, therefore, need to be considered proper rights because violation or breach *now* could destroy the child's ability to realize their right in the future. As Feinberg explains,

> The violating conduct guarantees *now* that when the child is an autonomous adult, certain key options will already be closed to him.[7]

Feinberg calls these "anticipatory autonomy rights" as they ensure that the future autonomous adult will be able to choose freely. For example, Feinberg argues that an infant who is currently incapable of walking has a right in trust to walk freely down a public footpath. This produces a duty not to interfere with the child's future means of locomotion or, to put it crudely, not to cut off her legs.[8] What is supposedly special about these "rights in trust" is that they impose duties on others before the right-holder is capable of exercising the right herself. Therefore, for our purposes, the young prepubescent girl would hold a right in trust for her future fully sexual self. The right would protect her from any action, such as genital cutting, that could interfere with her future self's enjoyment of sexual and reproductive autonomy.

There are two main areas of concern with Feinberg's theory. First that the right lies with the future adult and second that is difficult to quantify what constitutes an "open" future. The construction of Feinberg's rights in trust for the future adult is problematic. In Feinberg's example of the child who cannot yet walk, what is actually being violated is the future adult-self's interest in being able to choose whether to walk down the street or not. Feinberg seems to be suggesting that since an infant will *develop* the capacity to walk down the street, this creates a right held in trust. In this, it appears that what Feinberg is really constructing is a right held in trust by the child-self in order to protect the future *liberties* of the adult-self. One has a Hohfeldian liberty to walk down the street; it is a Hohfeldian liberty that can be exercised or not according to the choice of the liberty-holder. For this reason, it appears what is being protected is not the future adult's right at all, but the future adult's ability to exercise a liberty protected by a right that is actually held by the child.

Not only does this construction seem to confuse the relative importance and difference between claim and liberty, but the interests of the present child seem completely absent. It is not important what the child has an interest in, only the future liberties of the adult. This again seems to be missing something we want to get at, namely that the present child has relevant interests too. The child is not just a vehicle for getting the autonomous self to adulthood but a person with interests and claims themselves. In the female genital cutting example, it is not just the future women's choice of whether to have children or not that we are concerned with protecting, but also the present girl's interest in developing. This seems to suggest that the future interest problem is not about *future* interests at all but present interests to develop capacities and competencies into the future.

Putting aside the temporal problem to do with the construction of these types of rights, even if we are willing to accept Feinberg's idea of rights in trust, there is still a further issue to do with how we conceptualize an "open future." If we are to take the idea of an "open future" seriously, we must determine exactly how open that future must be. Arneson and Shapiro interpret the "open future" as requiring individuals to acquire "to the greatest possible extent" the capacity to choose between "the widest possible variety of ways of life."[9] Archard and Mills, however, have argued that a truly open future is impossible to achieve but also undesirable.[10] First, how can one quantify everything that is possibly available to the child? And even if one could, some choices necessarily preclude others. For example, if a child were to become a professional ballet dancer, the physique required would preclude them from competing in a heavy weight boxing competition. The preparation and training it takes for either of these futures would also be incompatible; one only needs to look at the training hours of young athletes to see that it would be virtually impossible for them to also pursue careers as professional musicians. Life and the choices we make are path dependent. Therefore, it is impossible to keep options truly open in the way Arneson and Shapiro suggest. Furthermore, the duty to expose children to these options and to keep their futures "open" could produce unreasonable burdens on parents.[11] Yet, perhaps most importantly, is it really in a child's interest to have *all* possible futures open to them? It may be sufficient to say that a child has a right not to have *significant* life choices closed to them and that they have a right to *a* particular or possible future.[12] Claudia Mills raises a similar objection, arguing that what is really important for children is the meaning gained from an in-depth experience, not a shallow "smorgasbord" approach to all careers, religions, and futures on offer.[13] The problem, then, is that Feinberg does not tell us what this open future actually consists of, and why a child might have an interest in it. So, there is a problem not only with his analytical construction of the right but also in his specification of *why* it is a right.

Feinberg's work has been incredibly influential. Much of the work addressing the future interest problem concentrates on either directly critiquing Feinberg, propping up his position, or applying his theory to new cases, especially in the case of new reproductive technologies.[14] Yet, in contrast, John Eekelaar argues that the right should not lie with the future adult but with the current child. Eekelaar argues that all children

> should have an equal opportunity to maximise the resources available to them during their childhood (including inherent abilities) so as to minimise the degree to which they enter adult life affected by avoidable prejudices incurred during childhood.[15]

Children, in this argument, have a right that produces a duty on society (including their parents) to ensure that they are no worse off than most other children in their opportunities to realize their life chances.[16] These, he calls, "developmental rights." Eekelar's account seems to be far closer to the construction and sentiment we are trying to capture. However, it is still underdeveloped. For example, what counts as equal opportunity, what kind of duties does the right create, and what kind of interest grounds it? Although Eekelaar's account is on the right track, it needs to be further fleshed out in order to properly address the concerns raised earlier.

To sum up, although the future interests problem seems to be a real issue in the definition of what constitutes an interest sufficiently important to ground a right, the usual solution to such problems is to appeal to Feinberg's work. However, "rights in trust" are lacking as they place the interest and right with the future adult and not the current child, contrary to our intuitive understanding. Other discussions of this issue place the right appropriately in the hands of the child but, up to this point, have not been adequately conceptualized.

Reconciling Rights and Future Interests

In order to reconcile rights and future interests, I argue that children have an interest in developing the capacities that, if they were not interfered with, the children would normally develop. This places the interest correctly with the existing child and not with the future adult. I argue that a child has an interest in the *development* of capacities now, and that this interest, therefore, founds a claim that produces a duty in others not to interfere or prevent the present development. In order to overcome the future interests problem for children's rights, we must first show why the right belongs with children now and not with the future adult they will become, and second why it is that such construction should be a right. These two questions are inescapably interlinked and I will deal with these two concerns together in order to support my assertion of a child's right to develop capacities.

It may be worth more clearly articulating *why* we need to offer a reason for placing the right with the present child and not the future adult. There may be those that doubt whether this is really a problem we need to overcome. Archard claims that there is no difference between placing the interest with the current child or the future adult as arguably they are one and the same person. He argues, discounting the metaphysical issues posed by Parfit,[17] that child and adult are merely distinct temporal stages of a single individual. Child and adult have, thus, the same interest in development.[18]

This may be true, but only serves to displace the underlying question. When asking "why does a child have an interest in developing in the future?" we cannot simply answer—"for the same reason that adults do." This simply begs the bigger question as to why anyone, including a child or adult, has an interest in developing in the future.

I argue that the interest can be isolated in the following way. First, it seems uncontroversial that children (and adults) have an interest in *being* in the future, in at least *a* future state—that is to say, existing. Therefore, it cannot be true that we cannot have interests in future states. As stated earlier, at the most basic level, a child has an interest in life and, therefore, others have a duty not to end this life. It is true that some individuals may have lives so full of pain and suffering that they may consider nonexistence better than existence, and so have no interest in any future state at all. Yet, these individuals represent an exceptional case with a distinct theoretical literature.[19] In any case, the existence of such individuals does not falsify the proposition that one can presently have interests in future states. It is, therefore, conceptually possible to have interests not just in the present but also in the future.

Why then do children have interests in specific future states, such as being able to bear children? As Mills demonstrated, it cannot be that we have a right to *all* possible future states, as this would be unreasonable and undesirable. Instead, I argue that these rights exist on the following basis: children have an interest in being free from interference in developing core capacities.

Capacities and Competencies

Children have an interest in developing capacities and competencies due to their *potential* to develop. As I argued previously, capacity is a counterfactual ability. One has the capacity to A when one has all the relevant skills internal to that person to A. Competence, on the other hand, is one's *actual* ability to A. Competence is the capacity to A plus the relevant mental states (such as knowledge and intention) necessary for successfully doing A. There are also two additional identifiable concepts—latent capacities and ableness. Ableness refers to the competence of the agent plus external conditions to actually do the act. For example, a piano player may be competent in playing the piano but must actually have a piano present in order to do so. Latent capacities, however, consist of the capacity to develop a capacity. It is the acquisition of these latent capacities and capacities proper that set children apart. The relationship between these four concepts can be seen in Figure 6.1.

With this distinction of terms now in mind, let us consider the prepubescent girl's interest in developing the capacity and competence to bear children. The capacity to have children refers to the relevant skills internal to a person, such as the secondary sexual characteristics, fertile gametes, and a well-nourished body. One's competence to have children refers to knowledge and intention, in this case the knowledge that conceiving a child involved sexual intercourse.[20] Ableness to fall pregnant refers to external conditions such as the necessity of a willing, fertile man. Our prepubescent girl, therefore, lacks the *capacity* to have children in the strict sense, as

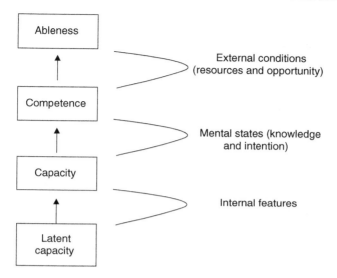

Figure 6.1 Relationship between ableness, competence, capacity, and latent capacity

she lacks the secondary sexual characteristics. However, unlike a man, for example, who also lacks the secondary sexual characteristics, our pre-pubescent girl has the primary sexual characteristics. She, therefore, has the capacity to develop the capacity to become pregnant. This second-order capacity we can call the "latent capacity."

Genital cutting can destroy the child's latent capacity to bear children. We can, therefore, say that the girl, by virtue of her latent capacities, has a present interest in being free from interference in these latent capacities and this produces a duty in others not to act in such a way that will destroy them. Furthermore, actions that interfere with the development of latent capacities into capacities proper would constitute a violation because it is a form of harming. Genital cutting is not simply an action that removes a capacity that a child has not developed yet, therefore, causing no detri-ment; it is an action that actively removes the child's latent capacity—their potential to develop the capacity to bear children or enjoy sex. By essen-tially keeping children in a state of childhood, one harms their interests by removing their potential to leave it.

Therefore, the young girl has a right to develop her capacity to bear children free from interference actions (such as genital cutting) from oth-ers. This is because she holds the latent capacity to acquire this capacity, and interference with this process of development would constitute harm.

At this point, the arguments laid out above present a case for why children have a present right to develop capacities that produce strong negative duties of noninterference. In the next section, I consider whether this can be extended to include positive duties such as assistance in developing capacities.

Positive Duties

The arguments laid out above seem to work well in cases where a child can be expected, all other things being equal, to develop the relevant capacity, such that the relevant right produces strong negative duties of noninterference. But does this type of claim-right also produce positive duties to assist in the development of certain capacities? In many cases, children are not going to develop certain capacities by themselves and, yet, we think they have some sort of claim to assistance in this development. Let us now complicate the picture of a simple negative right to develop capacities with a case that has received much attention in the area of children's rights—that of congenitally deaf children and cochlear implants.[21]

Consider a child who is born with congenital deafness. Such children have structural differences or damage to their inner ear usually caused by genetic factors and are unable to hear from birth. Congenitally deaf children not only are without the ability to hear, but often also have severe difficulties in learning written and spoken language.[22] Written and spoken language is essential for modern life, something that we may consider that children have a right to develop. However, it is not enough simply to impose a duty of noninterference with respect to those with congenital deafness, since they will not develop the capacity to hear, speak, and understand the spoken language unaided. In this case, the congenitally deaf child is most unfortunately cast into the same category as the turtle we discussed in Chapter 4, who lacks both the capacity and the competence to speak Russian. While lacking the underlying capacity to develop the capacity for hearing, the deaf child in this scenario holds no antecedent rights.

Yet, unlike the case of the turtle, congenitally deaf children can be given cochlear implant surgery that will allow them to hear. Studies show that cochlear implants given to children allow these children to develop the same level of spoken and written skill as other hearing children. The failure to give congenitally deaf children cochlear implants could then produce a future interest problem, as it is an omission that could interfere with the development of capacities in the future. Just as genital cutting may prevent girls from bearing children in the future, so does the failure to give a child cochlear implants irreversibly prevent them from fully participating in the written and spoken language. The difference is that while secondary sexual characteristics will develop on their own, for congenitally deaf children, hearing will not. Therefore, simple negative duties of noninterference are insufficient to guarantee the right.

It would be easy to leave the discussion here by concluding that future interests can produce only rights with concomitant duties of noninterference that are relatively easy to fulfill. Yet, this would be counterintuitive—it seems that so long as society is capable of assisting those with congenital deafness, it may be under a duty to do so. Why, then, do we have rights that ground not only noninterference with the development of our future capacities but also assistance in development of these capacities? We must show that children have an interest not only in retaining the latent capacities they already have, but also in acquiring capacities proper they would not develop unaided.

One option may be to adapt the work done by Norman Daniels on the importance of "normal human functioning" in healthcare allocation. Daniels argues that we have a duty to restore individuals to the level of "normal human functioning" or "species typical normal functioning" to guarantee equality of opportunity to access Rawlsian primary goods.[23] Normal human functioning or normal species functioning is a concept that originated in the field of biology, in particular through the work of Christopher Boorse.[24] Daniels adapted the concept to specifically mean "functioning that is exhibited by a majority of member of a species."[25] Daniels argues for the distribution of healthcare resources according to a baseline of functioning considered normal for the human species. He deals primarily with questions of distributive justice—what kind of healthcare services will exist in society, who will get them and on what basis?[26] However, his answers to these questions draw on some important principles about what we think is important in treating people, and these principles may be just as applicable in the context of rights theory. In fact, Daniels himself argues that his distributive justice theory of health care can be seen to support and properly sculpt right-claims, for such a theory would tell us which kinds of right-claims are legitimately viewed as rights. It would help us specify the scope and limits of justified right-claims.[27]

Therefore, by applying the concept of normal human functioning, we can argue that children have a right to core capacities that are essential to normal human functioning. This right produces duties of assistance in others to help children develop or acquire these capacities. Since the capacity to hear is essential to developing the competence to understand, speak, and write the written language, it can be considered a core capacity essential to normal human functioning. A child, therefore, has an interest in cochlear implants in order to acquire the core capacity for hearing. This is true despite the claim that congenitally deaf children lack the latent capacities to develop the capacity to hear unaided.

Critics have argued, however, that the normal human functioning approach focuses overly on *mode* of functioning and not functional *outcomes*.[28] For example, consider Hannah who has been born with partial upper arms. She can type with upper arm prostheses but finds them painful, so prefers to type with her feet. Critics claim that a normal human functioning approach would see normal as typing with one's upper arms and, therefore, seek to restore this rather than recognize the alternative functioning outcome of feet typing.[29] I do not think this is a fair criticism. I have used the concept of normal human functioning in terms of *capacities*. A right to a capacity does not impose any obligation to *use* that capacity. It may be correct that Hannah has the choice to feet type if she wishes; however, it may also be correct that if she chose otherwise then other people would, therefore, hold a duty to assist this. What becomes important is ensuring that right-holders have the core capacities to make the types of choices they wish about functioning and that they are not denied the capacity for normal human functioning.

Constraints on These Rights

One advantage of adopting a normal human functioning model for determining core capacities and rights is that we are now well placed to answer some of the challenges posed to the alternative model—Feinberg's right to an open future—that were introduced at the beginning of this chapter. The two criticisms leveled against a child's right to an open future were that a truly open future imposed unreasonable obligations on parents and the State, and that even if it were possible to ensure a truly open future, the outcome is probably undesirable.[30] I will deal with these two objections in turn.

Mills argues that the "inescapable finitude of life" renders it is impossible to truly keep our options open.[31] Even if we are able to approach this kind of openness, the type of duties it would impose on parents are simply unreasonable. It would necessitate taking children to all sorts of sporting activities, allowing them to learn several languages, several musical instruments, and even gain experience and knowledge of each spiritual tradition, something, she points out, all too many parents do try to attempt! This smorgasbord approach does indeed seem unreasonable and the reason lies with interest theory itself. An interest only constitutes a right when it is sufficiently important to impose duties on others. Although it may be true that if you speak both English and Spanish you may gain a benefit, it is easy to imagine that the additional benefit would decrease with each language one learns, since there are relatively few areas of human life that would actually be improved by such pan-linguism. Therefore, the benefit a child would get from being exposed to all of these things would simply not constitute an interest of sufficient importance to ground a right.

The normal human functioning model further narrows this requirement. This chapter has established a child's right to develop their latent and capacities proper. However, most of what Mills is concerned with in her objections are clearly competencies, not capacities. There is an argument to be made that in guaranteeing the development of certain latent capacities and capacities proper, an individual will be in the position to acquire and develop competencies as they choose. The normal human functioning model also tells us which capacities a child has a right to. These are clearly the capacities that allow the child to achieve normal human functioning; therefore, this type of right would not impose the type of unreasonable duties discussed by Mills. The right to the core capacities, however, must still have correlative duties that are reasonable and achievable. For some capacities, such as hearing, the duty (cochlear implant surgery) is achievable. For other capacities, we may not yet have the technology to assist in the same way. Furthermore, there may be many other capacities we would like a child to have but which do not fall within this core of normal human functioning. These might include the capacity to become a great leader, or the capacity to be creative and use one's imagination.[32] However, no matter how desirable we might consider these to be, we would not consider that a child has a right to them. Capacities that are impossible to achieve, or are not always clearly in the child's interest, or that would impose unreasonable duties, are not capacities that would ground rights.

The second objection listed by Mills was that a truly open future is undesirable because being exposed to this "smorgasbord" approach misses what is truly valuable about these experiences; the child would become a "Jack of all trades and Master of none."[33] As Raz points out, it is not about the number of choices one has, but the quality of these choices. It becomes clear by the capacity-based rights model offered above that what we are concerned with is not the number of options per se but one's ability to achieve any of these options in the most basic sense.

Therefore, by adopting a normal human functioning model to guide our judgment about what rights a child has, we impose certain constraints that neatly align with one of the core principles of interest theory—that the interests that ground rights are those sufficiently important to justify imposition of duties on others. There may be capacities that we would like children to have and competencies we would like them to develop or we might even see as beneficial to have. However, these are not necessarily rights if they are not sufficiently important to impose duties on others to guarantee them.[34]

The previous discussion concludes that children have a right to develop certain core capacities. This right produces a duty of noninterference in those capacities children will normally develop and also, in some cases, a positive duty of assistance. These capacities are in the child's interest to develop, due to their latent capacities and also the benefit of acquiring these capacities to achieve normal human functioning. However, if we are to hold this statement to be true in regards to congenitally deaf children and the cochlear implant case, we must address some further counterarguments.

Some Objections

The question about cochlear implants is not one of rights theory alone. There is a history of strong objection to cochlear implant surgery by those in the Deaf community.[35] These objections can broadly be broken into three issues: first, that Deaf people have an equally high quality of life as hearing people and, therefore, deafness is not a disability; second, that trying to "cure" Deaf people through cochlear implant surgery sends a strong message to society that their lives are less valuable; and finally that if Deafness is understood as culture and not as a disability, then Deaf parents have a right to bring up children in their own cultural tradition—that is, without cochlear implants.

Here, I am only going to deal with the first objection as this bears directly on the assumption that the capacity to hear is of benefit to children and, therefore, an interest that can ground claims. I do not deny that there may be genuine concerns arising from the second objection, which can be broadly called the argument from "Expressivism."[36] The concerns in the third objection deserve to be dealt with thoroughly elsewhere. The approach I take here gives us the answer that Deaf parents should not be able to refuse cochlear implants for their children. This argument is one based wholly on the consideration of a child's right to develop certain core capacities and does not consider cultural identity. There may be cultural considerations that override this capacity-based right. However, even the most ardent of advocates admit that there are "genuine and difficult" concerns regarding the rights of parents to choose a cultural identity for their children that may substantially reduce their opportunities.[37] The argument offered below is an account of one such concern.

Deafness as a Disability

Throughout the 1980s and 1990s, many Deaf communities began to argue that deafness should not be understood as a disability. They argued that those living within the Deaf community are not disadvantaged, that in fact they benefit from access to the community support. Davis writes,

> Deaf pride advocates point out that as Deaf people they lack the ability to hear, but they also have many positive gains: a cohesive community, a rich cultural heritage built around the various residential schools, a growing body of drama, poetry and other artistic traditions, and, of course, what makes all this possible, American Sign Language.[38]

The reporting of a good quality of life despite popular assumptions is not unique to Deaf people. There also exists a broader "disability paradox." The problems can be essentially stated as follows—why do many people with serious and persistent disabilities report that they experience a good or excellent quality of life when to most external observers these people seem to live an undesirable daily existence?[39] Albrecht and Devlieger's study reported how those facing severe disabilities had a high quality of life despite often lacking the capacities necessary for normal human functioning. Therefore, Deaf advocates argue, if Deaf people consistently report a high quality of life, applying the "normal human functioning" model gives a false standard of what is necessary to live a good life. Participating in Deaf culture is just as valuable.

In addition, many consider that any disadvantage that the Deaf community experiences is the product of an unaccommodating society. For example, the community in Martha's Vineyard, Massachusetts, has a high rate of hereditary deafness. In the late nineteenth century, one in every 155 people on the island were deaf, almost 20 times the average for similar-sized communities.[40] As a result, the majority of the community could speak American Sign Language, and Deaf people participated fully in all forms of political and social life. The Deaf communities claim that this example shows how "disability" disappears with social adjustment.[41] The proper approach should not be to "fix" the target of discrimination in society, but society itself. As Roslyn Rosen, President of the National Association of the Deaf, has stated,

> In our society everyone agrees that whites have an easier time than blacks. But do you think a black person would undergo operations to become white?[42]

It follows from this line of argument that congenitally deaf children do not need cochlear implants, but that they do need proper societal support.

Protecting Core Capacities

Essentially, the objection raised above argues that demonstrating that Deaf people have a high quality of life shows us that children do not have an interest in cochlear implant surgery to acquire a capacity to hear. In this final section, I argue that this is not the case; we can hold these two claims simultaneously—Deaf people have a high quality of life and children have an interest in acquiring the capacity to hear.

It may not be the case that our specific goals in life, whatever they may be, will always be achieved less readily if we fall short of normal human functioning. However, it is the case that achieving normal human functioning has a tendency to make our lives go better; at the very least, it provides us with the opportunity, the equality of access to our goals or, as Daniels puts it, to the Rawlsian primary goods. It is an unfair comparison to compare the individual as they would be as a hearing person and the individual as they would be as a non-hearing person. We can, however, compare the category of non-hearing people and the category of hearing people. Although non-hearing people may live self-reported high-quality lives, it still remains true that they face numerous challenges to their lives that hearing people do not face. The same applies for the broader disability paradox. The study by Albrecht and Devlieger demonstrates that those with a disability often adapt to their situation. However, this relative happiness is again asking the wrong question. It is not whether one can live a good life with the disability, but whether having a certain core capacity would be in a child's interest.

In addressing this, it becomes clear that we cannot *just* have a cultural understanding of deafness. *Even* if society were changed so it was even easier for Deaf people, those who could both sign and hear would still be at an advantage. When considering the Martha's Vineyard's argument, it is worth pointing out that at the time in the 19th century, the major industries for the island were farming and fishing, occupations where oral or written communication skills were not necessary for success. It is questionable whether such a seamless integration would be still possible today. It cannot be denied that competence in understanding, speaking, and writing the spoken language is an advantage in modern life and that the capacity to hear is essential to acquiring these competencies. Denial of cochlear implants to children may, therefore, constitute counterfactual harming. According to Feinberg, the counterfactual test harm exists if B's interest is in a worse condition than it would be had A not acted as he did.[43] It is even possible to *improve* B's condition while still counterfactually harming her. Suppose I go to see the doctor with a serious throat infection and, instead of prescribing me antibiotics, he sends me away with painkillers. The painkillers make me feel better but do not address the infection. By failing to prescribe me antibiotics, my doctor has adversely affected my interests even though I am better off from his actions than I would be had he not acted at all. Not allowing a child access to cochlear implant surgery can be seen as counterfactual harming in this sense. A child may be happy and healthy growing up deaf and using sign language, but their interests are still harmed by the loss of opportunity to acquire the core capacity of hearing.

Although, as was pointed out earlier, it is impossible to keep *all* options open for a child, this does not mean that talk of open or closed options or choices is completely meaningless when applied to individual cases. For example, choosing to give a child cochlear implants leaves open the options of (a) developing skills in the spoken language, (b) taking the implants out and choosing to be deaf once the child has reached the age that they can do so, and (c) learning sign language and participating in Deaf culture. Research does suggest that it may be more difficult to acquire competence in sign language while simultaneously learning spoken language, but it is not impossible.[44] This breadth of choice is considerably more "open" than those that would be available if cochlear implants surgery were not undertaken. Although the child will have access to Deaf culture as described above, without the implant it is highly unlikely that a deaf child will be able to learn the spoken and written language and that their ability to participate in majority society will be severely restricted.[45]

Despite individual stories and evidence that one can live a valuable life in the Deaf community, when considering the rights of the child, it is still in their interest to have the capacity to hear. Ensuring that children have the capacity still allows for the option of removing the cochlear implant later in life. Therefore, it seems possible to hold the two claims simultaneously, first that Deaf people have a high quality of life and second that it is in the interests of children to acquire the capacity to hear. This interest of children to acquire this core capacity should be taken into account when considering claims that Deaf parents have a right to bring their children up in their own cultural tradition.

Conclusion

This chapter has presented the future interests problem of children's rights. It examined the dominant solution to the problem—Feinberg's right to an open future—but found it insufficient. Such a right does not acknowledge the importance of the interests of the present child and fails to properly distinguish what constitutes an open future. The chapter then offered an alternative understanding of the future interests problem. I argued that it was not about *future* interests but about *present* interests in developing capacities. The right belongs to the child now, as children have an interest in developing their latent capacities. Others have a duty not to interfere or destroy a child's latent capacities.

I then examined whether the right not only had a correlated duty of noninterference but also had a duty to assist in the development of certain capacities. In doing so, I considered the controversial case of cochlear implant surgery for congenitally deaf children. I argued that children have a right to assistance of the development of their capacities, but not of all capacities. A useful way of determining which capacities are sufficiently important to constitute a right is the adoption of the normal human functioning model. Children, therefore, have rights to certain core capacities that allow them to achieve normal human functioning.

Finally, I considered some objections to my position on cochlear implants presented on behalf of the Deaf community. Although I cannot present a full analysis of the "deafness as culture" argument here, I have argued that the right to cochlear implants as established by a child's right to the acquisition of certain core capacities presents a compelling case. Any cultural objection will have to overcome this argument in a more substantial way in order to establish that Deaf parents have a justified power to bring their children up within a cultural identity that clearly restricts the development of core capacities. The difficulties presented in this chapter surrounding the cochlear implant case are indicative of the difficulties in protecting the capacities and futures of children. However, if there ever were a goal for rights, especially children's rights, this would seem to be it.

A Right to Know

On a Friday night, I go to a bar to meet a friend who has told me she has had a terrible week and needs to unwind.[1] When my friend arrives, she is wearing a very ugly dress; it accentuates all the wrong features and makes her look unattractive. After greeting me, she says "Do you like my dress? I just bought it today!" I smile, tell her she looks fantastic, and buy her a drink. In this, I *pretend* to like her outfit and *pretend* she looks good when in fact the truth is quite the opposite. Yet, in withholding the truth from her I have done her no harm, in fact I may have even done her some good. If I told her that she looked a wreck she may have sunk into further depression and failed to enjoy her night out; by choosing to tell her she looks fantastic I have spared her of the harm that may have resulted from learning the truth.

For many Australian parents of children conceived using donated gametes, this is a very persuasive logic.[2] If the child is never told that they were donor conceived then they are saved from any psychological damage, or "genealogical bewilderment," that may arise from the knowledge that the people that have raised them are not their genetic relations. No harm, no foul, right?[3] Why does a child have a right to know they are donor conceived if such knowledge will cause them harm and being separated from this knowledge will protect them from such harm? It seems that the no harm, no foul rule presents a strong argument against openness in cases such as these. In order to explain why a child has a right to know their genetic parents, we must not only show why it is important that a child, once knowing they are donor conceived, has access to information regarding their donor, but also show why it is important that children are told of the nature of their conception in the first place.

In this chapter, I will first give some background by briefly outlining the differing legislative positions across the States and Territories in Australia and highlighting the recommendation by the 2011 Australian Senate Legal and Constitutional Affairs References Committee report on Donor

Conception Practices in Australia (hereafter Senate Inquiry Report) for separate but uniform legislation across the country. The Senate Committee's recommendations, taken with the respective legislation of the States and Territories, indicate strong support for non-anonymous donation throughout Australia, based on a child's right to know their genetic parents.

I will then consider the three most commonly cited reasons for moving to a system of non-anonymous donation:[4]

1) that children have an interest in knowing their true medical and genetic history;
2) that children have an interest in knowing their genetic family in order to avoid concerns of consanguinity; and finally
3) that children who are aware that they are donor conceived suffer psychologically when they are denied information about their origins and identity.

An appeal to this third reason, arguably the most convincing of the three, is open to the response that children should, therefore, not be told about the nature of their conception at all. It is difficult to resolve this problem by referring to traditional ideas of harming.

Therefore, in order to support the position that children have a right to know their genetic parents, we must show that children have a right to be told of their genetic origins in the first place. I will explore two alternative arguments in support of this latter claim. First, nondisclosure generates strong risks for the donor-conceived child. Second, even if these risks could be mitigated, children have a right to be treated with respect, and truth-telling about information regarding one's life course is intimately tied up with respect for an individual's identity. I conclude that the second argument constitutes good cause for rejecting "no harm, no foul."

If the "no harm, no foul" principle does not hold, then Australian governments may have an obligation not only to allow access of donor-identifying information to donor-conceived individuals but also to ensure these individuals are informed of their status as right-holders in the first place. I argue that if a child's right to know their genetic parents does indeed imply a right to disclosure then governments may have to ensure or enforce this disclosure.

Australia and Anonymous Donor Conception

Donated gametes are sperm or eggs donated from a third party to produce a pregnancy through artificial reproductive technologies (ART). In ART, pregnancy is achieved by intracervical insemination or intrauterine insemination of donated sperm, or less commonly through in vitro fertilization (IVF) using donated sperm or eggs, or both. Sperm and egg donation can be done directly between individuals, but for the purposes of this discussion I will focus primarily on gamete donation facilitated through clinics. Preserving the anonymity of gamete donors in ART procedures in Australia was the norm until very recently. Secrecy and donor anonymity were initially considered essential for legal, social, and policy reasons; however, these once persuasive reasons have lost their resonance.

Legally, donor anonymity was necessary to allow the donor-conceived child to be properly seen as the legal child of the social parents.[5] Anonymity not only gave the social father rights over the child but also protected the donor from incurring any legal duties toward the child.[6] However, in the 1970s and 1980s legislation was enacted by all Australian States and Territories, protecting the legal status of children conceived by donor conception.[7] This removed the legal rationale for secrecy. A second reason for secrecy arose from negative public attitudes. Donors were viewed with suspicion, especially as donation involved masturbation. The close association in people's minds with eugenic practices, as well as the perceived shame of infertility, added to negative perceptions.[8] However, public attitudes have largely changed. Indeed, fertility technology is now seen as a treatment which couples have a right to access. The third and final argument for preserving anonymity claims that without anonymity to protect donors, rates of sperm and egg donation would drop, thereby denying many infertile couples access to treatment.[9] However, this argument too has lost resonance. In Sweden, the first country to move to an open system of gamete donation, donation rates initially slumped when anonymity was abolished in 1985, but they soon rose back to normal levels.[10] The Australian State of Victoria has seen a similar trend.[11] However, I will briefly return to this objection in more detail at the end of this chapter.

Just as the reasons to preserve anonymity have largely fallen away, the reasons *against* anonymity have grown stronger. There is now a community of adult donor-conceived individuals who argue that they have a right to know their genetic parents.[12] In response to the advocacy of donor-conceived individuals and the removal of countervailing considerations, in 1988 Victoria became the second jurisdiction in the world (following Sweden) and the first in Australia to adopt a non-anonymous system of gamete donation, whereby children were allowed access to the identity of their donors. Since then, many countries have adopted similar systems.[13]

Legislation in Australia Today

The current legislative position within Australia is characteristically fragmented. The regulatory framework of ART has been described as "a patchwork... lacking cohesion and order."[14] There is no Commonwealth legislation governing donor conception in Australia and there is considerable debate regarding whether the Commonwealth is constitutionally empowered to legislate in this area.[15] At present, each State and Territory has the legislative power to regulate gamete donation; however, only four states, Western Australia (WA), South Australia (SA), New South Wales (NSW), and Victoria (Vic), have done so. There remains no legislation in Tasmania (Tas), Queensland (Qld), the Northern Territory (NT), or the Australian Capital Territory (ACT).

Among the States that do have legislation, the approach and direction differ greatly. Victoria, WA, and NSW all recognize a child's right to know their genetic parents and do not allow clinics to accept anonymous gamete donations. Victoria and NSW allow donor-conceived individuals, aged 18 and over, to access identifying information regarding their donor by contacting the respective State registers. WA allows donor-conceived individuals aged 16 and above to access identifying information after they have completed compulsory counseling. Importantly, WA, Vic, and NSW explicitly interpret a child's right to know their genetic parents as encompassing a right to *identifying* information regarding their donor, and recognize a state responsibility to enable access to this identifying information. SA legislation does not explicitly state that a child has a right to know, though this is implicit within the requirement to adhere to the National Health & Medical Research Council (NHMRC) guidelines, which specify that "persons conceived using ART procedures are entitled to know their genetic parents"[16] SA has not, however, undertaken the responsibility for enabling access to this information through the establishment of a register.[17] At the moment, individuals must contact the clinic directly.

Although there exists no Commonwealth legislation, the Commonwealth still exerts some influence over the regulation of gamete donation within Australia. The NHMRC, Australia's leading statutory body on health and medical research, was established by Commonwealth legislation.[18] The *Prohibition of Human Cloning for Reproduction and the Regulation of Human Embryo Research Amendment Act* 2006 establishes that all clinics operating in States or Territories where no existing legislation exists must still comply with the NHMRC guidelines and the Fertility Society of Australia's Reproductive Technology Accreditation (RTAC) Code of Practice (2010) in order to obtain accreditation. ACT, NT, and QLD do not have legislation regulating donation, although they are subject to NHMRC Guidelines as indicated above. The NHMRC guidelines specify that "persons conceived using ART procedures are entitled to know their genetic parents"[19] Therefore, even where there is no explicit legislation it is implicit through the registration process that all children in Australia have a right to know their genetic parents. Significantly, in ACT, NT, and Qld, as in SA, it is left to the donor-conceived individual to identify and contact the correct clinic to obtain identifying information.

Australia is also a signatory to the United Nations Convention on the Rights of the Child (CROC), which has been invoked by theorists as a potential additional basis to support a child's right to know their genetic parents. Article Three, the primary guiding principle of the Convention, states that parties must act in the best interests of the child. Furthermore, Article seven states that children have a right to a name and nationality, and Article eight states that children have a right to the preservation of their identity. Yet, there is debate regarding whether CROC really can support a donor-conceived child's right to know their genetic parents. Blair argues that CROC does not support an unequivocal right of access, as the original intent of the drafters was not to encompass reproductive technologies.[20] Others have argued, however, that the combined force of articles within CROC provides a basis for such a right.

In February 2011, an inquiry by the Australian Senate's Constitutional and Legal Affairs Committee produced a set of recommendations that overwhelmingly supported legislation against anonymous donation and reiterated a child's right to know their genetic parents. However, the committee noted that the varied approaches between States with legislation and the lack of legislation in some jurisdictions were leading to confusion and in some instances breaches of the child's right to know.[21] It recommended separate but uniform legislation across all the jurisdictions, facilitated through the then named Standing Council of Attorneys General (SCAG).[22] It seems clear, then, that the Commonwealth Government will continue to support a system of non-anonymous gamete donation. A clear basis for non-anonymous donation needs to be established if Australia is to introduce uniform legislation. In order to clarify the duties that governments hold in protecting a child's right to know, we must be clear about the basis for this right. In the next section I identify the three main arguments that ground a child's right to know their genetic parents.

A Child's Right to Know

In order to properly understand the duties that lie with the State, we must identify why a child has a right to know their genetic parents. As argued in the first part of this book, the interest theory of rights allows children to be properly understood as right-holders. If a right is understood as a claim that is grounded in an interest, held by a claim-holder that is worthy of protection and, therefore, creates a duty in others. Therefore, we must identify what interest of the claim-holder (the donor-conceived child) is of such sufficient importance that it creates a duty to allow them access to identifying information about their genetic parents. In short, what interest grounds this right? In this section, I will consider the three main reasons cited in support of a child's right to know their genetic parents: the importance of genetic and medical history, the risk of consanguinity, and psychological harm.

Genetic and Medical History

People have an interest in accessing genetic and medical information about their genetic parents. It is in a child's interests to have knowledge of congenital diseases or traits that run in her (genetic) family. This is important for diagnosing and treating diseases, and also for making fully informed family-planning decisions.[23] False assumptions regarding one's medical history can lead to an individual being misdiagnosed, unknowingly forgoing important care, or undergoing unnecessary treatment.[24] This concern seems to constitute an interest worthy of protection.

However, even if this interest is of sufficient importance to ground a right, the duty it produces would not necessarily entail *knowing* one's donor. This interest can be protected without revealing identifying information about the donor. Indeed, information about the donor's medical and genetic history is already released to the families of most donor-conceived individuals before the treatment begins. Clinicians often consider that they have met reasonable demands about genetic histories by the careful screening of potential donors for a great variety of heritable diseases and characteristics.[25] For example, the Californian Cryobank provides a quarterly catalog of donors detailing information from blood type, medical history, hair color to the highest education level attained. In Australia, the social parents are allowed access to the medical and genetic history of the donor, while still being denied identifying information.[26] Even if this nonidentifying information had not been previously provided, or an unexpected situation arose whereby genetic testing of the donor was needed, this could be done without revealing the donor's identity.

So one's interest in genetic and medical history can ground a right to relevant *nonidentifying* information, but it is not clear why this interest would be sufficient to allow children access to *identifying* information, to *know* their genetic parents. This interest would be most appropriately protected by building more detailed donor profiles rather than revealing the donor's identity. The comprehensive genetic screening undertaken by clinics is usually far more detailed than an individual's own knowledge of their family health history.[27] Therefore, the child's claim to the genetic and medical history of their genetic parents cannot alone be the basis for identifying information about one's genetic parents.

Consanguinity

Many donor-conceived children are concerned about the risk of unknowingly forming a sexual relationship with their genetic half-sibling. Consanguineous relationships can increase the risk of serious genetic disease in resultant children.[28] If consanguineous couples do have children, they should undertake genetic counselling and screening, a process that most couples will only undertake if they are aware they are consanguineous. In addition, consanguinity may have adverse legal consequences. In Australia, the *Marriage Act* 1961 (Cth) states that marriage is void when it is between a half-brother and sister.[29] However, the chances of a consanguineous relationship occurring seem to be very low. In evidence given to the Australian Senate Inquiry, one witness stated, " ... there is no adjective which accurately describes just how tiny this chance really is."[30] Yet, this remains a real concern for donor-conceived individuals. As noted by another witness,

[i]t is not just the issue of consanguineous relationships, which are statistically unlikely; it is the psychological impact on the child who, for a fellow, will be wondering about every girl he sees, "Is she my half-sister?"[31]

Yet, if we take this as a legitimate interest, albeit one based in being psychologically secure rather than statistical importance, again there exist many ways to address this concern without providing donor-conceived children with the identity of their donor.

Currently, within Australia, there are limits to the number of families that may receive gametes from a single donor. In Western Australia and New South Wales, this limit is set at five families, in Victoria it is ten.[32] This restriction is designed to reduce the statistical possibility of individuals forming consanguineous relationships, although there has been some criticism about inconsistent enforcement of these limits.[33] Yet, even if limits on the number of families to whom donors can donate prove ineffective, other steps can be taken to address these concerns. In the United Kingdom, long before the removal of anonymity, donor-conceived individuals could contact the Human Fertilisation and Embryology Authority (HFEA) and request information about whether their prospective partner is a genetic relation. The Authority would then check the register and let the donor-conceived individual know without revealing the identity of the donor.

Given the statistical rarity of consanguineous relationships and the fact that they can be prevented by revealing nonidentifying information regarding the relation between two donor-conceived individuals, this interest does not seem sufficient to ground a right to access identifying information about one's genetic parents. It cannot ground a child's right to *know* their genetic parents.

Psychological Harm

The most persuasive basis for a child's right to know their genetic parents is that lack of access to identifying information about an individual's donor can lead to psychological harm. Most donor-conceived children report a feeling of loss of identity, and what has been termed "genealogical bewilderment" when they are not allowed access to identifying information regarding their genetic parents. For many donor-conceived children the importance of knowing their donor does not lie in issues of medical history or consanguinity, but rather in a deeper understanding of who they are and where they sit in the world in relation to others. One witness told the Australian Senate Inquiry,

> I cannot begin to describe how dehumanizing and powerless I am to know that the name and details about my biological father and my entire paternal family sit somewhere in a filing cabinet . . . with no means to access it. Information about own family, my roots, my identity.[34]

Another man, conceived by donated gametes in the 1970s, described the feelings and trauma he had lived with his whole life,

> After having children of my own and holding them in my arms, I came to realize what my conception had truly deprived me of. I had lost kinship, my heritage, my identity and my health history. This realization was crushing, depressing and immensely painful . . . the consequences of my conception had profound implications and affected me deeply without my even knowing it, and it is something that will negatively impact on me for the rest of my life. Every day I have to get up and look at a face in the mirror that I do not know. As a teenager, I struggled constantly with my sense of self and identity.[35]

In 1964, Sants demonstrated that adopted children may develop psychological difficulties regarding identity if information about their origin and details of their genetic parents were not made available.[36] Further studies have confirmed that for adoptees, not knowing their biological origins led to an incomplete sense of self which resulted in low self-esteem and a threat to their identity.[37] Many commentators argue that the findings arising from the study of adopted children apply equally to children conceived by donor gametes, and as we now have conclusive evidence of this harm we should work to prevent it occurring again.[38] Others, however, have disputed this claim. Shenfield and Turkmendag et al. maintain that the position of adopted children is dissimilar to donor-conceived children as adopted children are abandoned whereas donor-conceived children are *wanted* and are usually genetically related to one of their social parents.[39] Nevertheless, emerging research about the experiences of donor-conceived children supports the contrary view. The first study of adult donor-conceived individuals found a diversity of negative experience resulting from not knowing their genetic parents. Participants reported feelings of "genetic discontinuity," shock, deceit, mistrust of family, abandonment by donor and practitioners, frustration and loss due to lack of information.[40] Although their study is of a relatively small sample size and participants were recruited from donor support groups, the evidence is growing that access to identifying information regarding one's genetic parents is essential to a child's mental health.[41]

Unlike concerns about medical and genetic history or consanguinity, one's interest in being free from psychological harm cannot be remedied by nonidentifying information about the donor. The very harm arises from a lack of knowledge about the donor's identity. Providing identifying information will allow donor-conceived individuals the opportunity to place a name, a face, a person in a space that was once empty. It allows individuals the opportunity to contact and know their donor, to complete their family history, and to fulfill their own sense of identity. Many donor-conceived individuals, having been presented with the opportunity to contact their donor, have reported a sense of fulfillment, contentedness, and even enrichment in the new family relationships they have formed.[42] As Turner and Coyle reported, donor-conceived individuals expressed a

> need and a right to know who their donor fathers are and, if possible, to have some sort of relationship with them. It seems, therefore, that for these donor offspring, "non-identifying" information might not be sufficient to meet their identity needs.[43]

Therefore, the interest in being free from psychological harm seems to present the most convincing argument that an individual has a right not only to information about their donor's medical and genetic history, or about who they might be related to, but also to information about who their donor actually is.

"No Harm, No Foul"

Yet, if one's right to know one's genetic parents is grounded in an interest to be free from psychological harm, surely a more effective way to protect children from this harm is not to tell them about the nature of their conception at all. When one has *a* sense of identity and genetic history that seems to be so important for the psychology of an individual, does it matter that this genetic history and identity is false? Just as my friend may have a better night not knowing that she is wearing an ugly dress, a donor-conceived child may lead a better life not knowing that their social parents are not their genetic relations. The best way to protect an individual's right to be free from psychological harm seems to be not to tell them of the nature of their conception at all.

Indeed this seems to be the most common reaction from parents. Worldwide, disclosure rates are very low. It appears that legislating the child's right to know does not necessarily communicate the message to potential parents that they have an obligation to tell their child of their genetic origins. In the United Kingdom, where there is a legal right to access identifying information, only 5 percent of parents have informed their adolescent children about their genetic origins. Similar rates exist in Italy (0 percent), Spain (4 percent), and the Netherlands (23 percent).[44] These low rates are not necessarily due to the short time the legislation has been in force. Sweden's legislation was introduced in 1985, yet in 2000 still only 11 percent of parents had informed their children of the nature of their conception. A 2004 study indicated that by then 46 percent *intended* to tell; however, this still falls below a majority of parents.[45]

The option of keeping a child's genetic origins secret is often not available to parents of adopted children. Gamete donation, however, offers the opportunity of a pregnancy that appears to the child and to outsiders to be a product of natural conception.[46] Obviously, this is only true for heterosexual couples; same-sex couples must necessarily be open about the nature of the conception. Therefore, in the following I will be primarily concerned with heterosexual couples who choose to keep the involvement of donated gametes a secret.

Inadequacy of Arguments from Harm

It is difficult to refute the "no harm, no foul" principle by appealing to traditional ideas of harming. Not disclosing the nature of a child's conception does not seem to constitute harm to the child. Traditional notions of harming are most commonly expressed in the "harm principle," famously articulated by John Stuart Mill, holding that "the only purpose, for which power can be rightly exercised over any member of a civilized community against his will, is to prevent harm to others."[47] It follows that if no harm is caused to others by your actions, then you have no reason not to engage in that action.

What, then, is harm and how do we tell when it has been caused? According to Feinberg, harm must lead to some kind of adverse effect on its victim's *interests*—distinguishable components of a person's good or wellbeing.[48] To demonstrate the way in which harming works, Feinberg introduces the idea of an interest graph. To set back an interest is to reverse its course on the graph, to thwart an interest may be to stop its progress without necessarily putting it in reverse, and to impede an interest is to slow down its progress without necessarily stopping or reversing it.[49] For an action to constitute prima facie harm, it must satisfy the "worsening test," that B's interest is in a worse condition on the interest graph than it was before A acted.

Nondisclosure fails to satisfy the worsening test. Studies seem to indicate that donor-conceived children are not harmed when they are *not* told about the nature of their conception. Indeed, they might benefit from ignorance about the nature of their conception. In the comparative studies conducted by Golombok, four groups of children—conceived naturally, by donor insemination (DI), by IVF, and adopted—underwent standardized tests and observational procedures. The children conceived by donor conception were not told of the nature of their conception. The quality of the parent–child relationship in DI families, IVF families, and adoptive families emerged as *better* than in the control group of natural conception families.[50] This suggests that a child's interest in being free from psychological trauma would measure highly on the interest chart when they do not know the truth about their conception. Telling them of the truth would almost necessarily lead to a downward trend in this interest, whereas concealing the truth would allow the interest to continue, up or down, as it would if the child were naturally conceived.

Yet, not all harms are simple worsening harms—in order to show conclusively that the action is not harmful we must also show that it fails the "counterfactual test." The counterfactual test states that harm exists if B's interest is in a worse condition than it would be had A not acted as he did. To use Feinberg's example, suppose the hot favorite for the Miss America contest is detained on the eve of the competition, and that if she had competed she would certainly have won the prize of a million dollars. She is no worse off than she was before the detention, but she is much worse off than she would have been if she were not detained.[51] It is even possible to *improve* B's condition while counterfactually harming them. In the previous chapter, I discussed the case of a doctor prescribing painkillers which improve a patient's condition, but still harming the patient by negligently not prescribing antibiotics.

Is the child's interest in being free from psychological trauma worse off than it would have been if their parents decided to disclose the nature of their conception? As we have seen, knowledge of one's status of being a donor-conceived person often brings negative psychosocial consequences. However, we must acknowledge that this might not always be the case. Indeed, some donor-conceived children born to same-sex partners are well balanced and secure in their identity.[52] Yet, in the pure comparison between the two counterfactuals' respective positions on the interest chart, the position of the nondisclosure situation will still sit comfortably higher than the disclosure situation. We are comparing a harm-free existence to one where the child will inevitably have to deal with a difficult situation—even if some children deal with it relatively well. So the nondisclosure action fails the counterfactual test as well as the worsening test.

At this point, we must take time to address the objection that the definition of harm offered above is too narrow as it relies on harm being understood in experiential terms. Harms can occur when we are not aware of them.[53] Consider, for example, that my colleague's work is badly mistranslated into another language in a way that grossly misrepresents his views. This mistranslation causes damage to his reputation in another country, to the point that one university decides not to offer him a prestigious invitation. Even though my colleague is unaware of the mistranslation, the resulting damage to his reputation, or the lost opportunity, he has clearly been harmed as his interest in advancing his career has been set back. This constitutes a case of non-experiential harm. However, in our case of nondisclosure, the very harm we are trying to avoid is one that only arises from knowledge or awareness. Unlike the mistranslation case, which involves a clear setback in concrete interests, it is still unclear what interest is being set back when one is unaware of one's genetic origins. It cannot be that I am harmed when I am unaware of my genetic origins simply because I have an interest in being aware of my genetic origins—such an argument would attempt to pull the case for disclosure up by its bootstraps. Unlike the mistranslation case, we cannot identify an independent harm that exists without the child's knowledge.

If the right to know one's genetic parents is grounded solely in one's interest in being free from psychological harm, then the availability of the total nondisclosure option seems to render the right nugatory. Social parents may point to the "no harm, no foul" principle and argue that they can protect the child by keeping the nature of their conception a secret, rather than disclosing the donor's identity. So, while even though a child may have a legal right to access identifying information about their donor, they will not know that this information even exists unless they are first told by their parents that they are donor conceived. Therefore, in order to continue to support the notion that donor-conceived children have a right to know their genetic parents we must find some way to overcome the "no harm, no foul" principle and show that children also have a claim to be told the nature of their conception.

Risk of Harm and Respect

In this section, I present two arguments that may support the right to know, independently of traditional notions of harming. First is the argument that children have a claim to be told the truth because they have an interest in not being exposed to the *risk* of harm in nondisclosure; and second that disclosing the truth about the nature of the child's conception is a form of respectful behavior toward the child and that the child has an interest in being treated with respect.

Risk of Harm

The risk of harm, as opposed to harm itself, may offer a credible grounding for a child's interest in being told the truth about their genetic origins. The risk of a donor-conceived child finding out about their conception from someone else is quite high. In Golombok's study 89 percent of parents had not informed their child about the nature of their conception, but 53 percent had told other people.[54] A New Zealand study found that 75 percent of couples had informed others of the nature of the conception of their child.[55] Even when doctors and clinics had advised couples not to, most had told someone else.[56] Even if they are not directly told, donor-conceived children may pick up on signals caused by secrecy as they grow older.[57] Baran and Pannor reported that donor-conceived children often feel like they "do not fit in . . . because of differences in physical features, characteristics and talents."[58] Furthermore, McGee argues that as genetic technology becomes more advanced, genetic screening (which may inadvertently reveal paternity) will become more and more common, further increasing the risk of discovering the nature of one's conception.[59]

Not only is the risk of harm high, but the gravity of the potential harm increases as the child becomes older and is not told of their genetic origins. Children who are told early have neutral or positive responses.[60] In Australia, Johnson and Kane's research shows that people who are informed they are donor conceived from a young age have a clear and stable sense of self-identity.[61]

Many support groups recommend that, in order to reduce the risk of harm, children should not need to be "told" of their conception, rather they should simply always have known. They argue that children should grow up with this knowledge rather than being told in a way that makes it seem unusual. From a very early age, it can be woven into your child's understanding of who she is—even if you feel she is too young to understand. As mentioned earlier in this chapter, individuals who are told later in life are far more likely to report feelings of stress and psychological trauma.

We may (and do) prohibit risky behavior because of the high likelihood that harm will arise. For example, dangerous driving, such as speeding or running a red light, is usually harmless; yet, we prohibit this risky action in order to prevent potential harm. Similarly, we may say that nondisclosure is likely to cause harm later if the donor-conceived individual discovers the truth; therefore, we should prohibit nondisclosure. This may give us good reasons to engage in truth-telling behavior, but it does not explain why the donor-conceived individual has a *right* to know of the nature of their conception. For no individual has a right to be free from others' reckless driving unless that driving ultimately results in harm. If I am standing on the side of the road as a car speeds past me, I cannot impose a duty on that driver nor seek compensation from him because of the *risk* that he could have hit me.[62] The prohibition on dangerous driving does not ground rights in individuals nor is it based on their individual claims.

In fact, the prohibition on nondisclosure could be seen simply as a way of *mitigating* the risk of harm arising from finding out later in life. If so, then we must consider whether the risk could be mitigated in other ways. The risk argument is based on the assumption that there is a high likelihood that the child will find out. One response to this may be simply to try harder to ensure that the child never finds out. For example, one could require potential parents to sign a confidentiality agreement and attend counseling to ensure they are able to conceal any unwanted "signals." We could even ensure that clinics providing genetic screening for health purposes are prevented from revealing paternity issues that might also arise.

So while the risk of harm argument may provide strong moral imperatives to tell the truth, it seems insufficient to explain for why an individual has a valid claim to know the nature of their conception. And, perhaps most importantly, the risk of harm does not seem to properly capture what donor-conceived individuals themselves are expressing. Many people have said that even if they never found out they *still* think they had a right to know and that *still* somehow they would have been wronged. So in order to properly establish an individual's right to know the nature of their conception, we need a claim that exists even when there is *no* risk of the child being told.

Respect

The stories told by donor-conceived children place considerable emphasis on the element of deceit and lack of respect associated with nondisclosure. This seems to more closely reflect the wrong that donor-conceived individuals believe has been done even if they would never discover the deception. Children, therefore, may have a right to be told about their genetic origins not because of the potential harm of not telling, or the preventing of harm in not telling, but because deception of this nature constitutes a wrong in that it violates the respect owed to that child.

Consider the example of "pure" rape.[63] "Pure" rape is a case where a victim is raped but is not aware that it has happened: she may have been drugged at the time, is left with no physical injuries, and, because of her lack of knowledge of the act, suffers no psychological harm. In this case, is the act of rape wrong? Gardner and Shute argue that this in fact isolates the core wrong of rape, stripping it of the associated harms that usually accompany it.[64] Rape is wrong, according to them, because it involves treating the woman as something other than a person; it constitutes treating her as a thing.[65] Therefore, harmless acts can still be seen as wrongs. I believe the same is true for donor conception. By focusing on the case where the child does not know she is donor conceived, we can isolate the wrong without the distractions of collateral harms.

"Respect" captures this sense of "wrongness" that is independent of the consequences of the individual finding out about the nature of their conception. Respect is a mark of status owed to someone. Recognition of this value is expressed through behavior toward the subject of respect. Darwall identifies two types of respect: the first is "recognition respect" that is owed to members of a class simply and solely in virtue of their possession of some qualifying feature.[66] This kind of respect is of a fixed and determinate kind. The other form of respect, "appraisal respect," is respect that derives from a positive evaluation of persons or things by some standard. Importantly for our purposes, recognition respect restricts the type of morally permissible actions one can take toward the object of respect.[67]

It is recognition respect which is relevant to this argument; we owe the child respect not because of their life-achievements but because of their status as a subject worthy of respect. Truth-telling is a form of respectful behavior and, therefore, the individual child has a claim, based in respect, to know the truth about their conception. Some commentators have pointed out that children may not be due the same type of respect as adults.[68] This is because often the property that gives an individual the relevant status is that of autonomy or rational decision-making. Children, it is argued, do not have this property. In this sense, they are unable to form rational preferences and pursue them. Without this essential element of autonomy, children are not due recognition respect.

There are a number of responses to this objection. First, it may be that we owe respect not to the child, but to the adult that the child will become. In the previous chapter, I addressed the category of rights called "rights-in-trust" whereby the child holds rights in trust for the future adult, who will be a rational, autonomous agent. Under this argument, we may owe a duty to tell the truth of the nature of the conception to the child because this is a form of behavior respectful toward the autonomy of the adult they will develop into. There are a number of problems with constructing rights in trust, including metaphysical concerns regarding predictions of the autonomy of the future adult. However, one way to demonstrate that respect is owed to the child now, vis-à-vis the adult they will become, is to consider the case of a terminally ill child. Does a child who is going to die in five years have the same claim to be told the nature of their conception? It seems that a five-year-old child who is not told of their true genetic origins and who dies not knowing (and who was always going to die before becoming a fully autonomous agent) has been wronged in the same way as we think adult donor-conceived individuals have.

The wrong seems caught up somehow in the individual's identity. We need not insist that the essential property of respect is autonomy.[69] Although recognition respect is binary rather than scalar (unlike appraisal respect), the concept may admit different bases for recognition. For example, one can have recognition respect for the law by virtue of it being the law, or recognition respect for nature.[70] Recognition respect could also encompass respect for persons who hold their own identity. Children certainly form a sense of identity from a very early age. Children can understand that their social parents are important to them, who they are, and how they sit in relation to the rest of the world. Children in their middle childhood become increasingly aware of biology as an underlying characteristic of family relations and also rapidly begin to express greater curiosity about their origins.[71] For these reasons, children are due the same kind of respect as adults—as persons with a sense of identity. Failing to tell the truth about a child's genetic origins is, therefore, a morally impermissible action as it fails to respect that child's status as an identity-holding entity.

Two Claims—Two Legal Rights?

There are many reasons cited for why social parents should disclose the nature of the conception to the child: that the risk of later discovery remains, that family secrets are destructive, that secrecy reinforces the stigma of donor-assisted conception, and the previously examined medical and consanguinity concerns.[72] However, the most common and emotive reason is that a person simply has a right to know the truth about their conception and their biological parents. It may be far easier to construct a legal constraint around the broader non-rights-based reasons for ensuring disclosure, but organizations, politicians, and donor-conceived individuals themselves still come back to the right of the individual. While I acknowledge that those parallel tracks to outlawing nondisclosure may exist, I have sought to build a framework that does justice to the central right-claim. From the above analysis, it is clear that the child's right to know their genetic parents must be comprised of two distinct claims:

1) a child's right to be told about the nature of their conception based on their interest in being treated with respect; and
2) a child's right to access identifying information regarding their donor based on their interest in being free from psychological harm.

I will now examine whether these claims create only moral duties or whether they are sufficient to support legal prohibition on nondisclosure and legal entitlement to access identifying information.

The second claim is a strong claim with a solid basis in harm. There is a clear reason for legislating to protect this right and a clear legal tradition for legislating to protect from harm. The first claim, however, seems much weaker in two distinct ways. First, the concept of respect is not as solid as harm. Although I have offered a definition of respect, I have in no way offered a conclusive understanding of the concept. Respect is still based on something more intangible and, therefore, is harder to use it as a basis for legal regulation. Second, the claim to be treated with respect may create a moral duty in parents to be honest to their children; but is this really any different from other types of deception regarding paternity? Many children are not told the truth about the nature of their conception even when they are conceived naturally. Doctors conducting tissue typing for organ donation estimate that 5–20 percent of organ donors discover that they are genetically unrelated to the men believed to be their biological father.[73] Recent systematic review suggests that up to 9.6 percent of the naturally conceived population is unrelated to their presumed fathers.[74] Why then should we create a legal right to disclosure for children born by donor conception if we do not regulate truth-telling in other cases? If we, as a society, are content for the law not to interfere in the "marital infidelity" case, even though it is based on the same argument from respect, what further reasons support legislative interference in the donor conception case? I argue that the claim regarding donor conception can move from a weak moral claim into a strong legal right in three distinct ways.

First, the first claim to disclosure is necessary in order to protect and enable the second stronger claim to access of identifying information. As previously noted, one cannot know that one has a right to access identifying information about one's genetic parents unless one is first told that one was donor conceived. Therefore, the first weaker claim becomes a necessary part of the stronger second claim, for if we want to enable individuals to access their legislated right to identifying information then we must ensure that they are aware of the relevant facts.

Second, the first claim is also necessary to protect the previously mentioned concerns regarding medical and genetic history and consanguinity. Although these two concerns were inadequate to ground a right to identifying information, they may very well stand on their own, producing duties to gain access to genetic and medical nonidentifying information and nonidentifying information about one's siblings. Disclosure regarding the nature of one's conception is necessary to realize these additional interests. Not ensuring disclosure also infringes on the legislated rights of the donor themselves. In Victoria, the donor can approach the Victorian Assisted Reproductive Technology Authority (VARTA) requesting information about children resulting from their donated gametes. The Authority is required to contact the child for their consent to releasing the information. There is the possibility (given the high levels of nondisclosure) that the individual will not know of their genetic origins. Schneller notes " ... that this section of the Act is unworkable without the ability to ensure that parents inform their children of their DI conception."[75] In order to carry out its current obligations under the legislation, the State of Victoria has an interest, or even a responsibility, in ensuring disclosure takes place. In this sense, these additional interests of the child and of the donor act as parallel props for the claim that donor-conceived children have a right to be told the truth regarding the nature of their conception.

Finally, and perhaps most importantly, the claim is distinct and of greater significance than other children's claims to disclosure, because of the involvement of the State. Unlike the examples of private individuals who conceive a child and then conceal its paternity, the state is involved in the creation and conception of donor-conceived children. The Commonwealth provides funding for ART processes, including donor conception, through the Medicare scheme. Ten items are listed on the Medicare Benefits Schedule relating to ART, attracting a 75–85 percent rebate. Additional funding for ART procedures is provided through the Extended Medicare Safety Net (EMSN), which provides a rebate for those who incur out-of-pocket costs for out-of-hospital services. In addition to funding the practice, the States, Territories, and Commonwealth play an important role in regulating it through legislation and guidelines.

The State's involvement in the conception of these children may cause it to acquire duties toward them that it does not hold to children at large. This principle is not a new one. The Commonwealth has made two high-profile public apologies to children who were removed from their families, from Indigenous communities, or the United Kingdom, and relocated elsewhere in Australia. The State's involvement in these practices of removal produced special duties, which it was seen to have breached. Therefore, it may be that the State is complicit in the deception of children conceived using donated gametes through State-funded medical procedures conducted at State-regulated clinics if it does not take steps to ensure disclosure. This would arguably constitute unconscionable action by the State.

To return to an objection raised at the start of the chapter, in legislating a right, governments must also consider wider public policy considerations. Turkmendag et al. argue that legislating a child's right to know fails to take into account the rights of the would-be parents. The removal of anonymity, it is argued, causes a drastic drop in the rate of gamete donation, therefore, infringing on the would-be parent's right to conceive. This argument seems to have much resonance throughout the debate; however, it is unclear that there is any evidence supporting it. As mentioned previously, donation rates have risen again in Sweden and Victoria, but, furthermore, there is clear evidence that the rate of donations has *not* dropped in the United Kingdom since removing anonymity; in fact, the number of first-time donors has actually increased. Even if there was a shortage in gamete donations there is a strong argument that this outcome is more acceptable than knowingly creating individuals who will never be able to know their genetic parents and, therefore, subject to the psychological harm outlined earlier, especially when it is unclear on what basis would-be parents claim a right to procreate that creates a duty to assist in the process, rather than a duty simply not to interfere.

The combined force of these three arguments, but especially that of State involvement, demonstrates that a child's right to disclosure and a child's right to access not only creates moral duties in their social parents but also imposes two distinct duties on the State to use its legislative power. First, the State should ensure that donor-conceived children are aware of their status and nature of their conception; and second it should allow donor-conceived children access to identifying information regarding their donor. These would correspond to legal rights in each donor-conceived individual. It is important to recognize that the framing of the legal rights in this way does not mean that the state has a duty to ensure that the donor forms a relationship with the donor-conceived child. Once the child has access to the information, the State cannot force the donor to interact with the child. The law "may be able to destroy human relationships; but it does not have the power to compel them to develop."[76]

Finally, it is worth noting that just as the second right bolsters the strength of the first, the reverse is also true. If the second right, to know identifying information about one's donor, is based purely on harm, then does it cover a child's right to know the "true" identity of the donor? For example, a child may be told that they are donor conceived, and their donor may in fact be a famous mass-murderer. At the time he donated his sperm, the donor seemed a respectable young man but a few years later he was uncovered and sentenced to a life in prison in a very public trial. Clearly, telling the child the truth would harm them; is it, therefore, permissible in this case to lie? I argue not, because a child's right to be told the truth regarding the nature of their conception (grounded in respect) encompasses a right to be told the truth about the identity of their donor. So even though the right to identifying information regarding one's donor is primarily based in harm, it too is bolstered by the claim to be treated with respect.

Conclusion

In this chapter, I have argued that in order for a child to have a right to know their genetic parents we must first overcome the principle of "*no harm, no foul.*" This principle cannot be easily overcome by reference to traditional ideas of harm. However, I have argued that children should be informed of the nature of their conception, based on their right to be treated with respect. Truth-telling is a form of respectful behavior related to the importance of identity to an individual. Once we have shown that "no harm, no foul" does not apply, it follows that the child's *right* to know their genetic parents is comprised of two distinct claims: (1) the right to access identifying information regarding one's donor based on one's claim to be free from psychological harm arising from lack of access to identifying information; and (2) the right to be told about the nature of one's conception based on one's claim to respect as an identity-holding individual. The existence of this additional and separate claim to disclosure regarding the nature of one's conception produces new duties within the State. Unlike the case of other naturally conceived children, Australian governments are directly involved in the process of donor conception through legislation, regulation, and funding.

As it stands, no jurisdiction has legislated to compel parents to disclose the nature of their child's conception, nor taken steps to inform children independently. At the moment, clinics are under no direct guidelines to encourage parents to disclose the nature of the conception. If the State does not compel or encourage parents or clinics to disclose, and takes no steps to inform donor-conceived individuals directly, it may be viewed as complicit in the deception of these children. I argue that if "no harm, no foul" does not apply, the State must take steps to ensure that children are informed of the nature of their conception. It is unclear whether the Commonwealth has power to legislate in this area. Therefore, the best method to ensure disclosure seems to be to establish separate but uniform legislation through the process of the Law, Crime and Community Safety Council. There are many ways in which the States and Territories can ensure disclosure, such as annotating birth certificates, notifying the child directly, or mandating counseling to couples who receive State assistance. It is not in the scope of this chapter to examine which approach would be best—that is a project for future research—however, it is clear that a child's right to know their biological parents must encompass a right to be told about their genetic origins. A harmless action may yet still constitute a foul.

8

A Right to Medical Decision-Making

Jamie was born in Australia as a healthy boy but, since the age of two, began to identify as a girl. From very early on, at school, she was known as female, she dressed in girls' clothing, and her friends and family all treated her as if she were a girl. At the age of 11, Jamie began to experience the pubertal development of a 14-year-old and this caused her great distress as the prospect of developing facial hair and a deeper voice were contrary to who she felt she was. Cases such as these are not unusual. In 2011, Terry, who was aged 14 and born a girl, was taken to a hospital emergency department after his father noticed deep lacerations on Terry's chest. On further examination, it became apparent they were caused by Terry binding his breasts with electrical tape.[1] For both of these young adolescents, the Family Court of Australia authorized treatment of puberty-inhibiting drugs to prevent Jamie and Terry from going through puberty and experiencing further distress.[2]

In the previous chapter, I examined the future interests problem and a child's right to develop. I considered the question of whether Deaf adults should have the power to choose not to have their congenitally deaf children undertake cochlear implant surgery. Although this case is fraught in many ways, in one sense, it is clear—the decision for cochlear implant surgery must be made at a very young age in order to reap the benefits of the language "sensitive period." The young age of these children means they are incapable of participating in decision regarding their treatment. However, there are many other cases of medical intervention that do not happen so early and, therefore, must consider the agency of the child in the decision-making process.

The case of children such as Terry and Jamie is one such example. Clearly making a decision to stop the progression of puberty, and further deciding to change one's gender, is a significant decision. These types of cases raise important ethical questions of whether children or adolescents have the competence to make such decisions, and if so how should this be advanced in practice. It is cases such as these where we often see the realm of children's rights tested.

In this chapter, I provide a brief introduction to the ethics of medical decision-making and introduce some of the considerations that are at play when medical decisions are made for children. I, then, turn to the case of older children who are developing the competence to make rational decisions and examine how this developing competence is dealt with and respected. In order to demonstrate the difficulties of recognizing a child's developing right to participate in medical decision-making in practice, I examine whether children as young as 11 or 12 should be given puberty-inhibiting hormone treatment and whether they can ever truly understand and consent to such treatment. I conclude that it is cases such as these that bring out the complexities of how a child's competence interacts with the duty to protect their best interests.

The Ethics of Medical Decision-Making

When it comes to making decisions about medical treatment, or interventions with one's own body, most adults have two interrelated rights:[3]

1. a right to consent to medical treatment and
2. a right to refuse medical treatment.

These rights produce a duty in the medical practitioner not to progress with treatment (1) without seeking and confirming the consent of the patient and (2) if consent is withdrawn, the treatment is refused at any stage of the treatment. This claim on the part of the patient is based on their interest to have control over their own body and to determine the actions that are taken toward them.

In most countries, practitioners are required not just to seek consent *simpliciter* but to gain *informed* consent from the patient for the particular course of treatment.[4] Informed consent requires that the patient has all of the information necessary to make a sound decision and fully understand the consequences of their decision. Consider, for example, if I offer you a chocolate from a large chocolate tin, all I ask you is "would you like a chocolate?" and you take a chocolate happily. However, what I have not told you is that the tin of chocolates does not belong to me; it belongs to my colleague who is fundraising for their child's football camp. By taking and eating the chocolate, you now owe my colleague money for the chocolate. We would say that in this situation, your agreement to take the chocolate was consent *simpliciter*, but it was not informed consent, as you did not have access to all of the information relevant to make the decision. Indeed, if you had known that you had to pay for the chocolate, you may have chosen not to have it. Informed consent in medical decision-making works in much the same way. Patients should be informed of and understand all the known risks and consequences of a particular treatment and be able to make a decision to consent on the basis of this information.

Models of informed consent for adults presume that the patient is autonomous and has a stable sense of self, established values, and mature cognitive skills.[5] As discussed in previous chapters, very young children lack rational decision-making competence and, therefore, cannot have an interest in making the decision themselves. Decisions for very young children must, therefore, be made for them. In cases of medical treatment, the parents of the child hold the power to consent to medical treatment on behalf of the child.

When children are deemed incompetent, parents or guardians usually hold the role of surrogate decision maker. It has become common practice that the guiding principle when making medical decisions for children (indeed, many other types of decisions as well) is the best interest principle.[6] The principle of acting in the best interests of the child is enshrined in Article Three of the United Nations Convention on the Rights of the Child. The principle is designed to ensure that decision-making for children is not captured by the interests of others (such as the parents and the State) but undertaken from a child-centered point of view. The concept of the child's best interests, according to the UN Committee on the Rights of the Children, is threefold:

1. a substantive right to have his or her best interests assessed and taken as a primary consideration when different interests are being considered;
2. a fundamental, interpretive legal principle to guide legal matters that are open to more than one interpretation; and
3. a rule of procedure whereby the decision-making process must include an evaluation of the possible impact (positive or negative) of the decision on the child or children concerned.[7]

It is important to note that sometimes it is believed that the best interests principle will fall prey to the problem of maximizing the interests at the expense of others. This sees the best interest principle treated "as a literal and absolute commandment rather than a guiding principle."[8] As has been discussed previously, to maximize all of a child's possible interests would be near impossible and would impose unreasonable demands and duties on others that would in turn violate and limit their interests. It is not the case that once having a child, a parent's own interests, claims, and therefore rights are completely subsumed by the interests of their children.

Surrogate decision-making is not particular to young children; there are many individuals in society who are deemed incompetent to make decisions regarding medical treatment and for whom decisions need to be made on their behalf. These individuals include not only the severely mentally impaired (both adults and children) but also adults who were once competent and may now be in an incompetent state (such as the elderly, those with brain injuries or severe psychological dysfunction). The reason that surrogate decision-making for children is different from that of adults is because unlike previously competent adults, children do not have previously clearly articulated values and goals that can guide the decisions that others make for them.[9] For this reason, Buchanan and Brock argue that for incompetents who have never been competent, the best interests principle should be the primary guiding principle, rather than that of substituted judgment.[10]

While medical treatment decision-making for very young children holds many ethical questions, I wish to concentrate below on the case of slightly older children and adolescents who are beginning to acquire the competence to understand complex medical treatments and may be developing the competence to participate in decision-making about their health care. It is these cases where we can begin to unpick and further understand the complex nature of competence and rights.

Older Children and Adolescents

As children grow older, they begin to develop decision-making skills, the ability to reason and use complex concepts, the ability to imagine a future for themselves,[11] and consequently an understanding of death.[12] As these competencies develop, we can see that children will begin to acquire a matching interest in being involved in their medical treatment. This may particularly be the case for treatment of serious conditions and those that may have lasting consequences for their future lives, or be life-threatening.

However, as I have previously argued each individual is different, two children of the same age will not necessarily have the same competence to make choices. The development of this competence can depend on many factors, such as one's experience making decisions. Research shows that for young children, experience making decisions about simple matters facilitates the development of more sophisticated competence when making complex decisions.[13] It should come as no surprise that a young child who has been made homeless and encountered many situations where they needed to make difficult decisions in order to secure food and shelter will often be a more experienced decision maker, and better understand the potentially serious consequences of their decisions, than a child of a similar age who has always had all aspects of their life provided for them.

In fact, many adolescents have the decision-making of an adult.[14] This might include the ability to think and choose with a degree of independence, the ability to understand and communicate relevant information, and the ability to assess the potential for benefit, risks, or harms, and to consider the consequences and multiple options. Despite the fact that many adolescents have a developing competence in decision-making or indeed the equivalent competence of an adult, it is the case in most jurisdictions that children under the age of 16 are not judged competent to consent to medical treatment and instead the medical practitioner requires the consent of their parents.

When assessing the rights of children under the age of 16, the defining case is *Gillick vs West Norfolk and Wisbech Area Health*, which established the now widely used "Gillick competence."[15] The House of Lords' decision involved a mother of five girls challenging a circular issued by the Department of Health and Social Services in England, which authorized doctors to give contraceptive advice and treatment to girls under the age of 16 without their parents' consent. In this case, the question was whether children under the age of 16 are competent to consent to medical treatment such as the oral contraceptive pill. The Court found that

> As a matter of law the parental right to determine whether or not their minor child below the age of 16 will have medical treatment terminates if and when the child achieves a sufficient understanding and intelligence to enable him or her to understand fully what is proposed[16]

This established a principle, which is now widely accepted, that below the age of 16, a child can consent to medical treatment, without the consent of their parents, if they can demonstrate sufficient understanding and competence to make independent rational decisions. How this principle bears out in practice may be a different kettle of fish.[17] Indeed, in practice, it is not only the child's competence that is relevant to the assessment of whether a child has the right to consent to or refuse medical treatment; other considerations such as well-being must also be taken into account.

This balance between competence and well-being is articulated by Buchanan and Brock who argue that when setting a standard of competence in decision-making for children, we must balance three principles:

1. protecting the child's well-being;
2. respecting his or her self determination; and
3. honoring legitimate parental authority.

Accordingly, they argue that this demonstrates that we need a variable standard of competence for children.[18] By talking about a compromise and a balance, Buchanan and Brock are rejecting the two extremes of decision-making:

1. Minimally paternalistic stance where children only need to express a preference and this is sufficient to base a decision on. This stance fails to provide protection for the child's well-being and against harmful consequences of their reduced decision-making competence.
2. Objective stance where one can examine the situation and come up with an objective answer to what is in the child's best interests. This stance fails to acknowledge the emerging competence and distinctive conception of the good that children may hold.[19]

According to Buchanan and Brock, "there is no reason to believe there is one and only one objectively correct trade off to be struck between these competing values, even for a particular decision under specified circumstances."[20] Determining the proper trade-off, they argue, goes beyond an empirical investigation into a child's decision-making competence.[21] In this sense, when they speak of variable competence, they are drawing our attention to the balance between the importance of the interest (the benefit or harm that making the decision may result in) of the child's competence to make the decision and whether their interest in making the decision themselves is sufficient to override other interests.

At this point, it is useful to draw out the distinction between assent and consent, in order to demonstrate how in practice this balance is usually made. Consent is when one holds the decision-making authority, that is, the claim to make the decision that produces a duty on others to abide by this decision. Assent, however, is where the child agrees with the decision but lacks the claim to make the enforceable decision. I think that what Buchanan and Brock are actually talking about when they refer to "variable competence" is not competence in the sense that I have discussed in Part I, as in an actual *ability* to make decisions, but instead the *authority* to make decisions. You may recall that, in Chapter 3, I identified the distinction made by rights theorists between factual competence and legal competence. A child may be factually competent to make a decision but the law may not recognize her as such. In this sense, she lacks the legal competence. Assent is usually given when the child lacks the legal competence but respect is still being shown to the factual competence of the child.

However, in many cases, it may be that the actual factual competence to consent is never assessed if simple assent from the child patient is given up front. Competence is only assessed if assent is not given in the first instance. Medical decision-making for children has sometimes been described as a triadic relationship between child, physician, and parents.[22] The type of decision-making path that may occur is described in Figure 8.1.

As can be seen above, in many circumstances, if the child, parents, and physician all agree on the recommended treatment, then the assessment of a child's competence is skipped over altogether. Assessment of competence such as the standard laid out by *Gillick* may only be taken in situations where the child dissents.

In addition, it has been noted that, currently, circumstances where it is routine for a minor to consent to medical treatment without the consent of their parents do not seem to be based on any detailed analysis of the child's competence, but rather a policy decision that requiring parental consent would discourage children from seeking such treatment that is seen as prima facie beneficial, such as drug rehabilitation or contraception.[23] These are often the more high-risk situations. It is interesting to observe that these

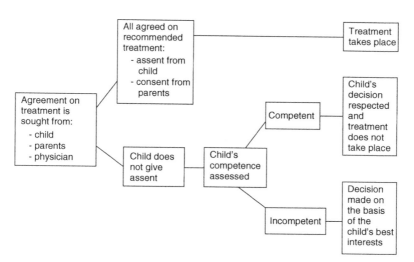

Figure 8.1   Decision-making pathway with child, parents, and physician

types of big choices are ones we think minors can make alone, but for a routine treatment such as getting your wisdom teeth removed, a young person under the age of 16 needs parental consent. It is clear why *Gillick* is a guiding principle: it is only a guiding principle when we think it counts, not for routine matters in the day-to-day life of children. Assessment of competence to see whether the child has a claim to make the decision without parental authority may not be as common as we would like to think it should be.

In order to draw out the complexities of these types of cases, I am going to consider the question of whether children under the age of 16 should be given puberty-inhibiting drugs and whether they have the competence to consent to such a decision.

Gender Dysphoria

Adolescents and children are applying for hormone therapy treatment at increasingly younger ages[24] and in increasing numbers.[25] As mentioned at the beginning of this chapter, there have been a number of recent cases where the Australian Family Court has granted permission for young children to begin puberty-inhibiting treatment.[26] It is believed that this increase is due to improved awareness of medical services available for children expressing a desire to change genders, rather than any increase in the incidence of the condition itself.[27] These children are generally described as having gender dysphoria.

Gender dysphoria is a condition where individuals experience their gender identity as being incongruent with their biological gender.[28] Those experiencing gender dysphoria express this desire in varying degrees from early childhood onwards.[29] This includes displaying characteristic behaviors of the opposite gender such as choosing different modes of dress, rejecting the types of games traditionally associated with their gender, and embracing the social norms and roles of the opposite gender. They often express a desire to have the genitalia of the opposite gender or assert they already have them. Desires and behaviors such as these begin well before puberty, and indeed in many cases, such as that of Jamie mentioned at the start of this chapter, they begin as early as two years of age.

It is worth noting at this stage that there is debate around this type of terminology. Many believe we should not regard children who express a preference to be identified as the other gender as having any type of "condition" as this pathologizes children. Instead, it is argued that this should be considered a variant of gender or sexuality.[30] I, like others, have sympathy for this position and agree that an overreliance on clinical diagnoses fails to acknowledge the other aspects of a person's life that are associated with their gender and sexual identity. However, my concern in this chapter is regarding the medical intervention that can assist to relieve some of the stress and anxiety in a person's life. Whether we choose to describe these experiences as gender dysphoria or sexual and gender variance, it remains true that the primary course of action for those that experience extreme stress and anxiety regarding their biological identity is a medical intervention. Therefore, I use the term gender dysphoria throughout the chapter when discussing the types of decisions being made about, and with, children in a medical context. I note that there is a broader context in which these individuals need to make decisions about their lives outside the medical sphere where the term "dysphoria" might not be as relevant.[31]

The use of the terms "Gender Identity Disorder" and "Gender Dysphoria" may also be prevalent because it is uncommon to refer to children experiencing these types of desires as transsexual; this term is often reserved for those of an older age. It is important to recognize that many of the children who display these types of behaviors associated with gender dysphoria will not grow up to be transsexuals. Some may be homosexual and some may choose to reject gender altogether. The Dutch experience, where most of the research into gender dysphoria in children has taken place, tells us that 80–95 percent of the prepubertal children with what was then called Gender Identity Disorder no longer experience it in adulthood.[32] Other studies state that only a quarter of children with gender dysphoria under the age of 12 will become transsexual adults.[33]

There is little agreement about the explanation for why some children and adolescents experience gender dysphoria. Research has shown that there are often multiple factors at play including psychological, biological, familial, and sociocultural ones.[34] There is some suggestion in two recent twin association studies that there is a heritable component.[35] However, what is clear is that gender dysphoria cannot be managed by external influences alone. Attempts at so-called "re-education," even when these attempts are begun as early as the first year of life, do not work.[36]

Along with displaying characteristics of the opposite gender and desiring to live as the opposite gender, those individuals with gender dysphoria also suffer from emotional and behavioral problems as well as a high rate of psychiatric comorbidity.[37] It has been pointed out that many of the problems these young people struggle with are the consequences, not the cause, of their gender dysphoria.[38]

Therefore, the search for treatment for these individuals is often urgent. Young people facing this type of distress cut themselves, threaten to cut, or remove their genitalia and are at risk of suicide. But, to add to the uncertainty and debate regarding the causation of gender dysphoria, there is also debate regarding the appropriate course of treatment characterized by reluctance and discomfort. For many years, the view held by clinicians was that this was something that warranted no treatment at all. For example, one clinician stated that he found it hard to understand how the belief of a man, "that he is a woman trapped in a man's body, differs from the feelings of a patient with anorexia nervosa that she is obese despite her emaciated cachetic state. We don't do liposuction on anorexics. So why amputate the genitals of these patients."[39] In the following section, I will set out the debate regarding treatment for individuals experiencing gender dysphoria and will draw out the issues regarding whether children have the competence to consent to this type of treatment.

Conservative "Wait and See" Stance

The traditional response in many countries, up until fairly recently, has been for clinicians to recommend that the child wait until they are old enough to legally make their own decision regarding treatment.[40] By waiting, clinicians argue that they avoid the ethical questions regarding whether a child has the competence to make the decision themselves or whether parents or clinicians can ever successfully make such a decision on the child's behalf.

Indeed, waiting until the child can choose for themselves would be a sound argument in many other cases. For example, it used to be the case that on the birth of a baby with abnormal genitalia (such as a micro penis or an enlarged clitoris), doctors would recommend surgery so that the child could live life as a "normal" child of either gender. In a famous case of twin boys,[41] a routine circumcision operation went horribly wrong and permanently damaged the penis of one of the children. It was decided that the boy should undergo surgery to remove what was left of his penis and his testicles and be raised as a girl. The case and the published results were lauded as proof that gender is malleable and socially constructed.[42] However, on subsequent follow-up by other researchers years later, it was discovered that the child had always felt uneasy as a girl and had now decided to live life as a man, undergone penile reconstruction surgery, and was happily married.[43] Indeed, this was the case with many other individuals who had undergone similar reassignment surgery when very young.[44] These stories would point to caution, as making the choice for the child before they were capable of doing so themselves led to the wrong choice being made.

As stated earlier, longitudinal studies show us that the type of experiences and desires of those individuals with gender dysphoria may turn into many different choices and outcomes later on in that person's life.[45]

Therefore, some clinicians have argued that it needs to be shown that the condition or desires of the individual are irreversible before any body-altering treatment can be initiated.[46] Diagnosis of gender dysphoria must rely on a subjective psychological report of the person as there is no clear diagnostic technique, and this again sees many clinicians counseling caution in undertaking any treatment. This goes to the maxim—do not harm and when in doubt, do nothing. The prevailing risk adversity surrounding medical interventions dictates you should wait until you are sure before intervening.

The Case for Early Intervention

Other clinicians argue that choosing to wait until the individual is legally capable of consenting (between the ages of 16 and 18 in differing jurisdictions) is not a neutral choice that avoids harm; instead, they argue that it may cause harm. The treatment course they recommend is a two-stage process, outlined below.

Stage One: It is constituted of the administration of gonadotrophin-releasing hormone analogs (GnRHa). GnRHa blocks the secretion of sex hormones such as estrogen, progesterone, and testosterone and, therefore, inhibits the development of secondary sex characteristics and the onset of puberty. For boys, these characteristics include the lowering of the voice and development of facial and body hair. For girls, this includes the suppression of breast development and commencement of the menstrual cycle. This stage is largely reversible in that once GnRHa treatment is stopped, puberty and the development of the secondary sex characteristics will recommence. This stage is usually commenced before an individual begins puberty, anywhere between 11 and 14 years of age.

Stage Two: It includes the administration of cross-sex hormone treatment, often called hormone replacement therapy. For male-to-female transitions, this most commonly includes the administration of estrogen, which stimulates the development of breasts, redistributes body fat, and often thins the skin and lightens the body hair. For female-to-male transitions, testosterone is administered resulting in the deepening of the voice, the development of facial and body hair, and increased musculature and decreased fat. Many of these changes are reversible, but many are not. For example, once an individual's larynx has changed shape and their voice has deepened, ceasing the hormone replacement therapy cannot reverse this. Similarly, the development of breasts may need surgery to be fully removed. Cross-hormone replacement therapy is usually commenced once the individual has reached 16 years of age. The decision for full sex reassignment surgery is usually not taken until the individual is 18 years or older; however, there are cases of it occurring earlier, such as Jackie Green, who recently became the youngest British transsexual to undergo surgery on her 16th birthday in Thailand.[47]

The Amsterdam Gender Clinic for Adolescents and Children was one of the first treatment centers to begin to prescribe hormone blockers before legal adulthood. The Dutch protocol that was developed there, and has subsequently been adopted by many other treatment centers, states that one is eligible for suppression of endogenous puberty (stage one) when the individual

- clearly meets the criteria for gender dysphoria;
- has suffered lifelong extreme gender dysphoria; and
- are psychologically stable and live in a supportive environment.[48]

The first retrospective studies of adolescents who underwent stage one hormone-blocking therapy found that post surgery, gender dysphoria decreased, body satisfaction increased, and the individuals were psychologically functioning in the normal range and did socially quite well.[49] Indeed, studies found that these individuals functioned better psychologically than transsexuals who were treated in adulthood.[50]

On this evidence, the Dutch protocol now allows those over the age of 12 to access stage one hormone treatment if the need can be clearly demonstrated and the individuals can meet the above criteria. It has been argued that starting intervention earlier and in this two-staged approach has a number of advantages, including the following.

Better Diagnosis

The administration of hormone blockers such as GnHRa will allow a clinician to assess the seriousness of the gender dysphoria experienced by a patient and whether they believe the dysphoria will continue into adulthood. Many have argued that the treatment is a helpful diagnostic aide as it allows the individual space and time free from distress and anxiety to discuss with their doctor and psychologist any problems that possibly underlie the wish to change genders. Without the time pressure of the development of secondary sex characteristics, hormone-blocking therapy can be considered as "buying time" to allow for an open exploration of the various options available to the patient.[51] It also allows clinicians to be sure they have the time to fully explain and have the patient understand the consequences and risks of cross-hormone therapy.

Provides Relief

In addition to allowing a better diagnosis, preventing the onset of puberty brings important temporary relief to those individuals who are suffering deep distress about the prospect of developing non-reversible secondary sexual characteristics such as voice deepening or the development of breasts. Early intervention allows individuals to be free from the anxiety and stress of feeling like they are trapped in another gender. For many people, the feeling that they are the wrong gender results in difficulties connecting socially and romantically, and this, in turn, can prevent other types of social and emotional development. The anxiety around going through puberty often takes precedence over other concerns in life.[52] Allowing these children access to puberty-inhibiting treatment allows them the space to be temporarily free from that emotional baggage in order to engage in their lives in other ways. Many clinicians and their patients report an immediate cessation of their suffering on beginning puberty blockers.[53]

Many children, including Jamie, live successfully as the other gender at school and in society before puberty without others knowing they are actually biologically of the other sex. This ability to live a "normal" life is compromised when they begin to develop secondary sex characteristics and cannot so easily "blend in." These young people often experience verbal and physical harassment and do not feel safe at school. Transgender children often experience rejection, discrimination, and abuse.[54] Homophobic and transgender bullying is common in schools. Indeed, 89.2 percent of lesbian, gay, bisexual, and transgender youth experience verbal bullying.[55] In addition, children who are victims of this type of bullying are five times more likely to not attend school and twice as likely not to pursue further education.[56] This clearly has implications for their success later in life. Administration of puberty-inhibiting drugs often provides relief from this type of discrimination.

Decreases Risk Later in Life

This type of early intervention not only brings immediate relief but can also reduce the type of risk-taking behavior that these individuals engage in throughout their lives. Experience shows that development and psychological functioning can forever be hampered by shame about one's appearance.[57] High risk-taking behavior is not uncommon among this cohort of young people. These individuals characteristically engage in high levels of sex work and drug and alcohol abuse, and often attempt to or commit suicide.[58] They are susceptible to depression, anorexia, and other social phobias.[59] Prevention of the commencement of puberty can result in a reduction of these experiences.

Delaying intervention can also have negative consequences for other areas of their health care. It can result in a distrust of healthcare professionals and the rejection of medical care that has lasting consequences throughout their lives.[60] On learning that they cannot access treatment, people will often seek to purchase hormones over the Internet or on the black market and, therefore, putting themselves at risk of the consequences of not properly administering this type of therapy. There have also been instances of individuals risking surgery overseas.

Better Results for Future Surgical Interventions

Finally, prevention of the development of secondary sex characteristics results in better results for sex reassignment surgery later in life. Surgery is often less involved and less invasive. For example,, in female-to-male transitions, if puberty is inhibited and cross-sex hormones have been successful, invasive surgery such as double mastectomies does not need to be undertaken. In addition, for male-to-female transitions, those individuals who have not undergone puberty will not have experienced the growth spurt and muscle development that are associated with male puberty. It is much more likely that they will easily be able to physically resemble a woman.

Research shows that psychological issues later in life can arise postoperation when it is difficult for transsexuals to successfully pass in their new gender.[61] To have to continue to explain or be reminded of their transsexualism can bring anxiety and depression.[62] Research has found that the age of the individual when they began treatment is a major factor differentiating two groups of male-to-female transsexuals, one with and one without postoperative regrets.[63]

Before going further, it is worth considering the argument posed by Dr Russell Viner that puberty blockers cannot be truly reversible and, therefore, are not as harmless as we believe.[64] Viner has argued that blockers have the irreversible outcome of denying the child the experience of puberty in the natural phenotype, and that it is irreversible that the natural development has been interrupted at a particular point in time. Therefore, blockers are not truly reversible.

However, as Giordano rightly points out, "of course when something happens no one can undo reality."[65] It is true that it is irreversible that the hormone blockers have been given or not,, but not true that they are not reversible in their effect. In this sense, the adjective in Viner's argument is predicated on the wrong subject. For example, an eyebrow pencil is reversible in the way that an eyebrow tattoo or cosmetic surgery is not; however, the fact that the act of using the eyebrow pencil cannot be undone does not change the fact that the effect of the eyebrow pencil can be reversed.[66] The reversibility of the effects of puberty-blocking hormone therapy is the same.

These arguments, better diagnosis; relief; reduced future harm; and better sex change outcomes, provide a compelling case for why it is not appropriate to wait until an individual reaches legal adulthood to commence treatment. Waiting to commence treatment causes individuals harm and puts them at the risk of future harm, whereas early commencement of treatment reduces the risk of harm and has a number of long-term benefits. However, this approach is still open to a number of challenges, not least of all the previously highlighted argument that children as young as 11 do not have the competence to consent to such a treatment, and indeed, such a choice cannot be made on behalf of the child.

The Argument from Incompetence

Despite the compelling arguments for the benefits of early intervention through the administration of puberty-inhibiting hormone treatment, many argue that children lack the competence to make a medical decision such as this. Clinicians fear that the risk of postoperative regrets will be high and the treatment will have unfavorable physical, psychological, or social consequences.[67] It is believed that children and adolescents generally lack the emotional and cognitive maturity needed to consent to treatment that will have lifelong consequences. In addition, many clinicians point out that children experiencing gender dysphoria often have below-average social skills, behavioral development, and psychiatric comorbidities. It is argued that these children are, therefore, "particularly susceptible to the temptation of a supposedly rapid solution to all of their problems."[68]

Cohen-Kettenis, one of the foremost researchers in this area and the founder of the Amsterdam clinic, argues that, on the contrary, there is no ground for the assessment that a child or adolescent with gender dysphoria cannot be competent to make a judgment about puberty-inhibiting drugs. She argues that most of the statements regarding this seem to be based on assumptions rather than research.[69] In response to these types of arguments based on the incompetence of the child, clinicians put in place a detailed procedure for assisting choice by children. This type of procedure is not unlike the type of steps one might go through with an adult who wished to undergo hormone replacement therapy.

It should be noted that children between the ages of 12 and 16 still need parental consent to undergo the treatment but understanding and competence on the part of the child must be demonstrated in most cases in order for the treatment to go ahead and for clinicians to be confident that stage one and stage two hormone treatment is the right type of treatment for that individual. The steps taken to ensure that the appropriate level of understanding and decision making is taken include

- assessing the general and psychosexual functioning of the individual;
- informing the individual that there is a chance that hormone therapy might not happen and asking them to consider the consequences of not undergoing hormone therapy. This is often a good diagnostic tool for how important the treatment is to the individual; and
- requiring the individual to live as the other gender for a period of time. For young children, this can happen before puberty-blocking hormones are needed, but for older children, this might need to happen at the same time as puberty blockers. This real-life experience (often called the RLE phase in the literature) requires the patient to live in the role of the desired gender and to appreciate in vivo the familial, interpersonal, educational, and legal consequences of the gender change. They are required to tell key people in their life including teachers and classmates and to choose a new name if appropriate. This is done in concert with continued psychological and psychiatric involvement and can last anywhere from 6 months to two years.

At the end of this process, those treating the child need to be confident that the individual has demonstrated knowledge and understanding of the effects of the puberty blockers, cross-sex hormone treatment, surgery, and the social consequences of sex reassignment.[70] In fact, the administration of puberty blockers may allow children and adolescents to make a *better* decision about the non-reversible cross-hormone treatment, as, instead of feeling distressed regarding the onset of puberty, they are given the time to explore in an open way whether cross-hormone therapy is actually the treatment of choice for their gender problem.[71]

Risks

However, some have argued that even if it can be shown that a child is competent and understands the consequences of the decision, it is impossible for them to truly make such a decision in a truly rational and independent sense because the risks associated with the treatment are too high. As discussed, the second stage of treatment includes non-reversible changes that will forever impact an individual's life, and it may be argued that the irreversibility of this treatment lends increased moral weight to the decision.

In addition, there are a number of side effects to the treatment. In early pubertal boys, the hypogonadotrophic state induced by GnHRa will block the development of fertility; however, the development of fertility is likely to resume if the treatment is stopped or not undertaken for a prolonged period of time. In older boys, fertility will regress. Therefore, young children and adolescents often need to consider freezing sperm (or going off the blockers for a time to develop fertility and then freeze sperm) in order to preserve the option of having biological children later in life. For girls, GnRHa will stop the menstrual cycle and, therefore, prevent fertility.[72] Prolonged hormone blockers and cross-sex hormones will result in sterility.

In addition, there is a risk of reduced bone density. As much of the bone density growth occurs during puberty, there is a risk that these individuals will have reduced bone density and will be at risk of osteoporosis later in life.[73] Some argue that these types of risks mean that even if the child is competent, they cannot consent to such a treatment by themselves.

This view was confirmed by the Family Court of Australia in the case of *Re Alex*.[74] The Court determined that Alex (who was born a girl) could not consent to the proposed stage one and stage two hormone treatment.[75] This was the case although Alex was 13 years old, and evidence from his treating psychiatrist stated that Alex had a very clear understanding of the treatment options and a clear understanding of the consequences of the treatment.[76] Nicholson CJ applied the standard of *Gillick* competence in regards to Alex and found that Alex demonstrated the standards as outlined by *Gillick*. However, Nicholson CJ drew a distinction between the treatment being proposed (stage one and stage two hormone therapy) and that in the case of *Gillick* (oral contraception) and stated "it is highly questionable whether a 13 year old could ever be regarded as having the capacity to consent to a procedure which would change his sex."[77] Despite this finding, the Court did determine that the treatment (both stage one and stage two) was in Alex's best interests and authorized the treatment.

The argument that there are types of procedures that, even if one is able to demonstrate competence in rational decision-making, one can never give their consent to (but authorization can be given by an independent body such as the Family Court) is a worrying proposition. The argument in this case seems to be that the risks are so high that you can never consent to it by yourself. However, if this were the case, then surely it would also stand for adults who wished to undergo hormone replacement therapy. The risks of such a non-reversible therapy would similarly exist for them. In this case, it seems it is not the assessment of the competence that is at stake but rather the age of the individual. As I have argued earlier, this failed to recognize that competence is task specific and particular to each individual.

Others have argued that as the treatment is still relatively new and knowledge in this space is still developing, some of the side effects are unknowable and it is impossible to consent to something that is unknown. However, this argument cannot hold when seen in the context of our broader treatment of both children and adults.[78] If one cannot consent to unknown risks, this would mean that no one could consent to research or potentially experimental treatment. What is needed for informed consent is for the decision maker to understand the known risks and that unknown risks potentially exist.

Orthodox decision-making states that the rational decision maker under conditions of risk will maximize expected utility. The utility is the expected benefit (probability × magnitude) minus the cost of harm (probability × magnitude). A rational decision maker will choose the option with the greatest net benefit or smallest expected net harm. When making decisions in situations of uncertainty, a chooser cannot assign probabilities or may know there are some harms that cannot be envisioned.[79]

Decision-making under these circumstances is necessarily going to be difficult: one cannot know definitively the outcomes of treatment versus non-treatment. However, this issue does not disappear if the clinician or the parents make this decision for the child. Deciding to wait until the child is older is not a neutral decision. It is a decision in itself and it has consequences for the child. If this is a decision made under uncertainty, then why is it more legitimate for a parent or clinician to make this decision instead of a child? For many individuals who are experiencing gender dysphoria, the assessment that hormone treatment is in their best interests is not a difficult assessment to make.

It may be that in these types of situations, it is unhelpful to consider informed consent or the competence to consent as being something that either exists or does not, at any one point in time. We know that competence for children and adults is fluid and developing. Cohen-Kettenis argues that "It will be clear that in the case of a complex treatment such as SR [sex reassignment], informed consent is not given at a single point of time. Rather, it is a process during which the adolescent is progressively more able to understand what the decision is all about."[80] The development of competence in children may, therefore, mean we must rethink how the traditional concept of informed consent functions.

The Authentic Self

A more ethically challenging opposition to the early administration of stage one and stage two hormone therapy is that a child or young adolescent cannot make the decision to undertake puberty suppression because they have not yet gone through the necessary development to become their full self yet. Korte *et al* argue that gender dysphoria has a "highly variable and plastic course," and this is due to the psychosexual development of the patient not yet being complete.[81] They go on to state that

> A treatment of this kind changes the individual's sexual experience both in fantasy and in behavior. It restricts sexual appetite and functionality and thereby prevents the individual from having age-appropriate (socio-) sexual experiences that he or she can then evaluate in the framework of the diagnostic-therapeutic process. As a result it becomes nearly impossible to discover the sexual preference structure and ultimate gender identity developing under the influence of the native sex hormones.[82]

Under this argument, any decision made by the individual before they have gone through puberty is necessarily influenced by the fact that they have not yet gone through puberty. Korte *et al* argue that the type of hormonal changes and experiences one goes through during puberty will change the way in which one might make decisions about one's gender and will make it difficult to discover one's "authentic" gender identity. As some individuals do not want to change sex later on and instead identify as homosexual, this type of hormone therapy, Korte *et al* argue, may intervene with a patient's development as a homosexual.[83] In fact, they argue that hormone therapy may lead to a consolidation of gender dysphoria and transsexualism, and even in cases where the treatment is retrospectively successful, "one cannot necessarily assume that the patient's transsexualism was pre-determined matter at the onset."[84] So, when studies such as those arising from the Amsterdam clinic find that none of the patients who took puberty-blocking hormones decided to stop treatment and indeed they were all very happy with the results of their decision,[85] this cannot be seen as a success in its own terms.

This argument seems to be predicated on the assumption that your "authentic" self, the one that you would "naturally develop" without the interference of puberty-inhibiting drugs, is more worthy than the other self that you would become when taking the treatment, even if that self is one where you are happy in your gender identity. Korte *et al* are essentially arguing that young children cannot make this type of decision before puberty because they have not become fully themselves yet.

However, research indicates that although it may be true that only one-quarter of children who experience gender dysphoria under the age of 12 will become transsexual adults,[86] the majority of those who continue to experience transgenderism in adolescence (from 12 years onwards) *will* become transsexual adults.[87] Furthermore, Cohen-Kettenis argues that there is no evidence from brain research to support the contention that the brain needs to be fully exposed to the hormones of puberty of the sex one is born in, in order to demonstrate that gender dysphoria will continue into adulthood.[88]

There is also a broader ethical question that underpins this type of discussion—can it be right to interfere with spontaneous development? In this sense, the transgender child case is the opposite of the child undergoing cultural female genital cutting. When I discussed female genital cutting when considering a child's right to develop, I argued that the child's future interest in being able to have children themselves later in life should be retained even if the child does not have this capacity to do so now. What is it about the case of gender dysphoria that seems to recommend the opposite course of action? It is here that understanding rights as being grounded in interests becomes very important. As we outlined in Part I of this book, interests are particular to the individual. An assessment of a child's interests must be done individually. While it might be the case that retaining the capacity to develop fertility and, therefore, reproduce in the future may be in the interests of most children, for some who experience extreme distress in their biological bodies, the development of secondary sex characteristics is a source of harm.

There is nothing inherently wrong with interfering with spontaneous development; if that were so, we would feel like there were important ethical questions to be asked about choosing to undergo corrective laser eye surgery as this would interfere with my development as a short-sighted individual. Clearly, the more important question in this regard is if the treatment is in the best interests of the child, and the child's opinions and preferences including their capacity to consent are an important part of this assessment. For example, if we return to the case of the girl and cultural female genital cutting, we might imagine a scenario where the young girl grows up in a culture that highly values this practice and, therefore, she expresses a desire to have it done. At this point, we need to balance the child's competence to make decisions with the risks and harm that may arise. Whereas hormone-blocking treatment seems to clearly reduce harm, undertaking genital cutting seems to bring about harm.[89]

It might be argued that if the problems faced by those with gender dysphoria are primarily social (in terms of bullying and discrimination), then surely it is not appropriate to seek to solve a social problem with medical intervention. However, gender dysphoria, unlike female genital cutting, is not just a social or cultural problem. Gender dysphoria is a severe condition where children routinely threaten self-harm, to cut and remove their genitals, or to commit suicide. This type of deep distress and self-harm can occur even in situations where they have complete support and understanding from their family. Just like we cannot cure depression by just being nicer to someone, the feeling of disconnect with one's body that is felt by those with gender dysphoria does not go away when others accept your condition.

Balancing Harm and Competence

The case of children experiencing gender dysphoria clearly demonstrates how difficult it can be to realize children's rights in practice. The balance between a child's interests and their developing competence to make decisions for themselves is a tricky one where every moment that passes and every experience often means new and developing competencies for that child. In particular, the seriousness of the desires and symptoms experienced by these children can put them at risk of serious harm if the right treatment path is not followed.

Increasingly, it seems that people are recognizing that children and adolescents do have a right to make medical decisions relative to their competence and the risks or harms of the decision they are making. We might be able to conceptualize this relationship as two parallel continuums—one from low risk or harm to high risk and harm, and one from low decision-making competence to high decision-making competence (Figure 8.2).

As discussed in the previous chapter, for an action or situation to constitute a prima facie harm, it must satisfy the "worsening test," that B's interest is in a worse condition than it was before A acted. However, not all harms are worsening harms. In order to show conclusively that the action is not harmful, we must also show that it fails the "counterfactual test." In this comparison, the worsening is not between the present and past condition of the subject, but rather the two counterfactual conditions that the

Figure 8.2 Two continuums of harm and competence

subject may be in response to action or inaction. For example, a doctor may choose to treat an individual with gender dysphoria with intensive psychological therapy and anti-depressants. This treatment will make the individual feel slightly better than they did with no therapy; however, for many individuals, their condition is still worse than if they had undergone hormone therapy and had relief from their anxiety and depression. It is this assessment of harm that must be undertaken.

Competence, as discussed in Part I of this book, is task specific. Competence is one's ability to do a specific task. Therefore, the assessment of competence in decision-making must assess the child's competence to make that particular decision, not decisions in general. This is important as we saw some decisions are easier to make than others. Some decisions, such as, for me, the decision of whether to have another cup of tea or not, are easy. Tea brings me satisfaction, I enjoy it, it is a low-cost drink, and there are no down sides to consuming another cup. The assessment of utility is, therefore, easily done. Other decisions, such as whether to go for a run this afternoon or continue to work on this book, are harder. Exercise is good for me, it will extend my life and prevent certain diseases and conditions, but it is also tiring and takes motivation and effort; while I am exercising, I am generally not enjoying myself. Writing, on the other hand, will ensure that this book is finished sooner and I have undertaken a commitment to deliver it on time. However, finding the motivation to continue can be hard. In this situation, the assessment of utility is far more complex. It is easy to imagine how much more complex the assessment will be when choosing whether to undergo life-changing treatment.

Where an individual sits on these continuums may determine how much weight their interest to make their own medical decisions is given. This will essentially mean that the assessment is different and unique for each individual, each situation, and each point of time. For example, the risk of death is an irreversible harm and, therefore, the competence one must need to be shown may need to be very high in order to be confident in choices made by children to refuse life-saving treatment. It should be noted that a similar scale can probably be constructed for adult medical decision-making; however, the important difference is that even if an adult's competence in decision-making is still developing, it is far more likely to inhabit a smaller range than that of children.

On closer examination, it may transpire that the nature of duties can change depending on the changing capacity and competencies of the right-holder. For example, there has been recent discussion on what a doctor's duty to provide patients with medical information actually entails.[90] The nature of the duty—that is, to what extent and what type of information a doctor may have to provide—may differ in reference to the patient's competence. If I go for a surgery such as a knee reconstruction, my doctor cannot reasonably be expected to provide me with information about the procedure to the same level as his own knowledge. Now, consider that between then and now I gain a medical degree and have to go in for a different procedure. My right to be informed may now entail a very different type of duty. The surgeon may now have to provide me with much more detailed and specific medical information in order for me to give free and informed consent. Similarly, the corresponding duty may change again if my mental capacities decline. In this vein, Joseph Raz has identified the dynamic nature of rights.[91] By dynamic, Raz means that the corresponding duties may change over time. Children's rights may be more dynamic rights than others; as their capacities and competencies are continually developing, the corresponding duties to their claims may be dynamic and changing.

Although the assessment of competence and rights may be finely tuned and variable, for the purposes of setting standards by which these types of decisions are made, we often need to have a specific policy position on how we treat these types of situations, so that each case is not assessed from scratch each time. Such a framework has recently evolved in Australia regarding the decision to undertake stage one and stage two hormone treatment.

Up until recently, in Australia, puberty-blocking hormone treatment had been defined as "a special medical procedure" under the Family Law Act. A special medical procedure is one that parents cannot consent to on behalf of the child; instead, an external independent body (in this case, the Family Court of Australia) must make this decision in order to ensure it is in the child's best interests.[92] Rule 4.09(1) of the Family Court Act provides that when an application is filed for a special medical procedure, evidence must be given that the procedure is in the best interests of the child.

After receiving authorization from the court to undergo stage one and stage two hormone treatment, Jamie's legal team appealed to the full Federal Family Court not to challenge the orders of the Court but on a point of law. Specifically, the grounds of the appeal were

- that treatment of the condition described as "childhood gender identity disorder" with which Jamie was diagnosed is not a special medical procedure which displaces the parental responsibility of the appellants to decide upon the appropriate treatment for their child; and
- once the diagnosis of childhood gender identity disorder was established and the treatment approved, the treatment for the disorder

should not be the subject of a further application to the Court when the stage two is about to commence.[93]

The Court found that in terms of stage one treatment, an application to administer puberty-inhibiting drugs did not need to be made to the Court. The fact that stage one treatment is reversible meant that the treatment is low-enough risk to fall into the normal range of treatment that parents can consent to on behalf of the child. Bryant CJ stated that

> In my view, it is not, as the submissions of the public authority propose, the alteration of an otherwise healthy body to accommodate a psychological imperative, but rather it is the alignment of the body with the person's self-identity.[94]

Application to the court for stage one treatment may still occur when there is disagreement between the child, the child's parents, or the child's doctors as to the need for treatment.

However, due to the fact that stage two treatment was largely irreversible and, therefore, the risk was greater, the Court found that an application has to be made to the Court to consider whether a child is *Gillick* competent. If the child is found to be competent according to the standards of *Gillick*, then the court has no further role in the decision regarding the child's treatment and the child has the right to consent to or refuse treatment.[95] This recent development and application in subsequent cases[96] has sought to develop practical principles by which these types of cases can be decided and give consideration to the right of a child to be involved and make decisions regarding their own medical treatment, balanced against actions that are in their best interest.

Conclusion

What is clear is that considering children's rights, in terms of their best interests and their right to consent, is essential to fully understand the complex questions and considerations that are at play in cases such as these. When considered from the point of view of a child's interests, non-intervention is not a neutral option. It has clear lifelong consequences that can impact on the quality of life for those individuals who had to wait until after puberty to receive treatment. I believe that cases like this demonstrate the power that a full consideration of children's rights, including understanding how a child's competence interacts with their best interests, provides us with the right tools to begin to put the rights of children into practice.

9

A Right to be Loved

In 1974, Foster and Freed wrote in their article "A Bill of Rights for Children" that "a child has a moral right and should have a legal right,[1] to receive parental love and affection."[2] Such a legal right now exists in Israel, Japan, Mozambique, and the United States and appears in the preamble of United Nations Convention on the Rights of the Child (CROC): "a child should grow up in an atmosphere of happiness, love and understanding."[3] The assertion that children have not only a *moral* but a *legal* claim to love, with all the State power of enforcement that entails, seems to ask a lot more of the child/parent/State relationship than we currently conceive. The right itself is backed by scant philosophical debate.[4] Philosophical justification is needed, considering that the right presents significant issues for both the theory of rights and the moral and political status of children. Is love an appropriate concept to include in our international and domestic legal documents? Can we really impose a duty on others to love? Is protecting parental love the best way to protect children? The questions surrounding a child's right to be loved go to the heart of what it means to have a right.

Matthew Liao directly addressed this issue in his article "The Right of Children to Be Loved."[5] In the article, Liao seeks to provide a philosophical argument for why a child has a right to be loved. In this chapter, I will examine Liao's argument and in turn argue that children do not have a right to be loved. First, I will consider Liao's argument and examine the scientific literature—the study of "maternal deprivation" in humans and nonhuman primates, the study of social isolation of monkeys, and recent neuroscientific studies linked to deprivation in both human and nonhuman primates—that he uses to substantiate the central empirical claim. I argue that this literature fails to support the claim that love is a primary essential condition for a good life.

Second, I will argue that, even if the empirical claim could be substantiated, "loving" cannot be a duty. Loving cannot be a duty because the structure of rights necessitates that there be a real and achievable corresponding duty. There are significant problems with conceiving of emotions as duties. The emotional component of love may be an unachievable duty. I argue that the emotional aspect of love can be logically separated from treatment we deem desirable for the child, and in some cases, the emotion of love may bring about undesirable treatment. If the proposed right cannot fulfill its desired function, the justification for its existence may be severely undermined.

Having shown the central explanation for a right to be loved to be lacking, I will consider two alternative conceptions of the right to be loved, namely, the right to be loved as a manifesto right and the right to be loved as a claim-right against the State. Even given these alternatives, I conclude that the real objectives of the child's right to be loved can be achieved through other clearer rights and that, accordingly, it still cannot be said that children have a right to be loved.

Liao's Argument and Empirical Nonsense

Matthew Liao states that children have a right to be loved as a human right on the grounds that human beings have rights to those conditions that are primary essential for a good life. This is because

> by their nature rights secure the interests of the right holders by requiring the duty- bearers, to perform certain services for the right-holder or not to interfere with the right holder's pursuit of their essential interests.[6]

If we attach meaning and importance to the end (a good life), then we must attach importance to the "primary essential" means used to achieve this end. In this, Liao draws on James Griffin's defense of human rights.[7] As children are human beings, they, therefore, have rights to those conditions that are primary essential for a good life. Liao defines parental love as

> To seek a highly intense interaction with the child, where one values the child for the child's sake, where one seeks to bring about and to maintain physical and psychological proximity with the child, where one seeks to promote the child's well-being for the child's sake, and where one desires that the child reciprocate or, at least, is responsive to, one's love.[8]

This love need not only come from the child's biological parents but can include other individuals such as foster parents and nannies. The "highly intense" aspect of this definition is designed to show us that love also has an emotional component that permeates all our dealings with the child. Parental love, defined in this way, is an essential condition for a good life for children, children have a right to be loved.

Liao's argument can be broken down to four steps:

1. Human beings have rights to those conditions that are primary essential for a good life.
2. Children are human beings.
3. Parental love, that is,

    a. seeking a highly intense interaction with the child,
    b. seeking to bring about and maintaining physical/psychological proximity,
    c. seeking to promote the child's well being for the child's sake,
    d. valuing the child for its own sake, and
    e. desiring reciprocity of love;
       is a primary essential condition for a good life.

4. Therefore, children have a right to parental love.

From this, we can see that Liao's argument rests on claim number three, that parental love, broadly defined as above, is a primary essential condition for a good life of children.

Interestingly, Liao explicitly wishes to argue that it is an empirical claim.[9] If this claim is not backed by evidence then Liao's conceptual framework of *a* right to be loved may stand but the content of the particular right will not. Liao seeks to substantiate this empirical claim by demonstrating that without love children suffer severe negative consequences. In doing so, he draws upon several broad branches of scientific literature: the study of "maternal deprivation" in humans and nonhuman primates, the study of social isolation of monkeys, and recent neuroscientific studies linked to deprivation in both human and nonhuman primates. However, none adequately support this empirical claim. It is beneficial to look closely at these studies as they not only expose the flaws in Liao's empirical claim, but also have implications for the broader concept of a right to be loved.

Maternal Deprivation

The broad base of literature that Liao draws on is the study of "Maternal Deprivation." Liao argues that

> children who did not receive love but only adequate care, became ill more frequently, their learning capacities decreased significantly, became decreasingly interested in their environment, failed to thrive physically

by failing to gain weight or height, suffered insomnia, were constantly depressed, developed severe learning disabilities...in one study, 37% of these infants had died by two years of age, compared with none in the adequately mothered control group.[10]

This does seem to be very strong evidence. It claims that adequate care was controlled for and that lack of love was the only relevant explanatory variable. The results are not only emotional but also measurable such as weight and height and most seriously, death. The evidence comes from a 1945 study by Rene Spitz entitled *"Hospitalism: An Inquiry into the Genesis of Psychiatric Conditions in Early Childhood"* and a 1946 inquiry by Spitz and Wolf entitled *"Anaclitic Depression: An Inquiry into the Genesis of Psychiatric Conditions in Early Childhood."* These are classic studies, part of a collection of work in the 1940s and 1950s that reformed the way in which foster homes operated and led to further understandings of childhood, development, and socialization.[11] However, they are inadequate to support the claim that love is a primary essential condition for a good life in children.

The literature on Maternal Deprivation is not restricted to the 1940s; in the 1960s and 1970s, the concept of maternal deprivation came under considerable criticism.[12] Reviews of the literature identified complex differences between "insufficiency of interaction implicit in deprivation" and the "discontinuity of relations brought about through separation."[13] Michael Rutter has suggested that the literature is in fact dealing with three distinct syndromes and the use of the phrase "maternal deprivation" is misleading.[14] Rutter suggests that they should be broadly characterized as Acute Distress from Loss, Experiential/Nutritional Privation, and Bond Privation. This neatly demonstrates the different variables that are at play in Liao's analysis.

Acute Distress

Acute Distress is suffered by young children removed from their families, often at the time of admission to hospital. Rutter argues that separation causes distress only in children older than six months, which indicates that distress is due to interrupting an important bond at a time when children have difficulty maintaining a relationship through absence.[15] This syndrome is best understood as the study of "loss." In the study *"Anaclitic Depression,"* children who had been with their mothers were separated from them for three to four months. The children showed a range of symptoms such as weeping, screaming, weight loss, and insomnia which Spitz and Wolf diagnosed as anaclitic depression.[16] The symptoms stopped when the child was restored to the mother. The only mention of love is in reference to the depression following the loss of their "love-object," referring to the subject of their attachment.

In this way "*Anaclitic Depression*" is a study of the effects of the *loss* of a mother or mother-substitute, not the effects of an unloving mother or mother-substitute. In addition, experimental studies have shown how distress may be reduced by provision of toys or by increased quality of care and changes in the hospital admission process.[17]

It is clear that separation from a "love-object" is different from a lack of love as defined by Liao. We would not be inclined to say that while our mother was traveling overseas that we were no longer loved by her. The acute distress suffered from separation seems to indicate the existence of a close relationship from which the loss of the missing person presents a cause for mourning, not the complete disappearance of love. Furthermore, the distress can be alleviated through high-quality institutional care. If lack of love could be reduced to separation alone, it would seem to imply the extreme claim that all children have a right to their parents' physical presence around the clock. The study of the distress from loss does not encompass Liao's claim that children who are not loved suffer negative outcomes.

Experiential/Nutritional Privation

Rutter's second syndrome, Experiential/Nutritional Privation, bears directly on Liao's claim that children suffering from a lack of love will fail to thrive both physically (reduced gains in height and weight) and cognitively (learning difficulties and disabilities). The study "*Hospitalism*" is an enquiry into the effects of prolonged institutionalization in infants. It compares two institutions, an institutional nursery where infants had access to the mother and a Foundling Center where the infants did not. The study observed that the mothers provided intense stimulation for the infants in the nursery, which was lacking in the Foundling Center. It concluded that the infants in the Foundling Center consequentially suffered physically and emotionally in their development.[18] "*Hospitalism*" was a study of deprivation of stimulation, where the lack of development in these children is due to insufficient human interaction, rather than a lack of love. In fact, Spitz argues that the care and attention given to the children by their mothers in the nursery did not constitute love.[19]

Review of the literature shows that physical developmental impairment is reversed by "increasing social, tactile, and perceptual stimulation without altering any other aspect of institutional life and without altering the child's separation from his family."[20] This seems to account for many of the observations in "*Hospitalism.*" The children in the Foundling Center did not have toys and were often placed alone in their cot for most of the day.[21] These children were deprived not only of any proper visual stimulation but also of any human interaction. In contrast, the children in the nursery not only had access to their mothers but were able to observe play in adjacent cubicles. These important differences led to controversy over whether the observable negative symptoms were attributable to the absence of a mother figure (what Liao might have termed "lack of love") or to "environmental deprivation."[22]

Liao's use of the study of rhesus monkeys shows the stark nature of the problem.[23] Liao argues that infant monkeys raised in maternal privation settings have hampered social cognitive and emotional development.[24] The study "*Total Social Isolation in Monkeys*" does not talk about "love" nor seek to measure the effect of an unloving relationship, but specifically seeks to measure the detrimental effects of social isolation. The young monkeys were separated from their mother at birth and raised in bare wire cages; they were devoid of any maternal contact or opportunity to form affectional ties with peers. In addition, some monkeys were in total social isolation, having been housed from birth until 12 months in a stainless steel chamber with no contact with any animal or human. They were then released into playrooms with two normal "control" monkeys. The symptoms exhibited were hostility to outside environment, self-harm, repetitive rocking movements, and inability to interact with normal monkeys. On release, the two that were in total social isolation went into emotional shock and refused to eat. One died five days later and the other was force fed. The autopsy showed that the infant monkey died of "emotional anorexia."[25] This case shows the extreme nature of experiential privation, but as it is concerned with highly specific sensory stimulation, it is of limited application to questions about the effects of lack of love.

It is important to note that the necessary visual, physical, and experiential stimulation can be given by someone who is not the primary care-giver or parent. This seems to indicate that experiential privation affecting physical development can be separated from the formation of attachment and bonds between child and care-giver. For example, more recent studies have focused on how lack of physical stimulation can affect the biochemical processes of growth hormone (GH) secretion, leading to psychosocial dwarfism.[26] The studies conducted on the effects of maternal touch and massage on young infants as a stimulant for growth continue to support the conclusion that the physical stimulation can be provided by someone who does not necessarily "love" the child.[27] In the study by Scafidi, Field, and Schanberg, the tactile and kinesthetic stimulation was provided by the investigator or a nurse trained in the procedure.[28]

It is apparent from these studies that visual/physical and experiential stimulation is important for the proper social and physical development of a child. However, in many cases someone who is not party to a loving relationship with the child can provide this stimulation. Despite showing that these elements are important for a child's development, the studies do not demonstrate that they need to be provided as part of a loving relationship in order to have the same positive consequences.

Bond Privation and Antisocial Disorder

Empirical studies demonstrate the more serious long-term effects of bond privation. While studies of Acute Distress showed the short-term effects of disruption in the bond creation phase, studies such as those by Hodges and Tizard[29] and Kaler and Freeman[30] look at the long-term effects of the lack of bond formation. Children who are prevented from forming bonds when young often exhibit antisocial behavior throughout their adult lives. Kaler and Freeman studied the cognitive and social development of Romanian orphans. Their study, however, was complicated by the added variable of experiential and nutritional privation as over 100,000 children were "warehoused with minimal food, clothing, heat or caregivers." Hodges and Tizard sought to control for the lack of visual stimulation by providing toys and interaction to the children who were growing up in an institutional setting.

Recent neuroscientific research has shown the chemical effects of the disruption of bond formation. In studies of infant rhesus monkeys and nonhuman primates, changes in the mother's foraging habits or differing rearing conditions could

> dysregulate the development of the brain biogenic amine neurotransmitter systems such as norepinephrine (NE), dopamine (DA), and serotonin (5HT); and the hypothalamic-pituitary-adrenal (HPA) axis; cause the development of adrenal glucocorticoid responses to be modified in negative ways.[31]

Changes in the complex neurochemical systems can have serious effects: serotonin and norepinephrine are widely recognized to be related to feelings of well-being (antidepressants raise serotonin and norepinephrine levels), dopamine is associated with our ability to experience pleasure, and glucocorticoid responses are strongly linked with stress.

This appears the strongest support for Liao's claim, for it seems that there is considerable evidence that the failure to form bonds in early childhood is linked to antisocial, attention seeking behavior and a reduced ability to form lasting relationships later on in life. It should be noted, however, that this disruption in the bond formation constitutes a very different arrangement from the previous cases. If we are to identify what is meant by "lack of love" we must be clear whether this is a child who is denied an opportunity to form a bond with their carer, a child who has formed a bond but who is routinely separated from their carer, or a child who has not formed a bond with their carer but the carer states that they "love" the child. It should also be highlighted that bonds may not be the same thing as love; it is generally recognized in attachment theory that attachment is not synonymous with love or affection.[32] What these studies seem to demonstrate is that the formation of an uninterrupted bond with the child's care-giver is an important part of their social development, and disruption of this bond formation can lead to negative affects on the child's neurotransmitter systems.

Is This Lack of Love?

From this evidence, we can conclude that short-term separations cause distress, but can be countered by improving institutional care and stimulation. Experiential or sensory privation can lead to a lack of physical and cognitive development but this can be reversed by increasing stimulation which need not necessarily be linked to the primary care-giver. Finally, children who grow up in institutions or are exposed to multiple changing care-givers can suffer lasting social consequences from the lack of bond formation in early childhood. The use of "love" in Liao's claim must, therefore, be replaced by these different variables. It may be disingenuous to state that "lack of love" will result in these negative consequences with no qualifier that what is being measured is different in each study. Many writers have rejected the use of "love" on the grounds that it introduces "mystical and immeasurable elements."[33] The controversy over whether variables such as privation, distress, and lack of "bond" development can properly be understood as "lack of love" serves to highlight that love is problematic to measure, as we often believe it to involve intangible elements.

The literature, therefore, fails to measure the effects of a lack of love in the way Liao suggests that it does. It fails to conclusively show that the desirable treatment identified by Liao, the provisions labeled a. to e. above, are essential conditions for a good life. What has been demonstrated is that intense social interaction, sensory and experiential stimulation is necessary for young children's normal development and long-term socialization. This could be interpreted as fulfilling provision (a) "seeking a highly intense interaction with the child" and (b) "maintaining physical and psychological proximity." Yet, the second finding of the literature, that separation from a "love-object" will cause distress, can only obliquely be understood as fulfilling provision (c) "promoting the child's well being for the child's sake" if we accept that a child's well-being includes always being free from distress. There is no support in the literature for provisions (d) "valuing the child for its own sake" and (e) "desiring reciprocity of love." It seems that these are assumed to be self-evidently primary essential conditions for a good life.

Liao has not made a serious case that there is a right to be loved, rather than just a right to some of the a. to e. provisions. The empirical evidence alone, however, has not shown us that there is no such thing as *any* right to be loved; if sufficient empirical evidence is found, the right may still stand. In part two of this chapter, I address the conceptual problems with the right, demonstrating that even with sufficient scientific literature the right does not exist.

Loving Is Not a Duty

Even if the studies are not adequate to support the empirical claim that parental love is an essential condition for a good life, it still may be that the structure of the child's right to be loved is correct. That possibility raises the question: if there was sufficient scientific literature to back up the claim that parental love was an essential condition of a good life, what form would this take as a right?

As I argued in the first part of this book, rights are generally understood to be Hohfeldian claims. The Hohfeldian framework stipulates that a claim always has a correlative duty and is specified by reference to the actions of the people who bear the correlative duty.[34] For example, I have a claim to my life and, therefore, you have a duty to refrain from killing me. A's claim creates a duty in B to (1) abstain from interference or (2) render assistance. The duty to love must, therefore, contemplate the existence of "love" as an action. If we return to the definition of parental love we can observe that, with the exception of the desire for reciprocity, all of the elements (seeking a highly intense interaction, maintaining physical/psychological proximity, promoting the child's interests, and valuing the child) are actions that the duty-holder would take toward the child. As actions we can rightly understand them as duties.

However, these actions could be simply defined as desirable treatment. Although such desirable treatment could be the consequence of one's love, it could also arise without love being present. For example, the carer of the child, such as a nurse or nanny, may promote the child's interests for the child's sake while not feeling love for the child. They may recognize that the child's interests are important and should be respected. Therefore, there is a distinct difference between desirable treatment simpliciter and desirable treatment that arises from a place of love in the duty-bearer. If we accept Liao's definition of parental love as it stands then really what we wish to say is that a child has a right to these specific actions that constitute desirable treatment.

However, Liao does not wish to limit the scope of the right only to the actions and behavior of the lover. He argues that the "highly intense" nature of parental love indicates that parental love is not just "behavioural or attitudinal but has emotional components" as well.[35] According to Liao, the duty-holder must not only show "the appearance of the emotions appropriate for the circumstances, but actually have the genuine emotions appropriate for the circumstances."[36] Therefore, desirable treatment simpliciter is insufficient. In order to fulfill a child's right to be loved, the duty-bearer must provide the desirable treatments plus the internal emotion. It must come from a place of love. This would be like saying I have a right to bodily integrity whose fulfillment requires people to *want* not to stab me, not just to restrain themselves from the action.

There is an alternative interpretation of Liao's definition of parental love, that the first three elements of parental love, a. to c., are *conative* rather than *affective*. Liao's definition of parental love is *seeking* highly intense interaction with the child, *seeking* to bring about and maintaining physical/psychological proximity, and *seeking* to promote the child's well-being for the child's sake. In this interpretation, a parent will have fulfilled their duty of parental love by *trying* and *seeking* to achieve these ends; they will be blameless if in trying to fulfill both the actions and the emotional aspect, they achieve neither. I am dubious of this interpretation for the reason that although it may offer a more charitable and achievable interpretation of the duty, I do not believe it is what Liao means. If the duty were truly conative then a parent's unsuccessful attempts would be enough to fulfill their obligations. What a child would have a right to is the *striving and seeking* to love rather than the actual outcome of love. Why then was Liao at all concerned with showing that the presence of love is of benefit to the child? It is clear from the discussion that what Liao wishes to protect is the actual presence of the a. to e. provisions plus the emotional content. Furthermore, provisions d. and e. are clearly not conative and require the duty-holder to actually desire reciprocity and to value the child for their own sake.

Therefore, in placing the conative interpretation aside, to argue that the emotional component is necessary is to argue that one has a right not only to the desirable treatment but also to the proper motivation. There are clear problems with defining parental love in this way, the most pressing being that if the duty does consist not just of actions but also of motivation, can the duty always be properly discharged? In order for the emotional component to be necessary, it too must be a primary essential condition for a good life; in other words, the desirable treatment alone must be shown to be insufficient. I will consider these two objections in turn: (1) Can loving, an emotion, be a duty? (2) Is the emotional component an essential condition for a good life?

The Command Problem

A duty will necessarily constrain the liberties of the duty-holder. The actions of constraint must not only be justified by the claim but also be reasonable and achievable. MacCormick infers that ascription of a right to an individual presupposes that there is some act or omission, performance of which will satisfy, protect, or advance some need, interest, or desire of that particular individual.[37] It is not clear that the emotion of love is an action that can be performed by all duty-bearers as emotions are traditionally assumed to occur without conscious control. They cannot be commanded. How then can the duty-holder reasonably discharge their duty?

Liao argues that it is untrue that emotions can *never* be commanded and sometimes they are successfully commanded. He argues that one can give oneself reasons to have particular emotions, therefore, demonstrating a level of control.[38] In addition to these internal controls, we can place ourselves in external circumstances we know will bring about certain emotions. Internal controls may include practices such as giving ourselves reasons to feel warmth and affection toward a child or removing impediments to feeling this emotion. For example, recognizing the fact that the unplanned nature of a pregnancy was not the resulting child's fault may remove impediments to loving the child. Liao argues that external controls might include getting enough sleep to help one be more affectionate toward the child. This example seems somewhat counterintuitive—that by simply having a good night's sleep one may wake up in the right place to experience the emotion of love. It is certainly true that it is easier to be affectionate and caring when one is not sleep deprived but surely this is true for all duties, whether they are to love or to help my little sister with her homework and patiently explain concepts such as "rights." Sleep may help with the expressions of love but it does not have effect on the motivation, the underlying love emotion.

Though the example of being suitably rested may be an ill-chosen one for Liao's purposes, it indicates the broader problem with this approach. I have serious doubts about whether Liao is actually offering an explanation of how one can command an emotion. It seems that these are simply *conditions* by which it is easier to fulfill one's duties. We have already dealt with the interpretation of conative duties. It may well be that parents have a moral obligation to *try* and love a child, many of us may be happy to concede this; however, this is distinct from a duty to actually love the child.

Liao is only talking about commanding the presence of love in any given time. It may be appropriate to draw a distinction between two ways in which emotions manifest themselves. There is the emotion we may feel in a particular moment and the overarching feeling of emotion that is always present. For example, there is a difference between the intense love I feel for a child when she takes her first steps or says her first words, and the emotion I feel when I get up at 3 a.m. to attend to her screams. In the latter case, I may still have the overall feeling of love for my child but I may not feel the intense feeling of love at that moment. The conditions that Liao sets out refer to cultivating the feeling of love in a particular moment in order to act in a loving and caring way toward the child. They do not seem to be concerned with building a loving relationship or the overarching feeling of love. I would argue that this is probably the case because it is harder to control or even know *how* one would control this broader type of emotion.

Therefore, it still seems unclear that the emotion of love is an appropriate object of a duty as loving is not an action but a reason for action. In this, I am making a double claim. A claim about love—that it is not only about actions—and a claim about rights—that they are only about actions or inaction.

What Does Love Add?

I have demonstrated the problems with conceiving of loving as a duty; now, I will turn to the question of whether the emotional component of Liao's parental love is necessary. It is unclear what sort of relationship is there between the emotion of love and desirable treatment. Why is the desirable treatment necessary to fulfill the duty but not sufficient? Liao is essentially making two claims, first that the desirable treatment (provisions a. to e.) are primary essential conditions for a good life and second that the internal emotion of love is a primary essential condition for a good life. If we return back to the empirical research cited earlier, we can observe that there is no mention of the necessity of the internal emotion of love from the duty-bearer. How then is the presence of the internal emotions within the duty-bearer beneficial to the right-holder? What does love add?

In order to test this we can take the example of an individual who behaves as if they loved a child, provides the child with the desirable treatment but in fact does not feel the internal emotion of love toward that child. They *pretend* to love the child. Does this pretence fulfill the duty to love the child? Liao argues no, that a child in such a situation would be unable to develop certain "primary essential capacities such as knowing how to love others and having a positive conception of self" from receiving pretended love alone.[39] His reasoning is that in practice it is hard to pretend to love someone for more than a short period of time and that soon the child would realize that it is pretence. This, however, is an argument demonstrating that *discovering* deceit and pretence will vitiate the fulfillment of the duty. It does not answer the question about whether the duty is being fulfilled during the period of pretence.

If the child is unaware of the love, does this change the way we think of the duty being fulfilled? Although a baby may be able to observe the external expressions of love, it is unlikely that they can perceive or understand the internal emotion of love that may be present in their parents. Given this, does it matter if the love is real or pretend? The analogous situation, Liao argues, would be where I am owed five dollars by my friend x. I have a claim to the five dollars; therefore, friend x has a duty to pay me back. x, however, repays me using a fake five dollar note. Liao argues that x has not truly fulfilled her duty. Even if I successfully use the fake note to buy something and never realize that it was fake, the element of deceit will constitute an abrogation of the duty as there is something morally wrong taking place. Therefore, my knowledge of the deceit or pretence is not relevant to the fulfillment of the duty.

In the example of lending money, I believe the opposite is true. Friend x had a duty to pay me back; he did so as the money fulfilled its purpose and I was able to purchase something. x has fulfilled his duty to me; however, in doing so he may have breached a duty to others, for example, to the government not to forge its currency. We can understand the morality of his actions as separate from the claim and duty relationship that constitutes a right. Similarly, if I pretend to love a child and the child is unaware that my actions do not come from a place of love, they may still receive all the benefit that the right was created to achieve. I find the suggestion, that it is morally wrong to show affection and care for a child even though you do not feel the internal emotion of love, somewhat jarring. For most cases, we are not discussing the deceit of someone who really hates a child but pretends to love it—such as an evil stepmother in a fairytale—but instead consider a dedicated health-care professional or foster parents who despite all their conscientious efforts, feelings of duty and respect, do not feel the emotion of love toward their child. Liao has failed to show that the internal emotion is necessary; he has not demonstrated that the desirable treatment by itself is insufficient.

There is an assumption that (a) love will always be coupled with these beneficial treatment and that (b) it will not be coupled with negative treatment. Both of these assumptions are flawed. The emotion of love may not always be coupled with beneficial actions; for example, many parents may not think it is appropriate (one may imagine for cultural, societal, or personal reasons) to be physically or psychologically close to their child; however, this would not necessarily mean that they love their child less. We could also conceive of a situation where one would love a child in silence and isolation such as a mother with postnatal depression. Similarly, autistic parents may be incapable of these outward expressions of love. In both cases, it seems intuitively wrong to claim that the children are not loved.

Not only can love be present without the desirable treatment, but the emotion of love may produce undesirable treatment. As we have observed, love is an emotion that often produces loving actions—yet, it can also produce harmful ones. The family courts are unfortunately littered with cases where horrible things are done to children in the name of love. Children are routinely beaten by parents who love them. A child's relationship with their parents is often defined by power and too often this power can be abused. Even in instances where parents may not be intentionally harming the child, actions done from a place of love in order to benefit the child may be harmful. For example, the Victorian-era father who beats his child while saying "This is going to hurt me more than you" need not be lying. Or parents who spoil their children with the sweets they never had when young, but who, therefore, cause the children to become diabetic. Many parents have followed bad childcare advice, not through viciousness but through love, believing that what they were doing was for the good of the child. In such cases, it would be difficult to argue that the parents did not love their child and, therefore, impossible to show that a duty had been breached.

Jeremy Waldron identified a similar situation in the case of marriage and posited the idea of rights as either "fall-backs" or "constant constraints."[40] Waldron argues that often the bounds of love and affection will be enough to generate the type of treatment one wishes. For example, money is shared between partners because they wish to be generous not because of a claim-right to equal property. However, the existence of these claim-rights is still necessary, despite the fact that a partner may not need to "stand on them." They are necessary as "fall-backs" if the relationship collapses. Fall-back rights are coupled with rights that act as "constant constraints." These constantly constrain the actions of the partners. For example, a wife may have a claim-right to bodily integrity that constantly imposes a duty on her husband not to beat her. Liao seems to understand a child's right to be loved as a claim-right of constant constraint, that parents should constantly love their child *because* they have a duty to do so. In fact, it may be better to conceive of the relationship as such—most often parents love their children and provide them with desirable treatment and children in this situation have no need to assert or stand upon their claim-rights. However, sometimes love may produce undesirable outcomes or fail to produce desirable outcomes and children's claim-rights to desirable treatment will need to be claimed and enforced. Throughout both situations there are claims of sufficient strength such as the right not be abused that constantly constrain parental behavior. Consider how this may work in practice in family courts; if a child's claim against their parents is cast in terms of love, then it is too easy for "bad" parents to counter criticism with the retort that they in fact love their children. Focusing on the actions rather than their motivations allows a clearer diagnosis of what is wrong with the relationship—it is not the failure of loving emotions, but the failure to translate these into beneficial actions toward the child.

The fact that love can go wrong does not disprove that it can be good, it simply demonstrates that "love" as an emotion is not universally connected with desirable treatment and Liao's a. to e. provisions. We have seen that children can benefit from caring treatment and intimate interaction without the emotional connection and, further, that actions resulting from this emotional connection may in fact be detrimental to a child. Therefore, the internal emotion of love is neither necessary nor sufficient for the child's best interests and does not constitute a primary essential condition for a good life.

Some Alternatives

The conception of a child's right to be loved outlined above clearly demonstrates empirical, structural, and normative problems. However, are there any conceivable alternative ways in which we *can* conceive of a right to be loved? Before dismissing the right to be loved altogether, I wish to address here two alternative interpretations, namely, the right to be loved as a manifesto right and the right to be loved as a claim-right against the State.

Love as a Manifesto Right

Joel Feinberg has argued that there is a well-established practice in international law where statesmen often speak of "rights" when they are really concerned with the natural needs of deprived human beings. For example, take the assertion that orphans *need* a good upbringing. We know that in many places there are not enough resources immediately available to bring about this outcome. In these cases, there are no determinate individuals who could actually hold the duty to provide the orphans with the goods they need; the claim, therefore, is not *against* anyone but an *entitlement to* some good.[41] The statesmen are, therefore, by referring to these basic needs as "rights," are urging us to see them as worthy of sympathy and consideration even though they cannot now be treated as rights proper that bring about duties within other people. Feinberg is willing to speak of these basic needs in a special "manifesto" sense of a right and recognize that they need not be correlated with another's duty. Manifesto rights are "the natural seeds from which rights grow."[42] A child's right to be loved may, therefore, be considered a "manifesto right," a fair use of rhetorical license. Understanding the right to be loved as a manifesto right would mean that the corresponding duty is not imperative. Without the necessity of a duty and duty-holder, many of the objections I have raised would no longer be relevant.

There are significant objections against allowing manifesto rights to be recognized as rights in any sense. For example, if rights do not necessitate a duty then we begin to lose the very political and moral weight that rights-talk holds. Rights may become nothing more than important goals. However, the idea of a child's right to be loved as a manifesto right can be countered without entering into potential objections of the concept, because the right to be loved cannot constitute a manifesto right. The important aspect of manifesto rights is that they are "laws that ought to be made" or in Feinberg's language, the seeds from which rights proper will grow. Manifesto rights are not considered "real rights" because their corresponding duties cannot be fulfilled due to a lack or scarcity of resources. The desire is that acquisition of resources will enable the manifesto right to become a fully fledged right with correlative duties. However, the impediment to the child's right to be loved is not one of scarcity. It is not the case that there is insufficient "love" to go around but instead that "loving" cannot *ever* constitute a duty. The impediment to the child's right to be loved is not solved by the passage of time. Therefore, the right to be loved cannot even be properly understood as a manifesto right.

Noninterference and Architecture

Almost all international declarations and domestic conventions are State centered; they are designed to regulate the actions of the State in regard to the individual, not the interpersonal actions of individuals. Given this aspect of international law, we should consider the possibility that a child's right to be loved is not a claim-right to receive love held against the child's parents or care-giver, but a claim-right against the State. A claim-right against the State could be understood in two ways: (1) a duty in the State not to interfere with that love and/or (b) a duty in the State to provide the architecture by which the love can be received.

The State's duty of noninterference may consist of provisions such as not doing anything to prevent the development of a loving relationship between parent and child. For example, the State should not forcibly remove children from their parents or primary care-givers except in extreme need, nor should the State lie or mislead either parent or child as to the nature of the separation. This was what happened in Britain and Australia throughout the 1920s to 1960s when 500,000 British children were removed to Australia. Not only were they removed but many families were told that their child had died and the children told that their parents did not love or want them anymore. Duties of noninterference such as these are tangible and able to be enforced.

In addition to duties of noninterference, the State may hold duties to provide the architecture in which a child could be loved. The State holds within its power the ability to modify institutional architecture to enable parental love to flourish. For examples, programs such as paid paternity leave would allow parents and children more time together to develop bonds of love. It could also include not separating children from parents in immigration decisions and providing adequate visiting time for parents of children who are jailed.

Many of the provisions identified above already exist in the UN Convention for the Rights of the Child without any reference to love. For example, Article Seven states, "the child shall . . . as far as possible, the right to know and be cared for by his or her parents." Articles Nine and Ten provide that a child shall not be separated from his or her parents against their will and give detailed explanation of the exceptions by which the separation may occur, including provisions for the State's responsibilities in the event of the detention, deportment, or death of the parents. Article 18 states that "State Parties shall render appropriate assistance to parents and legal guardians in the performance of their child-rearing responsibilities and shall ensure the development of institutions, facilities and services for the care of children" and Article 20 asserts that children temporarily or permanently deprived of their family environment are entitled to special assistance by the State. These articles explicitly set out the type of provisions that would make up the content of the State's duty of noninterference and provision of the architecture to allow love to flourish. CROC seeks to do this clearly and effectively by identifying the duty-holder, claim-holder, and action required without any mention of "love." A child's right to be loved as a claim-right against the State may be the most convincing way of interpreting the right to be loved but it is better expressed without mention of love. For this reason, I argue that the right to be loved does not properly exist in this context either, for really it is only a re-badging of a range of other claim-rights, some of which children already hold within law, others of which are still to be codified.

The provisions creating the architecture of love come closest to the policy suggestions that Liao himself makes in the final section of his paper. Liao speaks of developing "institutional arrangements that would adequately provide for children's various essential needs" such as compulsory parenting classes and changes to the current single family adoption scheme.[43] These two policy suggestions seem to be advocating the involvement of government in enhancing institutions to increase the possibility that more children are loved—in short to provide the necessary architecture. The policies he explores do not relate to a child's claim to be loved held directly against her parents or care-givers—the very theory for which he spent so long arguing. A quick look at the type of policies that would be needed in order to enforce such a right may provide good reason for why Liao avoids confronting it. Teachers or friends may have a responsibility to report the parents of any child they suspected was not being loved. However, how would a state teacher or friend establish the presence or absence of love? Would we accept a child's assertion that she is being loved? No, as Liao argues, because if she is mistaken in her belief, then the duty is still not being fulfilled. Maybe trained authorities could judge the presence of love in a parent–child relationship? Finally, if it were possible to identify a breach of duty it seems inconceivable that we could force a parent to love their child in the same way that we enforce other duties such as debt repayments. If there is no way to remedy the claim after it has been abrogated then maybe the only way to enforce the right is to prevent the breach from ever occurring. For example, we may envision that those who are deemed unable to provide proper parental love would not be allowed to have children. Prospective parents may need to sit some sort of "love test," the same way in which prospective adoptive parents are subjected to intense scrutiny, not just of their material ability to provide for the child but of their psychological endowments. In such a policy, autistic couples may well never be able to have children due to their inability to perform actions that the strict definition of parental love calls for. The objector may say that these examples are simply ridiculous; however, they are only ridiculous given the ridiculous nature of the right itself.

Conclusion

I am not seeking to argue that children should not be loved. Children should ideally be loved by their caregivers who genuinely care for the child's interests and combine this with loving treatment and respect for the rights of the child. Parental love is a particular and unique experience; it is something that is often cherished by those who grew up with it and by parents who feel it toward their children. It is almost always a desirable state of affairs.

Liao seeks to provide the philosophical basis for a statement many people may find self- evident—that children have a right to such love. I sought to demonstrate in this chapter that although many people may feel that it seems right that children should be loved, this does not equate to a right as a claim. Liao's argument fails to establish a child's right to be loved exists, as opposed to a simple right to desirable treatment. The scientific literature used to substantiate the claim that parental love is a primary essential condition for a good life is insufficient. It does not even show that Liao's a. to e. provisions are essential conditions. Instead, it shows that short-term separations cause distress, but can be countered by improving institutional care and stimulation. Experiential or sensory privation can lead to a lack of physical and cognitive development but this can be reversed by increasing stimulation which does not have to be linked to the primary care-giver. Finally, children who grow up in institutions or are exposed to multiple changing care-givers can suffer lasting social consequences from the lack of bond formation in early childhood.

Even if Liao had sufficient empirical evidence, loving cannot be a duty. Loving is a reason for action and not an action itself. This double claim states that the "emotional aspect" is not an action and that to include it in the discourse of rights is to misunderstand the nature of a duty. It is also unclear what the relationship is between the emotional aspect of parental love and the a. to e. provisions. I have shown that the emotional component does not always result in desirable treatment. A claim to love does not always achieve that which it is constructed to protect.

Finally, I considered two alternative interpretations of a child's right to be loved: love as a manifesto right and love as a claim-right against the State. Manifesto rights are defined by the understanding that they can become legal rights. The right to be loved is constrained by conceptual impediments, not issues of scarcity, and, therefore, can never become a fully fledged right. A child's claim-right against the State seems to be an interpretation that could be realized as a legal right. However, the United Nations Convention for the Rights of the Child lays out these provisions individually and in far more detail than any consideration of a right to be loved could accomplish.

Children's rights should be statements defining the relationship between the interests of the child and the duties to which they give rise. These duties are actions or inactions that are in some way able to be achieved by the duty-holder and are properly understood to lie both with the State and with individuals with whom the child frequently comes in contact. In this way, a child's rights begin to sketch out the relationships they have with the rest of the world, but are by no means an exhaustive description. There is much to be done in the area of children's rights. If one wishes to increase the effectiveness of the care and protection given to children, one should concentrate on establishing moral and philosophical grounding for rights that are currently given little attention by adults and the State—such as a child's economic rights and to fair political representation—rather than confusing rights with love.

10

A Future for Children's Rights

Michael King has argued that Convention on the Rights of the Child (CROC) is like the magical fairy Tinkerbell from "Peter Pan." Like Tinkerbell, the Convention possesses the power to change children's lives but in order to do so it depends on the people believing in its existence.[1] As lovely as this analogy is, it is simply not enough for people to just *believe* in the existence of children's rights. Belief is a hard subject to introduce into any social science project. One's belief in the power and existence of children's rights can be just as easily countered by someone else's belief in the superiority of the family, the subordinate status of children, and the denial of rights to children. How does one resolve a debate based on belief? Rights do not appear out of nowhere like magical fairies. Rights, as I have argued here, are not based on belief but justification. Rather than have an ultimately fruitless debate about belief in the existence of such rights, the proper approach is to have a debate about what it is that such rights are intended to protect and why or why not those things are worth protecting. Rights are human creations; they are powerful social and political tools for change.

This book began with the question—do children have rights? Despite the advancement of children's rights in law, such as the adoption of the CROC, national legislation, and regional charters protecting children's rights, there still exists an underlying disagreement about whether children have rights in a philosophical or theoretical sense. Addressing this disagreement and providing a theoretical basis for children's rights is necessary to properly understand how such rights function, the shape of their corresponding duties, and how to effectively implement them in policy and practice. In the introductory chapter, I stated that this book had three aims: first, to present a theoretical argument for why children have rights; second, to examine and unpack the role of the terms "capacity" and "competence" in rights theory and their application to children's rights; and finally, to demonstrate the power of a strong theory to bring children's rights from the realm of "slogan" into reality.

This book has addressed these three aims in two parts. In Part I, I developed the theoretical basis for children's rights and in Part II, I applied this theory to four contested rights for children: whether Deaf parents can deny congenitally deaf children cochlear implant surgery; whether children born using donated sperm and eggs have the right to know the identity of their donor; whether children with gender dysphoria can consent to puberty blocking hormone treatment; and finally, whether children have a right to be loved. These case studies illustrate the limitations and the power of rights for children. Throughout the investigation into why children have rights and the examination of these case studies, this book has also highlighted some important aspects of the nature of rights in general.

In this concluding chapter, I draw together the main conclusions from the previous chapters before examining how children's rights can be realized in public policy making. The conclusions I wish to discuss are (1) children have rights; (2) there is an important relationship between capacity, competence, and children's rights; (3) the nature of duties is relevant to children's rights; (4) children's rights are special claims; and (5) a strong theory of rights for children is important for translating rights into practice.

Children Have Rights

It should be clear by now that children do indeed have rights. They not only have rights in law they also have conceptually defendable rights in theory. Children have rights because they have interests that are of sufficient importance to be protected. These interests ground claims that produce duties in others to act or refrain from acting. Rights are, therefore, understood as Hohfeldian claims with correlative duties. I have argued that when I speak of rights I mean normatively justified claims. Some of these claims can (and should) be translated into legal rights. However, some of these claims function better outside a legal framework.

This book directly address Brennan's two-fold challenge of first demonstrating that it is conceptually possible for children to hold rights and second, providing evidence that children do hold particular rights. Part I of this book applied the Hohfeldian framework of rights to the two leading theories of rights, will theory and interest theory. The analysis demonstrated that children can hold rights under the interest theory of rights because children can hold claims. The simplest definition of interests employs a thin evaluative stance to distinguish between benefit and detriment. Interests, therefore, must be those things that are at the very least presumptively beneficial to the claim-holder. It is clear that children have interests that are presumptively beneficial, such as an interest in adequate nutrition. If children can hold interests, then it is conceptually possible for them to hold rights.

However, even if children hold interests, it may be that none of these interests are sufficiently important to justify the imposition of duties of others. Therefore, the second part of the book applied the theory of children's rights to illustrate how children can hold particular rights. Chapter 7 applied the theory of why children have rights to the question of whether children who are conceived using donated sperm and eggs have a right to know the identity of their genetic parents. I drew upon empirical evidence to argue that donor-conceived children have a genuine interest in being free from any psychosocial harm that might arise from being prevented from knowing the identity of their donor. This is a real interest held by real children that justifies the restriction of the Hohfeldian liberties of others through the imposition of duties. The right to know the identity of one's genetic parents is an example of why children are not only conceptually capable of holding rights, but actually do hold them. In this sense, this case illustrates what children's rights *can be*.

Capacity and Competence

The second major conclusion of this book is that a child's competence is relevant to the determination of their rights. I argued in Chapter 4 that there is a useful distinction to be made between the concepts of "capacity" and "competence." A capacity is a counterfactual ability. One has the capacity to A when one has all the relevant skills internal to that person to A. Competence, on the other hand, is one's *actual* ability to A. Competence is the capacity to A plus the relevant mental states (such as knowledge and intention) necessary for successfully doing A. The distinction provides a useful tool to engage in debates regarding the requisite threshold children may have to meet in order to hold rights. The precise use of language is relevant not only in philosophical debates but also in policy-making.

In the third chapter, I outlined the argument from incompetence whereby children are denied rights on the basis of their reduced capacities and competencies. For will theorists, the argument from incompetence takes the form of denying children the status of right-holder as they lack the power to waive or enforce their claims. Having drawn the distinction between capacity and competence, it becomes relevant to ask which is the correct threshold for will theory. I have argued that it is actual competence that is required in order to hold a power. This is a relatively high threshold for children (especially young children) to meet. Therefore, many children lack this power as they are incompetent in rational decision-making, and, therefore, cannot hold rights.

Interest theory, however, demonstrates that it is conceptually possible for children to hold rights. However, it is not conceptually necessary for a child to hold the *power* to enforce or waive their claim in order to hold a claim right. Children's rights can be enforced by others, such as their parents or the State, without the force of the claim being reduced. Therefore, it is not necessary for a child to be competent in autonomous choice to be the type of being that may hold rights. Yet, this does not show that children can hold *all of the* rights that we normally ascribe to adults. The type of rights that children can hold is constrained by their competence.

Although the argument from incompetence as it is employed by will theory can be overcome, a thorough analysis of interest theory demonstrates that capacity and competence still play a part in constructing the rights of children. A child must be competent in realizing the interest to which a particular claim pertains. This is necessary for the interest to be considered of sufficient importance to impose duties on others.

The concept of competence, therefore, restricts the type of rights that children can hold. They will not hold all the same rights that adults hold as they are in a period of developing their capacities and competencies. If the benefit of the right pertains to autonomous action that a child cannot yet do, they cannot have an interest that protects this action. For children, the rights that we will restrict are ones usually pertaining to physical or cognitive incompetence. For example, a newborn baby cannot have an interest in voting, but may have an interest in being treated well by the government. When acknowledging the distinction between capacity and competence, it appears that it is again actual competence that is required in order for a child to realize the benefit to which the claim pertains.

The analysis of competence in Chapter 3 demonstrates that it is "task specific." Competence in one area does not entail competence in another. Similarly incompetence in one area does not necessarily entail incompetence in another. For example, just as my competence in making a rational decision about what I would like to wear today does not necessarily entail competence in making complex medical decisions about a potential surgery, my incompetence at driving a large truck does not entail incompetence in driving a car. This makes sense in terms of the relationship between competence and rights set out above. It is the specific competence to realize the particular interest that is of concern.

In the introductory chapter, I argued that this theory of competence constraining rights is different from Brennan and Noggle's "role dependent rights." In their paper "The Moral Status of Children," Brennan and Noggle seek to reconcile three common sense assumptions regarding children. These are the "Equal Consideration Thesis"—that children are due equal moral consideration as adults; the "Unequal Treatment Thesis"—that we can prevent children from doing things that it would be illegitimate to prevent adults from doing; and the "Limited Parental Rights Thesis"— that parents can exercise limited but significant discretion when raising children.[2] In order to reconcile these, Brennan and Noggle convincingly argue that "granting equal moral consideration does not imply that each person has the same package of rights and duties."[3] As I have argued above, demonstrating that children can conceptually hold rights does not entail that they immediately hold all the same types of rights as adults; they may have a different "package of rights and duties." However, the reason that Brennan and Noggle give for this conclusion is importantly different from my own. Brennan and Noggle argue that the reason unequal treatment is consistent with equal consideration lies in the difference between *basic* rights and rights that are dependent on context.

Some rights are constructed from basic moral rights plus other factors. They depend in part on facts about the persons who bear them, facts about the relationships of which they are a part, facts about previous commitments they have made, and facts about the societies in which they live.[4]

Some of these contextual rights are dependent on the right-holders' "role" and if one does not play the role then one cannot hold the right. For example, Brennan and Noggle argue that many of our political rights derive from our role as citizen or voter, as children are not mature enough to play these role they cannot hold the rights. Contrary to this position, I have argued that rights turn on interests, not roles.

First, many of these role-dependent "rights" that Brennan and Noggle identify are Hohfeldian powers not claims. For example, a judge has the *power* to sentence someone to prison, that is, to change someone else's Hohfeldian relations. It may be true that these powers are bestowed on them because of their professional roles; however, they are not claim rights based on interests. Saying that children do not hold these powers is the same as saying that adults do not hold these powers—this does not tell us why children may hold different claim rights.

Furthermore, for the examples that are indeed claim rights, such as the right to vote (that has strong correlative duties that others not impede our rights to vote and that perhaps the government has positive duties to enable us to vote), these claims are not properly explained by pointing to roles alone. We do not have the claim right to vote because we play the role of "citizen" or "voter," we have the claim right to vote because we have an interest in voting. Maybe part of the explanation of why we have these interests is related to our role in society, but it is not the ultimate justification. Brennan and Noggle's theory is initially appealing because I think it is ultimately reducible to interests. Understanding rights as claims justified by interests constrained by competence not only explains those rights that are attached to roles but also the rights of children and adults generally. It allows us to maintain that children have rights but not all of the same rights as adults. Children have particular rights because they have interests that are of sufficient importance to impose duties on others. Children do not have other rights because they do not have the relevant interests; for some of these interests, the reason children do not have them is because they do not have the competence to realize the benefit to which the interest pertains.

Capacity and competence, therefore, have an important role in understanding rights for children. However, the analysis of the relationship between capacity, competence, and rights also sheds light on an aspect of rights in general. The requirement that the claim-holder be competent to realize the benefit of the claim is true not only for children, but also for adults. This aspect of rights theory, though, is often obscured when we only concentrate on the rights of adults, for adults are often in command of most of the core competencies. It is likely, however, that as adults we will lose and acquire new competencies throughout our lives that will influence our interests and, as a result, our rights. Arguments about how rights are constructed for children may be just as relevant for the elderly or other classes of people.[5] Establishing a strong theory as to why children have rights can, therefore, shed light upon the rights of adults as well as children as they develop and decline.

Duties

It is not just capacities and competencies that play a role in how a right is constructed. Rights are also constrained by whether the corresponding duty is reasonable and achievable. Part I of this book demonstrated that a Hohfeldian claim always has a correlative duty. The duty correlated with a child's claims must be reasonable and achievable in order for the claim to be sufficiently important to impose restrictions on the Hohfeldian liberties of others. The duty-holder, therefore, must hold the capacity or competence to fulfill the correlative duty.

This constraint becomes clear when considering a child's right to an open future in the second part of this book. Feinberg claims that children have a right to an open future.[6] For a child to have a truly open future, their parents may be required not to "close off" any potential future. However, to properly protect such a right we would have to impose significant duties on the parents and the State. It would be almost impossible to truly guarantee that no potential future at all will be closed off to a child. Some futures are simply incompatible: for example, one cannot complete the training to be a world-class ballerina without closing off other possible futures, such as becoming a weightlifter. Attempting to achieve as open a future as possible may result in parents taking what Mills calls a "smorgasbord" approach by exposing children to many experiences and skills.[7] These duties may be onerous on parents but they might also have dubious benefit. It is far more likely that what is important is the possibility of *a* meaningful future, the quality not the quantity. It is clear that the reasonableness of the correlative duties can constrain which interests are sufficient to ground rights.

A similar conclusion is reached when considering the question as to whether children have the right to be loved. In order for children to have a claim to parental love, there needs to exist a reasonable and achievable correlative duty. However, a child cannot have a right to be loved because "love" is not a duty that can be controlled or reasonably imposed upon people. This, though, does not preclude us from stating that parental love is a desirable state of affairs for children; it is just not something that can appropriately take the form of a right. This example demonstrates the limitations of children's rights. There may be things that we think are desirable outcomes but that we cannot construct, and therefore protect, through rights. So, while there is some truth to O'Neill's critique—that we only see part of the story by looking at rights—it is not fatal for children's rights.[8] Rights still remain powerful and useful tools for protecting the needs and interests of children. I will set out the case for their power below. However, it is reasonable to see rights as only part of the way in which we understand a child's moral status.

Finally, the emphasis on duties allows us to see how rights are not isolated elements, but rather sit within a matrix of relationships. Rights-based frameworks are often criticized as being atomistic, of being overly focused on the individual and ignoring the complex nature of groups, communities, and relationships.[9] Feminist critiques of rights point to the importance of relationships, especially for children.[10] Wenar's model of a molecular right demonstrates that rights must be seen as sitting within a web of Hohfeldian elements.[11] For example, I argued that parental love cannot be the object of a right but acknowledge that the combined effect of Hohfeldian elements can be used to create circumstances where relationships and love may thrive. The emphasis on a duty needing to be reasonable and achievable is not a drawback of thinking of rights in this way; instead, it should be seen as a strength. It recognizes that rights are held by individuals but sit in relation to other Hohfeldian elements; they impose duties on others and are restricted by the liberties of others. This tells us something not just about rights held by children but rights in general. Rights are social beings, they cannot exist in isolation, without other people to bear the duty, hold the claim, and realize the interest.

Children's Rights as Special Claims

In the first part of this book, I argued that it may be the case that a strict definition of a "child" is not necessary for a theory of children's rights. This is because what is important are the interests of the individual, constrained by their competencies. It does not matter whether an individual falls strictly into the category of "child" or "adult," but rather whether they hold interests that are of sufficient importance to justify the imposition of particular duties on others. One could conclude from this that we should do away with talking about "children" altogether when it comes to rights. Analytical political theory is the project of examining concepts, terms, and ideas and refining their use. By using the terms interests, capacities, and competencies when we speak of rights, we equip ourselves with a more precise language and avoid the value-laden term "child." These terms can be used to describe the rights of not only young human beings but also the middle aged and the elderly.

In addition, there are certain disadvantages of focusing on the term "children's rights"; the term leads us to believe that there is a fixed and determinable group of rights that is clearly assigned to a fixed and determinable group of people. From the discussion and arguments presented here, it is clear that this is not the case. It is almost impossible to determine a fixed definition of children that will reliably tell us who is and who is not a child, and that is not open to challenge. Even if such a definition did exist, rights may vary drastically in both content and form between different children. The interests of a small baby will be different from the interests of a 15-year-old and this is partly to do with the difference in their capacities and competencies. By focusing on the interests of an individual, we cut through these concerns. So, maybe the key conclusion of this book should be that children can hold rights but talking of "children's rights" is unhelpful. We should just simply talk of the rights of particular individuals regardless of what stage of life they are at.

While we could possibly do away with the term "children" when talking about rights, it might not be desirable when we consider the way in which rights work in practice. Rights are at their most powerful when they are effective social and political tools to protect those things we think are most important. Doing away with the term children altogether may not allow us to achieve this. Speaking simply of capacities, competencies, claims, and interests may be more precise but it is unlikely that people will stop referring to young human beings as "children." If we want these rights to "work," then they need to attach to concepts that people will use. Analytical political philosophy, therefore, cannot solely be about identifying stipulative definitions and concepts but also engaging with the use of "ordinary language" ultimately in order to make something that works. As I argued earlier, it can even be the case that some conceptions of children can be very effective in providing motivation to secure and protect their rights. So, although a definition of children is not necessary in the conceptual construction of rights it may be useful in translating them into policy, especially since I have argued that children are people with rapidly developing competencies.

Furthermore, I have argued that it is useful to define children as young human beings whose capacities and competencies are rapidly evolving, because this highlights an aspect of how rights for those that are children may work differently to those for adults. The distinction between capacity and competence allows us to recognize something special about children, that while they may not have the same developed competencies as adults, unlike other incompetents they have the *capacity* to become competent. In addition, children have the capacity to gain a capacity; these are "latent capacities." This becomes important when we begin to talk about the development of a child's capacities. It also allows us to refute claims made by traditional liberal political theorists that children are in the same moral category as others who are static in their incompetence.

The existence of these developing latent capacities, capacities proper, and competencies grounds special claims held by children. In Part II, I outlined the future interest problem, which stated that interest theory works best with clearly identifiable present interests; however, actions could be taken toward children now that could harm their *future* interests. In response, I argued that children have a present right to develop their core capacities. Core capacities are those they would normally develop or those that are important to achieving normal human functioning. Therefore, children hold claims to the development of particularly important capacities. This produces duties in others to assist in their development. It is true that adults may also hold these types of developmental interests; however, because children are defined by the rapid development of capacities and competencies it is likely that these types of interest will be a special feature of childhood. Therefore, despite the fact that a strict definition of child is not necessary for a theory of children's rights, a broad understanding of children as young human beings who are in a process of developing and acquiring capacities and competencies is useful for constructing rights for children.

In this book, I have argued that it is necessary for children to have the competence to realize the benefit to which an interest pertains. However, there may be cases where holding a capacity is sufficient to convince us that the interest is important enough to impose duties on others. For example, consider a claim right to be free from torture. I have argued that if a person could not feel pain then they may not have this claim. They may have a right to be free from torture based on other interests such as bodily integrity or freedom of movement; but the claim right could not be based on an interest to be free from pain, since the claim-holder lacks this competence.

However, imagine that we do not exactly know whether a particular person will feel pain or not, or whether the pain one person feels will be the same as the pain of another. An academic colleague of mine, for example, has suggested that torture techniques such as solitary confinement would not affect him in the same way as it would psychologically affect others. Consider, then, that we have two individuals, my colleague and a gregarious undergraduate student. For the potential torturer, the only way to know whether these two individuals will feel the psychological pain of solitary confinement is to subject them to it. This would be an unacceptable state of affairs for most of us, for we must run the risk of potentially violating a right in order to ascertain whether someone has a particular competence to possess the right in the first place. We do know, however, that both individuals have the *capacity* to feel pain and this capacity may be sufficient for us to justify a claim-right to be free from torture techniques such as solitary confinement. It may not matter in this situation that my colleague ultimately will not feel the psychological pain, because the act of establishing capacity is enough to justify awarding rights on capacity rather than competence.

Considering that it is often difficult to make a clear competence assessment for children who are in a period of rapid development, it may be the case that there are some rights that we are happy to attribute to children even if we do not know if they are competent to realize the benefit to which the right pertains. The interest is important enough to justify the imposition of limits on the Hohfeldian liberties of others. Future research may consider how and when knowing one's capacity to realize the benefit of an interest may be sufficient to impose duties.

Perhaps more controversially, examining the nature of duties and children's claims could lead us to ask if it is sometimes acceptable to infringe children's rights. Samantha Brennan has built upon the work of Judith Jarvis Thomson to suggest that there is a difference between infringing, violating, and overriding a right.[12] Infringements are any failure to accord a right, violations are morally unjustifiable infringements, and overriding rights consist of permissible cases of infringement due to the consequences at stake. Therefore, it is conceivable that caught up in the story about developing core competencies is some sort of assessment that some of the rights that children hold can be justifiably overridden to bring about positive consequences. For example, the international tennis player, Andre Agassi, has recounted the story of how his father trained him as a child. At the age of two, Agassi was running around the tennis court with a racquet taped to his hand. His father trained him tirelessly and at levels that pushed the young Agassi's psychological limits.[13] Despite this grueling upbringing, or more precisely only because of this grueling upbringing, Agassi enjoyed a career as an international tennis star. We do not have to agree that this particular treatment was justified by Agassi's later success to see that there can be later benefits from having burdens imposed upon them as children.

Success as adults is often path dependent; we may not be where we are today unless our parents had acted as they did when we were children. Could it be that such extreme behavior from parents is justified to bring about success? Are there rights that children hold against such treatment? Can they be justifiably overridden? I am not sure what these rights are or how such a system would function free from abuse, but these questions begin to get at the heart of how children's rights are concepts that can help us make sense of complex situations.

A Strong Theory

I began this book by arguing that it was not enough to point to the existence of children's rights in law, we must also show that rights for children are theoretically defensible. This is not just an exercise in theoretical consistency. A strong theory of rights for children is necessary to understand the nature of particular rights and the shape of the corresponding duties. It can strengthen and build upon existing legal jurisprudence and effectively assist to translate rights into reality.

The theory of why children have rights tells us what children's rights *are*. The main strength of interest theory is that it squarely focuses the attention on what the right is protecting. By identifying the relevant interest, we can identify the correlative duties and the shape the right takes. For example, the power of a clear theory of why children have rights becomes apparent when examining the child's right to know the identity of their donor. This right is often given as the justification for removing anonymous gamete donation. Investigating what interest grounds the right can tell us important things about how the corresponding duties should play out in reality. I examined the three major interests that are usually cited to justify a child's right to know the identity of their donor. These are a child's interest in knowing their own medical and genetic history; a child's interest in knowing their genetic family in order to avoid concerns of consanguinity; and a child's interest in being free from the psychological and social harms that can arise from being prevented from knowing the identity of one's genetic parents. If the right really does exist to protect the first two interests then this right can be fulfilled while simultaneously protecting the anonymity of the donor. For example, we can provide detailed medical and genetic history information without specific identifying information or we can provide specific information about whether an individual was or was not related to someone else without providing the identity of their genetic parents. However, to protect the third interest, the interest in being free from psychological harm, we must impose a corresponding duty to reveal the identity of the donor. In this sense, the theory of why children have rights properly guides our actions by shaping our duties.

In this case, identifying the interest that the right protects also tells us something more. If children have a right to know the identity of their donor they must also hold a separate but related right to disclosure, to be told that they are donor conceived in the first place. I argued that the involvement of the State within the gamete donation process produces duties in the State to ensure this disclosure. This aspect of a child's right has also been recently recognized by the Victorian Assisted Reproductive Treatment Authority (VARTA), which now sees part of its role as to provide public engagement to encourage and ensure disclosure. VARTA runs several "Time to Tell" campaigns and seminars each year. A theory of rights for children, therefore, makes it clear what our *specific* duties to children are—it guides how rights should be translated into policy. Arguments about *why* children have rights are also powerful in pushing back on the momentum that previously established rights possess. A striking example is the foreword to the Victorian Law Reform Committee's report, "Inquiry into Access by Donor-Conceived People to Information about Donors." The Chair of the committee stated that

> When the Committee commenced this Inquiry, it was inclined toward the view that the wishes of some donors to remain anonymous should take precedence—as they made their donation on that basis—and that identifying information should only be released with a donor's consent.
>
> Upon closer consideration, however, and after receiving evidence from a diverse range of stakeholders... the committee unanimously reached the conclusion that the state has a responsibility to provide all donor-conceived

people with an opportunity to access information, including identifying information, about their donors".[14]

Existing rights, such as the right to privacy or the right for the terms of a contract to be honored, have great force. This is because their justifications are often well known and well established. So, it is understandable that the law reform committee came to this area with the assumption that this existing right would be more powerful than the simple assertion that children have a right to know the identity of their donor. However, having been presented with the first-hand evidence of the harm that can arise when individuals are denied this information, the committee changed its mind. Identifying the interests of children is a powerful way to establish their rights in practice.

Finally, we need to know what children's rights *are* in order to know what they *are not*. In Chapter 9, I argued that children do not have a right to be loved. Although it may seem that spending the time arguing what are not children's rights is to engage in a game of building strawmen just to show how we can knock them down, knowing what children's rights are not plays an important role. To demonstrate this, we can consider a recent submission to the Australian Senate Inquiry re "Marriage Equality Amendment Bill 2010," by the organization "Doctors for the Family." The submission argued that

> The evidence is clear that children who grow up in a family with a mother and father do better in all parameters than children without.[15]

Following the release of the submission, there was much talk in the media of a child's "right" to be brought up by heterosexual parents in a stable relationship. Therefore, the argument goes, the debate surrounding same sex marriage or donor conception for same sex couples is not one of prejudice or discrimination but a question of protecting the rights of children.[16] Understanding why children have rights equips us with the tools to unpack such arguments. A strong theory of why children have rights forces us to identify the existence of the interest on which the claim right is based on. In this case, it needs to be made clear what interests of the child are supposedly furthered by having a mother and a father, and whether these interests are really sufficiently important to justify limiting the liberties of same sex couples to have children. However, the evidence seems to indicate that the opposite is true. Children born to same sex parents are well adjusted and suffer no detriment compared to those with heterosexual parents.[17] Understanding why children have rights is, therefore, essential to counter attempt to use rights as a rhetorical device and as a proxy for other social policy debates.

Public Policy and Children's Rights

At this point in the concluding chapter of this book, it is worthwhile to take some time to consider the implications that this understanding of children's rights has for public policy. The donor conception case, for example, is interesting as it shows us the power of rights theory to provide a way into new policy problems. The questions as to whether individuals conceived using donated sperm or eggs have these particular rights has only arisen due to the development and spread of new reproductive technologies. With the expansion of biotechnologies, theories of rights will play an important role in shaping our actions toward them. Rights push back on existing assumptions in public life by establishing justified claims and requirements for action.

Public policy has been notoriously hard to define.[18] Defined very broadly, public policy is the actions taken by the Government when seeking to influence or achieve a goal. The Government can seek to do this through making legislation, through amending or introducing regulation, or by changing the way in which the Government makes decisions or delivers services. In my experience, much of the day-to-day public policy making in the Government is done through subtle changes to the way in which it works, rather than wholesale legislative change. For example, a Government department may change the way in which it procures human services, such as maternal health care, in order to ensure better services are delivered and that mothers expecting babies receive the best care possible in order to ensure that the baby is healthy. Or the Government may decide that decisions regarding a child's care should be taken by a combination of different Government departments, not-for-profit service providers, and member of their family in a consensus style rather than directly by the child protection officers without consultation. Public policy is not only done when a decision is made by the government, it continues through the implementation of that policy decision. It is important to understand the more subtle way in which the Government can do public policy making in order to know how rights may be realized through Government action.

Given that public policy can be understood as the actions taken by the Government to achieve a social goal, it is clear that public policy will have an important role in making children's rights a reality. We might broadly conceive the types of actions that the Government takes toward realizing children's rights in three ways: the duties that the Government may directly hold toward children; actions to ensure that other rights can be effectively respected; and having the role of duty-holder of last resort.

Direct Duties

The Government may have duties that are held as a direct result of claims children hold against them. Many of these rights will be duties that are codified in some way. For example, Government departments that deliver services to children, such as out of home care, have a duty to hear complaints from children. This claim held by children produces a duty in departments to have appropriate processes in place to receive, hear, and appropriately deal with complaints from children. Other codified duties may include mandatory reporting of suspected child abuse, clearly based on a child's interest to be free from abuse. The Government may, therefore, ensure that their policies and procedures fulfill this duty.

Some of the duties that the Government may hold toward children are not clearly defined or codified. For example, we would be willing to argue that children have a right to education and that in most liberal democratic countries the corresponding duty to this claim—to provide children with education—is held by the Government. This duty might be fulfilled in many different ways and the decision on how to fulfill this duty is taken through the public policy making process. For example, a Government may build and run schools directly themselves, or they may choose to fund and manage independent schools, or they may provide scholarships to private schools. The Government may also take other steps such as developing a national curriculum, standards for teachers, or special events and programs to ensure that the right to education is protected. The debate we must have is, therefore, identifying what parts of the interest that grounds the right to education, and any other interests held by children, will dictate which policy approach best fulfills the duty and realizes the right.

Providing the Right Conditions

Rather than directly holding the corresponding duty, the Government may be able to take actions that provide the right conditions, incentives, and environment to ensure that the claims that children hold against others have the best chance possible of being fulfilled. As we have seen, many of the rights held by children create duties in their primary care givers. There may be conditions where it is easier or harder to fulfill this duty. Conceptually, we might see this as relating to ableness—the external conditions needed to complete an act. In this sense, parents may have a duty to provide appropriate care for their children. Governments can ensure that they have the ability to fulfill this duty by providing such supports as maternity leave, childcare rebates, or even housing support for those who have the need.

When I considered the rights of children born from donated gametes, I discussed the types of actions that the Government may take to ensure that children are told they are donor conceived. This may include providing appropriate information and counseling at the beginning of the IVF process and running education campaigns such as the Victorian "Time to Tell" campaign. In this instance, the duty to tell a child they are donor conceived may not rest directly with the Government; however, in order to ensure that harm does not come to children and their rights are fulfilled, public policy programs like those mentioned above can ensure that the parents are encouraged to disclose this information.

Enforcement and Duty Holder of Last Resort

The final way in which public policy may be important to protecting children's rights is by seeing the Government as the duty-holder of last resort when a child's right cannot be appropriately protected by their primary care giver. This concept is usually understood as *Parens patriae*. *Parens patriae* is Latin for "parent of the nation" and refers to the public policy power of the State to intervene and act as the parent of a child who needs protection. For example, when a child needs to be taken into care, the CEO of the child protection department will usually become the legal guardian of the child. This allows the Government to provide a crucial safety net for children's rights.

The Limits of Rights

However, there are instances where rights in the strictest sense do not work as public policy tools. I discussed this in Chapter 9 when considering whether children have a right to be loved. Another more contemporary example is the question as to whether drinking while pregnant should be criminalized in order to protect a child's right to be free from conditions such as Foetal Alcohol Spectrum Disorder (FASD). A recent study, undertaken by the Lililwan Project, found that 50 percent of eight-year-old aboriginal children[19] attending school in the Fitzroy Valley have signs of FASD. FASD is more widespread than many imagine. It is referred to as an "invisible disability" as it often goes undetected.

In order to address this, the Northern Territory Australian Government considered a proposal to introduce legislation allowing criminal prosecutions of pregnant women for drinking. The proposal is interesting as, on the one hand, there is clear and strong evidence that high alcohol consumption while pregnant leads to lower development outcomes in children and, on the other hand, prosecuting women for something the rest of society regularly abuses[20] seems to be a rather large step. The biggest consideration for these purposes is that the Northern Territory proposal is framed with reference to the rights of the unborn child. Attorney-General John Elferink told the ABC's Lateline that they were looking to "either prosecute or alternatively restrain [women] from engaging in conduct which harms their unborn child."[21] This proposal, therefore, raises some thorny theoretical problems about whether the unborn child can hold such a right, countered by some pretty heavy arguments regarding a woman's right to choose an abortion.

Understanding the basis for asserting that children have rights is central to examining the question of whether a fetus can hold rights. According to will theorists, children, especially young children, cannot meaningfully exercise freedom of choice; therefore, they cannot hold rights. We may still hold certain duties toward children to protect them, but these duties are not borne from rights. According to this account, if young children cannot hold rights, then certainly the fetus cannot hold rights. Therefore, any reference to a ban on drinking while pregnant that relies on the fetus's *right* not be harmed cannot be substantiated.

However, as I have argued here, according to interest theory, children's lack of capacity to make meaningful life choices does not mean that they do not hold rights at all. Instead, the enforcement and delivery of rights can be exercised by others on behalf of the child. Under this theory, we may begin to build an argument for a fetus holding a right not to be exposed to alcohol in utero. The damage caused by a pregnant woman's alcohol consumption is certainly high, and the interest that all children have in good health and development prospects may be considered important enough to impose a duty on pregnant women not to endanger the life prospects of as-yet unborn children.

But, while it may be theoretically possible for existing children to hold a right not to be exposed to alcohol, we need to ask whether a fetus is capable of holding rights. There are actions we can take toward the fetus, such as drinking, smoking, or taking illicit drugs that are harmful and there are actions we can take such as eating well, exercising, and staying healthy that are beneficial. Does this mean that these interests ground rights? Or indeed that a fetus is the type of being to hold interests?

The fear here is that by ascribing rights to a fetus would see these rights in direct conflict with a woman's right to access abortion. For if a fetus has a right not to be exposed to alcohol, surely it also holds a right not to be aborted. In response to this particular theoretical quandary, Julian Savalescu has argued that it is better to legislate not by reference to the fetus's interests but with reference to the future interests of the child. [22]

In this case, it is not that the alcohol is harming the fetus now, in utero, but rather by consuming alcohol, a pregnant woman harms the interests of the future born child. By this argument, abortion is not harming a current person but preventing a future person from coming into existence, in the same way that taking contraception prevents a future person from coming into existence. A person who has not come into being cannot be a rights-holder. Existing children, however, have an interest in not suffering from FASD and, therefore, pregnant women should take steps to protect the future interests of their children.

This approach, however, seems to be missing the point. Instinctively, we still want to say that the harm is not just magically done to the child the minute it is born; harm is done in utero. Perhaps, there is a way to articulate the problem that recognizes that drinking while pregnant will have negative consequences if the pregnancy is brought to term but which also acknowledges that abortion is a morally defensible choice. If so, it would seem to point us in the direction of concluding that rights are not the "right" type of language for this problem.

What we are dealing with is a public policy question. The Government is considering how to stop women from drinking while they are pregnant in order to reduce the number of children that are born with FASD. Resorting to rights as a way to achieve this public policy outcome seems ill conceived for the purpose. Even if we are able to theoretically defend this right, its recognition does not guarantee its realization; it simply punishes the duty holder (in this case, the pregnant woman) for failing to fulfill the duty that correlates to the right. Exposure to alcohol in the first trimester is the most debilitating for fetal development. It can affect organ and craniofacial development and produce cardiac and structural brain abnormalities. One imagines that once a successful prosecution of the pregnant woman has been pursued, the damage to the fetus is already done.

The only value in ensuring a fetus's right is respected, therefore, lies in prevention. We might argue that criminalization acts as a deterrent; however, it is unclear that the communicative value of this legislation would achieve this. Understanding *why* women drink alcohol while pregnant and providing them with the support they need to make the choice to stop drinking early in their pregnancy is the only feasible way to actually prevent harm to the child.

A better way to conceptualize this problem is to side-step talk of rights completely and, instead, to consider our duty to prevent foreseeable harm. For example, we have a duty not to drive a car while drunk. This is not because when we get in the car we are immediately harming someone. It is because there is a high likelihood that engaging in this behavior will lead to harm and we have a duty to avoid preventable and foreseeable harm and to refrain from risky behavior. This duty does not need to be based on the rights of others. It is similarly the case that drinking while pregnant, especially binge drinking and drinking frequently, is risky behavior involving foreseeable and preventable harm. Engaging in risky behavior when you intend to carry a pregnancy to term is a different kettle of fish, morally speaking, to choosing to have an abortion.

Rights are a powerful public policy tool but not one that works in every environment. In some cases, rights muddy the waters rather than bring clarity. By doing so, they lose the very potency that draws people to rights language in the first place. For those of us who have made a career in examining, explaining, and advocating for rights, it is a worrying conclusion to draw that sometimes when a right is theoretically identifiable, its recognition may not be the correct approach in a public policy environment. This is a politically, emotionally, and morally charged area and if public policy outcomes can be achieved without playing the rights card, we should choose to save that card for another round.

Public Policy Based on Evidence

Throughout this book, I have sought to draw upon scientific research and evidence when arguing about what is in a child's interests and what interests ground rights. I have engaged extensively with the literature that examines the psychological harm that can be caused when a child is denied the information about their donor parent. I have examined the evidence regarding whether love is something that can be commanded. I have sought research of the desires and fears of children with gender dysphoria who are staring down the barrel of puberty.

However, it is clear that public policy making is not always influenced by evidence on what is in a child's interest or what works best. Public policy making is famously beholden to emotions, public assumptions, and political imperative. An example of this is the Drug Abuse Resistance Education (DARE) program in the United States. DARE sought to address and reduce the use of legal and illegal drugs by young people by linking schools and law enforcement. The designers of the program believed that this innovative approach would be more effective than existing programs in preventing school-aged children from using drugs by using police officers as educational instructors to increase the credibility of the instructors and the programs for kids.

The program is political gold: it combines a prevention approach to drug use (rather than a tough punishment approach) with law enforcement, thereby preventing the Government implementing the program from appearing soft on crime. As such, DARE is continually trumpeted by consecutive Governments despite any evidence that it actually works. In fact, in a 2001 review of drug abuse prevention programs, the US Surgeon General placed DARE in the "Does Not Work" category. A 2003 Government Accountability Office study reviewed the existing body of literature on DARE and found no significant difference in drug use between students who had completed DARE and students who had not.

Although DARE programs have been cut in many areas in America, many still exist and advocates still believe it is effective. This is based on anecdotal evidence from individuals. This might bring us to a discussion on the role of protecting rights in Government. In many cases, Government cannot act in the very way I have advocated for here, that is, by taking each child, each right, and each assessment of their competence as distinct and separate from others. Public policy rarely has this type of finesse. It is *public* by its definition. Often, it tries to target cohorts and as much as possible devolve decision-making to the individual. However, by necessity, many things must be generalized.

At the start of this book, I discussed the necessity to adopt certain standards in order to achieve optimal outcomes across the board. For example, setting the speed limit at 50 km an hour means that we do not need to assess in each situation whether an individual driver is driving dangerously or would have the capacity to control the car if something happened. In this way, public policy making regarding children is often the same, and often it is age that is used. This applies to simple examples such as setting an age for children to attend school, instead of making an individual assessment of each child's competence. I also discussed previously how, although there is a general rule that children under the age of 16 need parental consent for medical treatment, in many cases this rule is broken in order to achieve a broader public policy goal such as encouraging children to access services such as drug treatment.

However, there are ways in which the individual interests and assessment of competence can be the central consideration. For example, many jurisdictions across Australia are moving to delivering services such as disability services in a patient-centered way. This approach involves assigning case managers to each individual to coordinate the services that an individual needs. This allows services to be tailored to an individual's needs. Public policy must, therefore, try and find the balance between the broad brush approach of what is best for all, and consideration of the interests of the individual.

The true challenge for children's rights then is to take the conceptual power of a solid theory of why children have rights, based on evidence of what interests a child holds, and to make public policy that seeks to protect and enable those interests. It is this challenge that I am lucky enough to be engaged in day to day through my work and is the reason I believe that Government can play a positive and important role in turning children's rights from a slogan into a reality, taking them from philosophy to policy.

Conclusion

Children have rights, if we understand rights as Hohfeldian claims with correlative duties. Specifically, children have rights because they have interests that are sufficiently important to ground claims that produce duties in others to do or refrain from doing particular actions. A child may not need to be competent in the enforcement or waiver of their claim, but they must be competent to realize the benefit to which the claim pertains. Furthermore, the correlative duty must be reasonable and achievable to justify constraint of the Hohfeldian liberties of others. Children are in a special category of right-holders due to their rapidly developing capacities and competencies. Their interest in developing particular core competencies can produce duties in others to assist in this development.

At the start of this chapter, I argued that belief in children's rights is not enough. A statement about what rights a child has should not be just an empty slogan, but should instead be a full and comprehensive statement about the interests of that child and the kind of duties the protection of these interests imposes on others. The power of the theory of children's rights presented here is that it necessitates that rights be *justified*—they must be based on interests that children have the competence to realize, that are of sufficient importance to impose duties on others, duties that are both reasonable and achievable. Rights cannot guarantee all desirable conditions for children, but they are powerful tools that can be effectively used to enact change and protect interests of the utmost importance. Understanding why children have rights presents pathways to translating rights from a "slogan without definition" into practical social and political instruments for change.

Notes

Chapter 1

1. Rodham, H. (1973) "Children Under the Law," *Harvard Educational Review* 43(4), 487–517.
2. Regional charters on the rights of children include the African Charter on the Rights and Welfare of the Child (1990) and the Charter of the Rights of the Arab Child of the League of Arab States. National declarations include The Children's Charter Japan (1950), Declaration of the Rights of the Child in Israel (1989), and Declaration of the Rights of Mozambican Children (1979). Regional human rights instruments protecting the rights of the child have also been adopted by the Council of Europe and the Organization of American States (OAS).
3. One example that has always struck me to have surpassed the usefulness of debate is the field of moral philosophy called (tongue firmly in cheek) "trolleyology"—hypothetical scenarios regarding an agent's acts or omissions. For example, I must choose whether to pull a lever to stop a runaway train (or trolley) from running over five men but will as a consequence kill one man. See Fried, B. (2012) "What Does Matter? The Case for Killing the Trolley Problem (Or Letting it Die)," *The Philosophical Quarterly*, 62(248), 505–529.
4. Wellman, C. (2002) "The Proliferation of Rights: Moral Progress or Empty Rhetoric?" in Gearon, L. (ed.), *Human Rights and Religion: A Reader*, Brighton: Sussex Academic Press, 368; Feinberg, J. (1970) "The Nature and Value of Rights," *The Journal of Value Inquiry* 4(4), 243–260; Fortin, J. (2005) *Children's Rights and the Developing Law*, 2nd Edition, Cambridge: Cambridge University Press, 12.
5. King, P. (1998) "Thomas Hobbes's Children" in Turner, S. M. & Matthews, G. B. (eds), *The Philosopher's Child: Critical Essays in the Western Tradition*, Rochester: University of Rochester Press, 395.
6. Moorhead, C. (1997) "All the World's Children," *Index on Censorship*, 2, 159.
7. Tobin, J. & Alston, P. (2005) "Laying the Foundations for Children's Rights," *Innocenti Insight Series* 05/19, available at: http://www.unicef-irc.org/publications/pdf/ii_layingthefoundations.pdf.
8. Palmer, T. C. (1992) "How Much Power Should a Child Wield Anyway?," *Boston Globe*, published August 16, 1992.

9. For a good overview of the different arguments underpinning human rights, see Dembour, M. (2010) "What are Human Rights? Four Schools of Thought," *Human Rights Quarterly*, 32, 1–20.

10. Rousseau, J. (2013) *Emile (1911)*, USA: Dover Publications Inc., 34.

11. Turner, S. M. & Matthews, G. B. (eds) (1998) *The Philosopher's Child: Critical Essays in the Western Tradition*, Rochester: University of Rochester Press, 1.

12. King, P. (1998) "Thomas Hobbes's Children," 65.

13. Hobbes, T. (2004) *De Cive, 1642*, Whitefish: Kessinger Publishing, 8.1, 160.

14. Archard, D. (1998) "John Locke's Children" in Turner, S. M. & Matthews, G. B. (eds), *The Philosopher's Child: Critical Essays in the Western Tradition*, Rochester: University of Rochester Press, 87.

15. Turner, S. M. & Matthews, G. B. (eds) (1998) *The Philosopher's Child: Critical Essays in the Western Tradition*, 137.

16. Foster, H. & Freed, D. (1972) "A Bill of Rights for Children," *Family Law Quarterly*, 6, 344.

17. Holt, J. (1975) *Escape from Childhood*, Harmondsworth: Penguin; Farson, R. (1978) *Birthrights*, Harmondsworth: Penguin.

18. Foster, H. & Freed, D. (1972) "A Bill of Rights for Children," 347.

19. Holt, J. (1975) *Escape from Childhood*; Farson, R. (1978) *Birthrights*.

20. Hafen, B. (1976) "Children's Liberation and the New Egalitarianism: Some Reservations About Abandoning Youth to Their Rights," *Brigham Young University Law Review*, 1976(3), 605–658.

21. Wald, M. (1979) "Children's Rights: A Framework for Analysis," *U.C.D. Law Review*, 12, 261.

22. Fortin, J. (2005) *Children's Rights and the Developing Law*, 5.

23. Ibid., 4.

24. Hafen, B. (1976) "Children's Liberation and the New Egalitarianism," 644.

25. Fortin, J. (2005) *Children's Rights and the Developing Law*, 6.

26. First-generation civil and political rights are often distinguished from second-generation economic, social, and cultural rights. The distinction is more historical than categorical. In the post Cold War world, most treaties now recognize that both types of rights are needed for effective implementation. Indeed, the CROC (1989) contains both types of rights and does not seek to distinguish between the two.

27. Fortin, J. (2005) *Children's Rights and the Developing Law*, 37.

28. See Alston, P. (1994) "The Best Interests Principle: Towards a Reconciliation of Culture and Human Rights," *International Journal of Law, Policy and the Family*, 8(1), 1–25; Hammarberg, T. (1990) "The UN Convention on the Rights of the Child—and How to Make It Work," *Human Rights Quarterly*, 12, 97–105; Parker, S. (1994) "The Best Interests of the Child—Principles and Problems," *International Journal of Law, Policy and the Family*, 8(1), 26–41.

29. Himes, J. R. (1995) *Implementing the Convention on the Rights of the Child: Resource Mobilization in Low-Income Countries*, The Netherlands: Kluwer Law International; Andrews, A. B. & Kaufman, N. H. (1999) *Implementing the UN Convention on the Rights of the Child: A Standard of Living Adequate for*

Development, Westport: Praeger Publishers; Tang, K. (2003) "Implementing the United Nations Convention on the Rights of the Child: The Canadian Experience," *International Social Work*, 46(3), 277–288.

30. As outlined in the 2002 UN Optional Protocol to the CROC on the involvement of children in armed conflict. The Optional Protocol outlaws the involvement of children in armed conflict, raising the previous age of 15 to 18. The definition of a child soldier as held by UNICEF includes children working as cooks, porters, messengers, and so on. The definition, therefore, does not only refer to child who is carrying, or has carried, weapons.
31. King, P. (1998) "Thomas Hobbes's Children," 396.
32. Brennan, S. & Noggle, R. (1997) "The Moral Status of Children: Children's Rights, Parent's Rights and Family Justice," *Social Theory and Practice*, 23(1), 53.

Chapter 2

1. Those countries that adhere to 18 as the age of majority include, for example, Australia, United Kingdom, and most countries of the European Union. However, other countries hold older ages for liberties such as drinking alcohol, for which the age is set at 21 years in the United States and 19 years in Canada.
2. Interestingly, in Australia a child can choose to register for a DefenceJobs Membership from the age of ten. This is access to an online portal and newsletter which allows members to games, media, and news. The membership is clearly a precursor to recruitment and no parental consent is necessary to sign up.
3. Archard, D. (2004) *Children, Rights, and Childhood*, 2nd Edition, London: Routledge.
4. Freeman, M. (1997) *The Moral Status of Children: Essays on the Rights of the Child*, The Netherlands: Martinus Nijhoff Publishers, 91.
5. Though in practice you do not get fined unless you are going 55 km per hour. However, it remains true that the legal speed limit is 50 km per hour not 51, 52, 53, or 54.
6. Schapiro, T. (1999) "What is a Child?," *Ethics*, 109(4), 717.
7. Archard, D. (2004) *Children, Rights, and Childhood*, 19.
8. Ariès, P. (1962) *L'Enfant et la vie familial sous l'anien régime*, Paris: Librarie Plon, 1960. Translated from the French by Robert Baldick as *Centuries of Childhood*, London: Jonathan Cape, 125.
9. The most comprehensive critique of his work is by David Archard in Chapter 2 of Archard, D. (2004) *Children, Rights, and Childhood*.
10. Cassidy, C. (2007) *Thinking Children*, London: Continuum International Publishing Group; Cunningham, H. (1998) "Review Essay: Histories of Childhood," *The American Historical Review*, 103(4), 1195–1208; Heywood, C. (2001) *A History of Childhood*, Cambridge: Polity Press; Pollock, L. (1983) *Forgotten Children: Parent-child Relations from 1500–1900*, Cambridge: Cambridge University Press.
11. Archard, D. (2004) *Children, Rights, and Childhood*, 22

12. Prout, A. (2005) *The Future of Childhood: Towards the Interdisciplinary Study of Children*, London: Routledge Palmer.
13. Smith, A. B. (2002) "Interpreting and Supporting Participation Rights: Contributions from Sociocultural Theory," *The International Journal of Children's Rights*, 10, 73–88.
14. Ibid., 77.
15. Morrow, V. (1999) "We are People too: Children's and Young People's Perspectives on Children's Right and Decision Making in England," *The International Journal of Children's Rights*, 7, 149; Heywood, C. (2001) *A History of Childhood*.
16. Alison, J., Jenks, C. & Prout, A. (1998) *Theorizing Childhood*, Cambridge: Polity Press.
17. Franklin, B. (2004) *New Handbook of Children's Rights*, Oxford: Routledge, 33.
18. Archard, D. (2003) *Children, Family and the State*, London: Ashgate Publishing.
19. Cassidy, C. (2007) *Thinking Children*, London: Continuum International Publishing Group.
20. Prout, A. (2005) *The Future of Childhood: Towards the Interdisciplinary Study of Children*, 2.
21. Archard, D. (2004) *Children, Rights, and Childhood*, 27.
22. However, unlike Rawls who sought to argue that only one conception of justice was the correct one, Archard does not adopt the stance that only one conception of children is correct. However, he does suggest that if there are better and worse ways of treating children then some conceptions of childhood will be more conducive to treating children well.
23. Martin, R D (1983) "Human Brain Evolution in an Ecological Context," *52nd James Arthur Lecture, American Museum of Natural History*, New York.
24. Walter, C. (2013) *Last Ape Standing: The Seven-Million-Year Story of How and Why We Survived*, Bloomsbury: Sydney, 23.
25. Ibid., 46.
26. Wong, A. H. C., Gottesman, I. I. & Petronis, A. (2005) "Phenotypic Differences in Genetically Identical Organisms: The Epigenetic Perspective," *Human Molecular Genetics*, 14(1), 11–18.
27. Bouchard, T. J., Lykken, D. T., McGue, M., Segal, N. L. & Tellegen, A. (1990) "Sources of Human Psychological Differences: The Minnesota Study of Twins Reared Apart," *Science*, 250, 223–228; Bouchard, T. J. & McGue, M. (2003) "Genetic and Environmental Influences on Human Psychological Differences," *Journal of Neurobiology*, 54, 4–45.
28. Fraga, M., Ballestar, E., Paz, M., Ropero, S., Setien, F., Ballestar, M., Heine-Suner, D., Cigudosa, J. C., Uroste, M., Benitez, J., Boix-Chornet, M., Sanchez-Aguilera, A., Ling, C., Carlsson, E., Poulsen, P., Vaag, A., Stephen, Z., Spector, T. D., Wu, Y. Z., Plass, C. & Esteller, M. (2005) "Epigenetic Differences Arise During the Lifetime of Monozygotic Twins," *Proceedings of the National Academy of Sciences of the United States of America*, 102(30), 10604–10609.
29. Compas, B. E., Connor-Smith, J. K., Saltzman, H., Thomsen, A. H. & Wadsworth, M. E. (2001) "Coping With Stress During Childhood and

Adolescence: Problems, Progress and Potential in Theory and Research," *Psychological Bulletin*, 127(1), 87–12; Anda, R. F., Felitti, V. J., Bremner, J. D., Walker, J. D., Whitfield, Perry B. D., Dube, R. & Giles, W. H. (2005) "The Enduring Effects of Abuse and Related Adverse Experiences in Childhood," *European Archives of Psychiatry and Clinical Neuroscience*, 256(3), 174–186.

30. Lupien, S. J., McEwen, B. S., Gunnar, M. R. & Heim, C. (2009) "Effects of Stress Throughout the Lifespan on the Brain, Behavior and Cognition," *Nature: Neuroscience Reviews*, 10, 434–445.

31. Walter, C. (2013) *Last Ape Standing*, 49

32. Fortin, J. (2005) *Children's Rights and the Developing Law*, 2nd Edition, Cambridge: Cambridge University Press, 10.

33. Schapiro, T. (1999) "What is a Child?," 738.

Chapter 3

1. Mill, J. S. (1985) *On Liberty (1859)*, London: Penguin, 13–14.

2. Brennan, S. (2002) "Children's Choices or Children's Interests: Which do their Rights Protect?" in Archard, D. & MacLeod, C. (eds), *The Moral and Political Status of Children*, Oxford: Oxford University Press, 53–69; Brighouse, H. (2002) "What Rights (If Any) Do Children Have?" in Archard, D. & MacLeod, C. (eds), *The Moral and Political Status of Children*, Oxford: Oxford University Press, 31–52.

3. Brighouse, H. (2002) "What Rights (If Any) Do Children Have?".

4. Griffin, J. (2002) "Do Children have Rights?" in Archard, D. & MacLeod, C. (eds), *The Moral and Political Status of Children*, Oxford: Oxford University Press, 19–30.

5. Hart, H. L. A. (1955) "Are There Any Natural Rights?," *Philosophical Review*, 64, 175–191; Wellman, C. (1985) *A Theory of Rights*, New Jersey: Rowman & Allanheld; Steiner, H. (1998) "Working Rights" in Kramer, M., Simmonds, N. & Steiner, H. (eds), *A Debate Over Rights: Philosophical Enquiries*, Oxford: Oxford University Press, 237–302.

6. For an overview of these debates: on children, see Archard, D. (2004) *Children. Rights and Childhood*, 2nd edition, London: Routledge; on group rights, see Shapiro, I. & Kymlicka, W. (2006) *Ethnicity and Group Rights*, New York: New York University Press; on animal rights, see Singer, P. (1975) *Animal Liberation*, London: Random House; on choices vs interests, see Kramer, M., Simmonds, N. & Steiner, H. (1998) *A Debate Over Rights: Philosophical Enquiries*, Oxford: Oxford University Press; on cultural relativity, see Macklin, R. (1999) *Against Relativism: Cultural Diversity and the Search for Ethical Universals*, Oxford: Oxford University Press; on the appropriateness of rights, see Taylor, C. (1985) "Atomism," *Philosophy and the Human Sciences: Philosophical Paper 2*, Cambridge: Cambridge University Press, 187–210.

7. Hohfeld, W. (1913) "Some Fundamental Legal Conceptions as Applied in Judicial Reasoning," *Yale Law Journal*, 23, 16–59.

8. Steiner, H. (1998) "Working Rights" in Kramer, M., Simmonds, N. & Steiner, H. (eds), *A Debate Over Rights: Philosophical Enquiries*, Oxford: Oxford University Press, 235

9. Kramer, M. (1998) "Rights Without Trimmings," in Kramer, M., Simmonds, N. & Steiner, H. (eds), *A Debate Over Rights: Philosophical Enquiries*, Oxford: Oxford University Press, 7–111; Raz, J. (1984) "Legal Rights," *Oxford Journal of Legal Studies* 4(1), 1–21.

10. Hohfeld used "Right" instead of "Claim" and "Privilege" instead of "Liberty." I use "Liberty" and "Claim" throughout this thesis, as do many other scholars. For an explanation of terms, see Kramer, M. (1998) "Rights Without Trimmings" in Kramer, M., Simmonds, N. & Steiner, H. (eds), *A Debate Over Rights: Philosophical Enquiries*, Oxford: Oxford University Press, 8.

11. Hohfeldian pairs can also be stated as opposites. For example, when there is a *claim* there is no *no-claim*; when there is a *duty* there is no *liberty*.

12. MacCormick, N. (1976) "Children's Rights: A Test Case for Theories of Right," *Archiv fur Recht-und Sozialphilosophie*, LXII, 305–316, reprinted in MacCormick, N. (1982) *Legal Rights and Social Democracy*, Oxford: Clarendon Press.

13. Kramer, M. (1998) "Rights Without Trimmings," 26.

14. Perry, R. (2009) "Correlativity," *Law and Philosophy*, 28(6), 537–584; White, A. R. (1982) "Rights and Claims," *Law and Philosophy*, 1(2), 315–336.

15. I do not seek to answer here as to whether all duties are Hohfeldian duties. I am inclined to think not and that Hohfeldian duties are one type of duties or obligations. However, space precludes this from being addressed in full in this book.

16. Brink, D. (2001) "Impartiality and Associative Duties," *Utilitas*, 13, 152–172; Dworkin, R. (1986) *Law's Empire*, Cambridge, MA: Harvard University Press.

17. Kramer, M. (1998) "Rights Without Trimmings."

18. Provided we think that my friend is under no duty not to lie to me.

19. Sumner, L. W. (1987) *The Moral Foundations of Rights*, Oxford: Oxford University Press.

20. Ibid.

21. Ibid.; Kramer, M. (1998) "Rights Without Trimmings."

22. Kramer, M. (1998) "Rights Without Trimmings," 69.

23. Wenar, L. (2005) "The Nature of Rights," *Philosophy and Public Affairs*, 33(3), 233.

24. For Wenar's original diagram, see Ibid..

25. Wellman, C. (1985) *A Theory of Rights*, New Jersey: Rowman & Allanheld.

26. Lyons, D. (1970) "The Correlativity of Rights and Duties," *Nous*, 4(1), 45–55.

27. Wellman, C. (1985) *A Theory of Rights*, 70.

28. Holmes, S. & Sunstein, C. R. (1999) *The Cost of Rights*, New York: W. W. Norton, 43.

29. Raz, J (1984) "Legal Rights," 8.

30. Schane, S. A. (1986) "The Corporation is a Person: The Language of a Legal Fiction," *Tulane Law Review*, 61, 563.

31. It could be suggested that it is not that truth telling is a form of respectful behavior, but rather it is more plausible that not being deceitful is a form of respectful behavior. It is correct that truth telling and not deceiving are two distinct claims; however, I argue in the second part of this book that in the context of donor conception disclosing the truth is what is required to fulfil the duty.

32. Raz, J. (1984) "Legal Rights," 1.

33. Wenar, L. (2005) "The Nature of Rights," 25.

34. Sumner, L. W. (1987) *The Moral Foundations of Rights*, 51.

35. Will theory is also referred to as choice or power theory throughout the literature. For consistency, I only refer to it as will theory throughout this thesis. It is sometimes problematic to talk of these theories in general as they differ between theorists. For example, Matthew Kramer's description of interest theory is somewhat different from that proposed by Joseph Raz. However, the differences do not outweigh the similarities and the core function of the different versions of the theory remain the same.

36. Steiner, H. (1998) "Working Rights," 238.

37. Hart, H. L. A. (1982) *Essays on Bentham: Studies in Jurisprudence and Political Theory*, Oxford: Clarendon Press, 183.

38. Steiner, H. (1998) "Working Rights," 240.

39. Wenar, L. (2005) "The Nature of Rights," 239.

40. MacCormick, N. (1997) "Rights in Legislation" in Hacker, P. M. S. & Raz, J. (eds), *Law, Morality and Society: Essays in Honour of H. L. A. Hart*, Oxford: Oxford University Press, 197.

41. MacCormick, N. (1982) *Legal Rights and Social Democracy: Essays in Legal and Political Philosophy*, Oxford: Oxford University Press, 154–166.

42. Kramer, M. (1998) "Rights Without Trimmings," 69.

43. Hart, H. L. A. (1955) "Are There Any Natural Rights?," 175–191.

44. Campbell, T. (1992) "The Rights of the Minor: As Person, As Child, As Juvenile, As Future Adult," *International Journal of Law and the Family*, 6, 2.

45. Hart, H. L. A. (1955) "Are There Any Natural Rights?," 82.

46. In civil law, the phrase sui juris indicates legal competence, a person who is of full age and full legal capacity (Butterworths Concise Australian Legal Dictionary (2001), 45).

47. Hart, H. L. A. (1982) *Essays on Bentham: Studies in Jurisprudence and Political Theory*, 184.

48. Simmonds, N. E. (1998) "Rights at the Cutting Edge" in Kramer, M., Simmonds, N. & Steiner, H. (eds), *A Debate Over Rights: Philosophical Enquiries*, Oxford: Oxford University Press, 226.

49. Raz, J. (1982) "On the Nature of Rights," *Mind*, XCIII, 192–214.

Chapter 4

1. The distinction and discussion presented here is based on work conducted by myself and J.C. Lau at the Australian National University. Thanks to Dr Lau for allowing this to be published here.

2. "Capacity" and "competence" in the Oxford English Dictionary (2010) *OED Online*. Oxford University Press, available at http://dictionary.oed.com.
3. Beauchamp, T. & Childress, J. (2001) *Principles of Biomedical Ethics*, Oxford: Oxford University Press, 69; Grisso, T. & Appelbaum, P. (1998) *Assessing Competence to Consent to Treatment: A Guide for Physicians and Other Health Professionals*, New York: Oxford University Press, 11.
4. Kim, S. Y. H. (2010) *Evaluation of Capacity to Consent to Treatment and Research*, Oxford: Oxford University Press, 18.
5. Buchanan, A. & Brock, D. (1989) *Deciding for Others: The Ethics of Surrogate Decision Making*, Cambridge: Cambridge University Press, 45.
6. Lansdown, G. (2005) *The Evolving Capacities of the Child*, UNICEF Innocenti Research Centre, Florence, 4.
7. This example is adapted from Lewis' illustration of an ape speaking Finnish, although the points we aim to make are quite different: Lewis, D. (1976) "The Paradoxes of Time Travel," *American Philosophical Quarterly*, 13, 145–152.
8. Our understanding of a CA here draws heavily from the philosophy of action literature. We are aware that CAs are not perfect—they suffer from problems regarding modalities—but we cannot solve those problems here. We employ a CA here because it does the work required to find a practical solution to how we can understand "capacity" and "competence," but we could easily vary our account to reflect an alternate theory from philosophy of action, such as a probabilistic analysis.
9. For debates surrounding different versions of CA, see Davidson, D. (1980) *Essays on Actions and Events*, Oxford: Oxford University Press; Peacocke, C. (1999) *Being Known*, Oxford: Oxford University Press.
10. This is a first glance of our understanding of competence. A more nuanced consideration is discussed below.
11. Buchanan, A. & Brock, D. (1989) *Deciding for Others: The Ethics of Surrogate Decision Making*, 18.
12. See, for example, Davidson, D. (1963) "Actions, Reasons, and Causes," *The Journal of Philosophy*, 60, 685–700, or McDowell, J. (2011) *Perception as a Capacity for Knowledge*, Marquette University Press, 34–36.
13. Applying a contextualist argument here should not be particularly difficult. We can be contextualists about all sorts of things, such as language and knowledge, so it follows that we could also be contextualists about abilities: Lewis, D. (1987) *Philosophical Papers*, Oxford: Oxford University Press, 13; Lewis, D. (1996) "Elusive Knowledge," *Australasian Journal of Philosophy*, 74, 549. Particularly the discussions on what it means for something to be "flat."
14. However, if the piano were suspended in the air, the pianist's vertigo would negate his ability to play, but not his competence. Even so, we are simply trying to give a general account of the concepts and, as such, can bracket off extreme examples such as this for the moment: Dowding, K. & van Hees, M. (2008) "Freedom, Coercion and Ability," in Braham, M. & Steffen, F. (eds.), *Power, Freedom and Voting*, Springer: New York 303–304.
15. We are grateful to William Bosworth for the suggestion of this example.

16. Another example may be cochlear implants; I discuss this example in Part II of this book.
17. Our use of competence is equivalent to Morriss' definition of "ability." We use the term "competence" for two reasons. First, it is already used throughout the rights literature and second, the term ability is not sufficiently distinct from capacity. See Morriss, P. (2002) *Power: A Philosophical Analysis*, 2nd edition, Manchester: Manchester University Press.
18. Ibid., 58
19. Dowding, K. (2006) "Can Capabilities Reconcile Freedom and Equality?," *The Journal of Political Philosophy*, 14, 323–336.

Chapter 5

1. Parts of this chapter were originally published in *Contemporary Political Theory*; see Cowden, M. (2012) "Capacity, Claims and Children's Rights," *Contemporary Political Theory*, 11(4), 362–380.
2. Buchanan, A. & Brock, D. (1989) *Deciding for Others: The Ethics of Surrogate Decision Making*, Cambridge: Cambridge University Press.
3. Cohen, H. (1980) *Equal Rights for Children*, Totowa, NJ: Rowman and Littlefield, 56.
4. Ibid., 48.
5. Archard, D. (2004) *Children, Rights and Childhood*, 2nd Edition, Oxford: Routledge, 26–27.
6. MacCormick, N. (1976) "Children's Rights: A Test Case for Theories of Right," *Archiv fur Recht-und Sozialphilosophie*, LXII, 305–316, reprinted in MacCormick, N. (1982) *Legal Rights and Social Democracy*, Oxford: Clarendon Press; Campbell, T. (1992) "The Rights of the Minor: As Person, As Child, As Juvenile, As Future Adult," *International Journal of Law and the Family*, 6, 1–23; Kramer, M. (1998) "Rights Without Trimmings" in Kramer, M., Simmonds, N. & Steiner, H., *A Debate Over Rights: Philosophical Enquiries*, Oxford: Oxford University Press.
7. Campbell, T. (1992) "The Rights of the Minor: As Person, As Child, As Juvenile, As Future Adult," *International Journal of Law and the Family*, 6, 12.
8. Federle, K. H. (1994) "Rights Flow Downhill," *International Journal of Children's Rights*, 2, 352.
9. Raz, J. (1984) "Legal Rights," *Oxford Journal of Legal Studies* 4(1), 205.
10. Kramer, M. (1998) "Rights Without Trimmings," 93.
11. Lyons, D. (1970) "The Correlativity of Rights and Duties," *Nous*, 4(1), 36–46.
12. For a more thorough dealing of the third-party beneficiaries' objection, see Kramer, M., Simmonds, N. & Steiner, H., *A Debate Over Rights: Philosophical Enquiries*, Oxford: Oxford University Press, 197–198.
13. There is a possibility that financial stress may be an important moral consideration for an employer when deciding whether an employee warrants a promotion. However, this is a different type of moral stimulus. It may be that this becomes a moral consideration for the employer when making a decision,

but this does not mean that there is a claim held by the employee's wife against the employer. External moral considerations can be taken into account outside of the realm of rights.

14. Wenar, L. (2005) "The Nature of Rights," *Philosophy and Public Affairs*, 33(3), 241.
15. Raz, J. (1986) *The Morality of Freedom*, Oxford: Clarendon Press.
16. Ibid.
17. Aristotle, *De Anima*, II.5, 417a22–417a30
18. Schellenberg, S. (2007) "Action and Self-Location in Perception," *Mind*, 116, 622–623.
19. Dowding, K. & Van Hees, M. (2003) "The Construction of Rights," *American Political Science Review*, 97(2), 288.
20. Such a distinction may follow the framework laid out by Dowding and Van Hees. Such a framework may be useful for addressing arguments such as the following: some may argue that the right to be free from pain still exists even if one cannot feel pain. The corresponding duty not to cause pain is easy to fulfill, as it is impossible to breach. Yet, we may ask whether these types of formal rights are worthy of the name. What does rights-talk gain from insisting that those incapable of feeling pain have a theoretical right to be free from pain? Further research can build on this to determine when rights materially exist.
21. Raz, J. (1984) "Legal Rights," 208.
22. MacCormick, N. (1976) "Children's Rights: A Test Case for Theories of Right."
23. Lopez-Guerra, C. (2010) "The Enfranchisement Lottery," *Politics, Philosophy and Economics*, 26, 21.
24. Ibid., 20.

Chapter 6

1. Singer, P. (1974) "All Animals are Equal," *Philosophical Exchange*, 1, 103–116.
2. Whitehurst, G. & Lonigan, C. (1998) "Child Development and Emergent Literacy," *Child Development*, 69(3), 848–872; Beck, S. & Guthrie, C. (2011) "Almost Thinking Counterfactually: Children's Understanding of Close Counterfactuals," *Child Development*, 82(4), 1189–1198.
3. This example is an extension and expansion of one given in Dena Davis's piece; Davies, D. (1997) "Genetic Dilemmas and the Child's Right to an Open Future," *The Hastings Center Report*, 27(2), 9.
4. Annas, C. (1995) "Irreversible Error: The Power and Prejudice of Female Genital Mutilation," *Journal of Contemporary Health Law and Policy*, 12, 325–354.
5. It may also be seen as less interesting than that of another "future" interest problem of a different sort, the nonidentity problem, discussed by Derek, P. in *Reasons and Persons* (1984) Oxford: Oxford University Press.
6. Feinberg, J. (1980) "The Child's Right to an Open Future," *Freedom & Fulfillment: Philosophical Essays*, Princeton: Princeton University Press, 76–97.
7. Ibid., 126

8. Ibid.
9. Arneson, R. J. & Shapiro, I. (1996) "Democratic Autonomy and Religious Freedom: A Critique of *Wisconsin v. Yoder*" in Shapiro, I. and Hardin, R. (eds), *Political Order*, Nomos, XXXVIII, New York: New York University Press, 412.
10. Archard, D. (2003) *Children, Family and the State*, Aldershot: Ashgate Publishing Limited; Mills, C. (2003) "The Child's Right to an Open Future," *Journal of Social Philosophy*, 34(4), 499–509.
11. Archard, D. (2003) *Children, Family and the State*, 32.
12. Ibid.
13. Mills, C. (2003) "The Child's Right to an Open Future."
14. See Brock, D. (2002) "Human Cloning and Our Sense of Self," *Science*, 296(5566), 314–314; Strong, C. (2003) "Two Many Twins, Triplets, Quadruplets, and So On: A Call for New Priorities," *The Journal of Law, Medicine and Ethics*, 31(2), 272–282; Davis, D. (1997) "What's Wrong with Cloning," *Jurimetrics*, 18(83), 83–90; Scully, J., Banks, S & Shakespeare, T W. (2006) "Chance, Choice and Control: Lay Debate on Prenatal Social Sex Selection," *Social Science & Medicine*, 63(1), 21–31.
15. Eekelaar, J. (1986) "The Emergence of Children's Rights," *Oxford Journal of Legal Studies*, 6(2), 170.
16. Ibid., 170.
17. Parfit raises objections surrounding the supposed moral significance of the continuation of identity. Why are problems involving the same person over time given more moral weight than different people? See "Reasons and Persons" (1984) Oxford: Oxford University Press.
18. Archard, D. (2003) *Children, Family and the State*, 33.
19. See Feinberg, J. (1986) "Wrongful Life and Counterfactual Element in Harming," *Social Philosophy and Policy*, 4, 145–178; Shiffrin, S. V. (1999) "Wrongful Life, Procreative Responsibility, and the Significance of Harm," *Legal Theory*, 5, 117–148.
20. Of course, one could fall pregnant by accident without knowing these things; however, if one wanted to fall pregnant and did not know *how*, the likelihood of them being competent in doing so, or doing so by accident, is very low.
21. For more detailed work on the congenitally deaf children and cochlear implant case, see Sparrow, R. (2005) "Defending Deaf Culture: The Case of Cochlear Implants," *The Journal of Political Philosophy*, 13(2), 135–152; Dolncik, E. (1993) "Deafness as Culture," *The Atlantic Monthly*, September, 37–52; Lane, H, & Grodin, M. (1997) "Ethical Issues in Cochlear Implant Surgery: An Exploration into Disease, Disability, and the Best Interests of the Child," *Kennedy Institute of Ethics Journal*, 7, 231–251.
22. There is significant evidence establishing that children who receive cochlear implants benefit in the form of improved language comprehension and production. See Tomblin, J., Spencer, L., Flock, F., Tyler, R.& Gantz, B. (1999) "A Comparison of Language Achievement in Children With Cochlear Implants and Children Using Hearing Aids," *Journal of Speech, Language, and Hearing Research*, 42, 497–511. Geers, A. E., Nicholas, J. G. & Sedey, A. L.

(2003) "Language Skills of Children with Early Cochlear Implantation," *Ear & Hearing*, 24(1), 465–585. Svirsky, M. A., Teoh, S. & Neuburger, H. (2004) "Development of Language and Speech Perception in Congenitally, Profoundly Deaf Children as a Function of Age at Cochlear Implantation," *Audiology & Neurotology*, 9, 224–233.

23. Note that at this stage, I do not deal with the question of whether individuals have rights to have their capacities raised *beyond* the normal human functioning level, that is, if we can make someone not only hear but hear better than anyone else. However, for a good discussion of human enhancement, see Savulescu, J. & Bostrum, N. (eds) (2009) *Human Enhancement*, Oxford: Oxford University Press.

24. Boorse, C. (1977) "Health as a Theoretical Concept," *Philosophy of Science*, 44, 542–573.

25. Daniels, N. (1985) *Just Health Care*, Cambridge: Cambridge University Press; Satz, A. B. (2006) "A Jurisprudence of Dysfunction: On the Role of 'Normal Species Functioning' in Disability Analysis," *Yale Journal of Health Policy, Law and Ethics*, 221–268.

26. Daniels, N. (1985) *Just Health Care*, 2.

27. Ibid., 5.

28. Satz, A. B. (2006) "A Jurisprudence of Dysfunction."

29. Ibid., 224.

30. Mills, C. (2003) "The Child's Right to an Open Future," 499.

31. Ibid., 499.

32. Capacities like these are set out in Nussbaum's "capabilities" list. Nussbaum, M. (1997) "Capabilities and Human Rights," *Fordham Law Review*, 66, 273–300.

33. Mills, C. (2003) "The Child's Right to an Open Future," 506

34. There even may be some capacities which we deem to be normal human functioning but we wish to prevent from developing; for example, many children who have gender disorder are given puberty-stopping drugs to prevent the development of secondary sexual characteristics. I cannot deal with this in full here, but it may be a fruitful place for future research.

35. Here, I follow other scholars and use the capitalized "Deaf" to indicate the broader Deaf community and culture and the lower case "deaf" to indicate the loss of hearing purely in the medical sense.

36. Edwards, S. A. (2004) "Disability, Identity and the 'expressivist objection'," *Journal of Medical Ethics*, 30, 418–420.

37. Sparrow, R. (2005) "Defending Deaf Culture: The Case of Cochlear Implants," *Journal of Political Philosophy*, 13(2), 140.

38. Davis, D. (1997) "Genetic Dilemmas and the Child's Right to an Open Future," *The Hastings Center Report*, 27(2), 12.

39. Albrecht, G. L. & Devlieger, P. L. (1999) "The Disability Paradox: High Quality of Life Against All Odds," *Social Science & Medicine*, 48(8), 977.

40. Groce, N. E. (1985) *Everyone Here Spoke Sign Language: Hereditary Deafness on Martha's Vineyard*, Cambridge: Harvard University Press.
41. Sparrow, R. (2005) "Defending Deaf Culture: The Case of Cochlear Implants," 137.
42. Davies, D. (1997) "Genetic Dilemmas and the Child's Right to an Open Future," 12.
43. Feinberg, J. (1986) "Wrongful Life and Counterfactual Element in Harming," 149.
44. Crouch, R. A. (1997) "Letting the Deaf Be Deaf: Reconsidering the Use of Cochlear Implants in Prelingually Deaf Children," *The Hasting Centre Report*, 27(4), 14–21.
45. Sparrow, R. (2005) "Defending Deaf Culture: The Case of Cochlear Implants," 140.

Chapter 7

1. This chapter was first published as an article in the *International Journal of Law, Policy and the Family*; thanks go to the editors for allowing it to appear in as a slightly revised version here. See Cowden, M. (2012) "No Harm, No Foul: A Child's Right to Know Their Genetic Parents," *International Journal of Law, Policy and the Family*, 26(1), 102–126.
2. The study by Turkmendag also indicates that this is persuasive logic for parents in the United Kingdom. Potential parents are concerned about the potential adverse affects of disclosure on a child's development. See Turkmendag,, I, Dingwall, R and Murphy, T. (2008) "The Removal of Donor Anonymity in the UK: The Silencing of Claims by Would-be-Parents," *International Journal of Law, Policy and the Family*, 22(3), 298
3. The phrase "no harm, no foul" was originally coined by American basketball sportscaster, Chick Hearn in the 1960s. The phrase indicates the rule of advantage play. If an action that is against the rules of the game does not affect the outcome of the game then no foul (wrong) has been committed and no punishment should be played out.
4. I use "non-anonymous donation" to refer to countries or States whereby anonymous donation is not allowed. This is not to be confused with other systems, which may be considered "open" as both anonymous and non-anonymous donations are accepted, such as the "double track" system recommended by Pennings. See Pennings, G. (2007) "The Double Track Policy for Donor Anonymity," *Human Reproduction*, 12(12), 2839–2844.
5. Throughout this chapter, I shall refer to the parents who are genetically related to the child as the "genetic parents" and the parents who are the legal guardians of the child as the "social parents."
6. Dewar, J. (1989) "Fathers in Law? The Case of AID" in Lee, R. & Morgan, D. (eds), *Birthrights: Law and Ethics at the Beginnings of Life*, London: Routledge, 115–131.

7. Status of Children Act, 1975 (Tas); Artificial Conception Act 1984 (NSW); Family Relationships Act 1984 (SA); Family Relationships Amendments Act 1984 (ACT); Status of Children Act 1984 (Vic); Artificial Conception Act 1985 (WA); Artificial Conception Act 1985 (Qld).

8. Firth, L. (2001) "Gamete Donation and Anonymity: The Ethical and Legal Debate," *Human Reproduction*, 16, 818–824; Daniels, K. & Taylor, K. (1993) "Secrecy & Openness in Donor Insemination," *Political & Life Sciences*, 12, 157–159.

9. In January 2011, the UK Human Fertilisation and Embryology Authority (HFEA) launched a public consultation regarding increased compensation for gamete donors. Submissions expressed the view that adequate compensation may be a method to address the gamete "shortage." See "HFEA launches public consultation on sperm and egg donation," http://www.hfea.gov.uk/6285.html accessed: 29/7/2011.

10. Daniels, K. & Lalos, O. (1997) "The Swedish Insemination Act and the availability of donors," *Human Reproduction*, 7, 1871–1874; Turkmendag, et al. (2008) "The Removal of Donor Anonymity in the UK," 288.

11. Blood, J., Pitt, P. & Parker, H. W. G. L (1998) "Parents' Decision to Inform Children of their Donor: Sperm Conception and the Impact of a Register which legislated to enable Identification of Donors," unpublished Paper, *Royal Women's Hospital and the University of Melbourne*.

12. Turner, A. J. & Coyle, A. (2002) "What Does it Mean to be a Donor Offspring? The Identity Experience of Adults Conceived by Donor Insemination and the Implications for Counseling and Therapy," *Human Reproduction*, 15, 2041–2051.

13. Countries that no longer support anonymous gamete donation include Sweden, the United Kingdom, Austria, Switzerland, New Zealand, Australia, Norway, and the Netherlands.

14. Szoke, H. (2003) "Australia—A Federated Structure Of Statutory Regulation of ART" in Gunning, J. & Szoke, H. (eds), *The Regulation of Assisted Reproductive Technology*, Aldershot: Ashgate Publishing Limited, 75–94.

15. During the 2010 Senate inquiry, the Attorney Generals' department declined to provide legal advice on whether there exists a Commonwealth power within the constitution that would allow the Commonwealth to legislate in this area. Also see Schneller, E. A. (2005) "The Rights of Donor Inseminated Children to Know Their Genetic Origins in Australia," *Australian Journal of Family Law*, 19, 228; Szoke, H. (2003) "Australia—a Federated Structure Of Statutory Regulation of ART," 75.

16. National Health and Medical Research Council (2007) "Ethical Guidelines on the Use of Assisted Reproductive Technology in Clinical Practice and Research," available at: https://www.nhmrc.gov.au/_files_nhmrc/publications/attachments/e78.pdf, Part B, 6.1, 25.

17. South Australian legislation has recently been amended to enable the establishment of a register in the future if desired.

18. *National Health and Medical Research Act* (1992) (Cth).

19. NHMRC Guidelines, (2007) Part B, 6.1, p25.
20. Blair, M. (2002) "The Impact of Family Paradigms, Domestic Constitutions and International Conventions on Disclosure of an Adopted Person's Identities and Heritage: A Comparative Examination," *Michigan Journal of International Law*, 22, 587.
21. Commonwealth of Australia (2011) "Donor Conception Practices in Australia," *Senate Inquiry into Donor Conception Practices in Australia*, Sec 2.3 at 7.
22. SCAG has since been transferred into the Law, Crime and Community Safety Standing Council and is now constituted of Attorneys General and Police Ministers across jurisdictions.
23. Dennison, M. (2008) "Revealing Your Sources: The Case for Non-Anonymous Gamete Donation," *Journal of Law and Health*, 21, 14.
24. Lamport, A. (1988) "The Genetics of Secrecy in Adoption, Artificial Insemination, and in Vitro Fertilization," *American Journal of Law and Medicine*, 14, 109–124.
25. Dennison, M. (2008) "Revealing Your Sources," 14; McWhinnie, A. M. (1995) "A Study of Parenting of IVF and DI Children," *Medical Law*, 14, 815.
26. NHMRC Guidelines, (2007).
27. Dennison, M. (2008) "Revealing Your Sources," 14.
28. Schull, W. J. (1958) "Empirical Risks in Consanguineous Marriages: Sex Ration Malformation and Viability," *American Journal of Human Genetics*, 10, 294–343.
29. Marrriage Act (Australia) (1961) Subsection 23(2).
30. *Senate Inquiry into Donor Conception Practices in Australia* (2011), 70.
31. Dennison, M. (2008) "Revealing Your Sources," 15.
32. Human Reproductive Technology Directions [WA] para 8.1; *Assisted Reproductive Technology Act* 2007 [NSW] s 27(1); *Assisted Reproductive Treatment Act* 2008 [Vic] s 29.
33. *Senate Inquiry into Donor Conception Practices in Australia* (2011) 73.
34. Ibid., 77.
35. Ibid., 77.
36. Sants, H. J. (1964) "Genealogical Bewilderment in Children with Substitute Parents," *British Journal of Medical Psychology*, 37, 133–141.
37. Brodzinsky, D. M., Schechter, M. D. & Henig, R. M. (1992) *Being Adopted: The Lifelong Search for Self.* Doubleday, New York; Krueger-Jago, M. J. & Hanna, F. J. (1997) "Why Adoptees Search: An Existential Treatment Perspective," *Journal of Counselling and Development*, 75, 195–202.
38. McWhinnie, A. M. (1995) "A Study of Parenting of IVF and DI Children"; McGee, G., Brakman, S. V. & Gurmankin, A. D. (2001) "Gamete Donation and Anonymity: Disclosure to Children Conceived with Donor Gametes Should Not be Optional," *Human Reproduction*, 16, 2033–2038; Dennison, M. (2008) "Revealing Your Sources."
39. Shenfield, F. (1994) "Ethics and Society: Filiation in Assisted Reproduction: Potential Conflicts and Legal Implications," *Human Reproduction*, 12,

1348–1354; Turkmendag et al. (2008) "The Removal of Donor Anonymity in the UK."

40. Turner & Coyle (2002).

41. Scheib, J. E., Riordan, M. & Rubiri, S. (2003) "Choosing Identity—Release Sperm Donors: The Parents Perspective 13–18 Years Later," *Human Reproduction*, 18, 1115–1127.

42. *Senate Inquiry into Donor Conception Practices in Australia* (2011), 78–80.

43. Turner, A. J. & Coyle, A. (2002) "What Does it Mean to be a Donor Offspring?," 2050.

44. Golombok, S., Brewaeys, A., Cook, R., Giavazzi, M. T., Guerra, D., Manovani, A., van Hall, E., Crosignani, P. G. & Dexeus, S. (1996) "The European Study of Assisted Reproduction Families: Family Functioning and Child Development," *Human Reproduction*, 11, 2324–2331; Golombok, S., Maccallum, F., Goodman, E. & Rutter, M. (2002) "Families with Children Conceived by Donor Insemination: A Follow up at Age 12," *Child Development*, 73, 952–958; Golombok, S., Brewaeys, A., Giavazzi, M., Guerra, D., MacCullum, F. & Rusi, J. (2002) "The European Study of Assisted Reproduction Families; the transition to Adolescence," *Human Reproduction*, 17, 830–840; Scheib, J. E., Riordan, M. & Rubiri, S. (2003) "Choosing Identity."

45. Gottlieb, C., Othorn, L. & Lindblad, F. (2000) "Disclosure of Donor Insemination to the Child: The Impact of Swedish Legislation on Couples' Attitudes," *Human Reproduction*, 15, 2052–2056.

46. In fact, this was one of the "selling points" of gamete donation. Dr Finegold explained that when presenting the reasons for preferring artificial insemination over adoption he would explain to prospective parents that, "To his friends, the husband has finally impregnated his wife ... in AI (Artificial Insemination) the child is never told." See Finegold, W. J. (1964) "Artificial Insemination," Springfield, IL: Charles C Thomas Publisher.

47. Mill, J. S. (1985) *On Liberty (1859)*, London: Penguin, 22.

48. Feinberg, J. (1985) *Harm to Others: The Moral Limits of the Criminal Law*, Oxford: Oxford University Press, 145–146.

49. Feinberg, J. (1987) "Wrongful Life and the Counterfactual Element in Harming," *Social Philosophy and Policy* 4(1), 147.

50. Golombok, S., Brewaeys, A., Cook, R., Giavazzi, M. T., Guerra, D., Manovani, A., van Hall, E., Crosignani, P. G. & Dexeus, S. (1996) "The European Study of Assisted Reproduction Families," 2324–2331.

51. Feinberg, J. (1987) "Wrongful Life," 149.

52. Vanfraussen, K., Ponjaert-Kristoffersen, I. & Brewaeys, A. (2000) "An Attempt to Reconstruct Children's Donor Concept: A Comparison Between Children's and Lesbian Parents' Attitudes Towards Donor Anonymity," *Human Reproduction*, 16, 2019–2025.

53. Archard, D. (2007) "The Wrong of Rape," *The Philosophical Quarterly*, 57, 371–393.

54. Golombok, S., Murray, C., Brisden, P. & Abdalla, H. (1999) "Social vs Biological Parenting: Family Functioning and the Socio-Emotional Development of

Children Conceived by Egg or Sperm Donation," *Journal of Child Psychology and Psychiatry*, 40, 519–527.

55. Daniels, K. & Taylor, K. (1993) "Secrecy & Openness in Donor Insemination," *Political & Life Sciences*, 12(155), 380.

56. Manuel, C., Chevret, M. & Cyzba, J. (1980) "Handling of Secrecy by AID Couples." In David, G. & Price, W. (eds), *Human Artificial Insemination and Semen Preservation*, New York: Plenum Press, 419–429; Lasker, J. N. & Borg, S. (1989) *In Search of Parenthood. Coping with Infertility and High Tech Conception*, Sydney: Pandora; Klock, S. C. & Maier, D. (1991) "Psychological Factors Related to Donor Insemination," *Fertility Sterility*, 56, 489–495.

57. Brewaeys, A. (1996) "Donor Insemination and Child Development," *Journal of Psychosomatic Obstetrics & Gynecology*, 17, 1–13.

58. Baran, A. & Panor, R. (2003) *Lethal Secrets. The Psychology of Donor Insemination Problems and Solutions*, 2nd Edition, New York: Amistad.

59. McGee, G., Brakman, S. V. & Gurmankin, A. D. (2001) "Gamete Donation and Anonymity: Disclosure to Children Conceived with Donor Gametes Should Not be Optional," *Human Reproduction*, 16, 2033–2038.

60. Daniels, K. and Lalos, O. (1997) "The Swedish Insemination Act and the Availability of Donors."

61. Johnson, L. & Kane, H. (2007) "Regulation of Donor Conception and the "time to tell" Campaign," *Journal of Law and Medicine*, 15(1), 125.

62. This remains true in Australia as seen in the recent asbestos miner case, *Amaca Pty ltd v Ellis; The State of South Australia v Ellis; Millenium Inorganic Chemicals Limited v Ellis* [2010] HCA 5. Although the appellants were found to be negligent and to have breached a duty or duties owed to the defendant, Mr Cotton, it could not be shown that Mr Cotton's lung cancer was a result of the appellant's risky behavior. Mr Cotton had no claim to be free from risky behavior without the risk eventuating into harm.

63. Gardner, J. & Shute, S. (2000) "The Wrongness of Rape" in Horder, J. (ed.), *Oxford Essays in Jurisprudence, Fourth Series*, Oxford: Oxford University Press, 193–217.

64. Ibid., 196.

65. Ibid., 203–204

66. Darwall, S. L. (1977) "Two Kinds of Respect," *Ethics* 88, 38

67. Ibid., 40.

68. Teitelbaum, L. E. (1998) "Children's Rights and the Problem of Equal Respect," *Hofstra Law Review*, 27, 799

69. It has not always been the case that respect for persons entailed that a "person" must be autonomous. See Lysaught, M. T. (2004) "Respect: Or, How Respect for Persons Became Respect for Autonomy," *Journal of Medicine and Philosophy*, 29(6), 665–680.

70. Darwall, S. L. (2000), "Two Kinds of Respect," 40.

71. Newman, J. L., Roberts, L. R. & Syre, C. R. (1993) "Concepts of Family Among Children and Adolescents: Effect of Cognitive Level, Gender and Family Structure," *Developmental Psychology*, 29, 952–962; Brodzinsky, D. M., Lang, R. &

Smith, D. W. (1995) "Parenting Adopted Children" in Bornstein, M. H. (ed.) *Handbook of Parenting*, Vol. 3 Status and Social Conditions of Parenting, Mahwah: New Jersey, 209–232.

72. See Baran, A. & Panor, R. (2003) *Lethal Secrets*; McWhinnie, A. M. (1995) "A Study of Parenting of IVF and DI Children"; Triesliotis, J. (1988) "Identity and Genealogy" in Bruce, N., Mitchell, A. & Priestly, K. (eds), *Truth and the Child: A Contribution to the Debate on the Warnock Report*, Edinburgh: Family Care.

73. Rothman, B. K. (1989) *Recreating Motherhood: Ideology and Technology in a Patriarchal Society*, New York: Norton; McEwan, J. E. (2003) "Genetic Information, Ethics, and Information Relating to Biological Parenthood," *Encyclopedia of Ethical, Legal and Policy Issues in Biotechnology*, 356–363.

74. Bellis, M. A., Hughes, K., Hughes, S. & Ashton, J. R. (2005) "Measuring Paternal Discrepancy and its Public Health Consequences," *Journal of Epidemiology and Community Health*, 59, 749–754.

75. Schneller, E. A. (2005) "The Rights of Donor Inseminated Children to Know Their Genetic Origins in Australia," *Australian Journal of Family Law*, 19, 233.

76. Goldstein, J., Freud, A. & Solnit, A. J. (1979) *Beyond the Best Interests of the Child*, New York: The Free Press.

Chapter 8

1. Strickland, S., The Hon Justice (2014) "To Treat or Not to Treat, Legal Responses to Transgender Young People," *Association of Family and Conciliation Courts, 51st Annual Conference*, Toronto: Canada, 23.

2. *Re: Jamie (Special Medical Procedure)*, 2011, FamCA 248; *Re: Sam & Terry (Gender Dysphoria)*, 2013, FamCA 563, 101.

3. It is also important to distinguish between consenting to medical treatment and refusing medical treatment when discussing how this may apply to parents exercising the power on behalf of the child. There may be important ethical considerations between the two. For example, we may be comfortable with a parent having the right to consent to medical treatment for a very ill newborn but are we comfortable with a parent refusing treatment? Such examples may be severely disabled or deformed newborns whose parents refuse correction of a lethal deformity, or children in need of life-saving treatment whose parents refuse it. (See Shaw, A. (1973) "Dilemmas of 'informed consent' in Children," *The New England Journal of Medicine*, 289(17), 885–890.) This consideration has become a widely discussed topic in terms of whether parents should be able to refuse vaccinations for their children. In any case, these types of decisions need to be made with the best interests of the child as the paramount consideration.

4. Faden, R. R., Beauchamp, T. L. & King, N. M. (1986) *A History and Theory of Informed Consent*, New York: Oxford University Press; Appelbaum, P. S., Lidz, C. W. & Meisel, A. (1987) "Informed Consent: Legal Theory and

Clinical Practice," *Systems and Psychosocial Advances Research Center Publications and Presentation*, See http://escholarship.umassmed.edu/psych_cmhsr/119/, paper 119.

5. Harrison, C., Kenny, N. P., Sidarous, M. & Rowell, M. (1997) "Bioethics for Clinicians: Involving Children in Medical Decisions," *Canadian Medical Association*, 15, (6), 825.

6. Buchanan, A. & Brock, D. (1989) *Deciding for Others: The Ethics of Surrogate Decision Making*, Cambridge: Cambridge University Press, 236.

7. UN Committee on the Rights of the Children, *General comment No. 14 (2013) on the right of the child to have his or her best interest taken as a primary consideration (art. 3, para 1)*, adopted 62nd session, January 14–February 1, 2013.

8. Buchanan, A. & Brock, D. (1989) *Deciding for Others*, 259.

9. Ibid., 234.

10. Ibid., 246

11. Koocher G. P. & De Maso, D. R. (1990) "Children's competence to consent to medical procedures," *Pediatrician*, 17, 68–73.

12. Matthews, G. R. (1989) "Children's Conceptions of Illness and Death" in Kopelman, L. M. & Moskop, J. C. (eds), *Children and Health Care: Moral and Social Issues*, Holland: Kluwer Academic Publishers, 133–146.

13. King, N. M. P. & Cross, A. W. (1989) "Children as Decision Makers: Guidelines for Pediatricians," *Journal of Pediatrics*, 115, 10–16; Lewis, M. A., Lewis, C. E. (1990) "Consequences of Empowering Children to Care for Themselves," *Pediatrician*, 17, 63–67; Yoos, H. L. (1994) "Children's Illness Concepts: Old and New Paradigms," *Pediatric Nursing*, 20, 134–145.

14. Weithorn, L. A. & Campbell, S. B. (1982) "The Competency of Children and Adolescents to Make Informed Treatment Decisions," *Child Development*, 53, 1589–1598; Lewis, C. C. (1981) "How Adolescents Approach Decisions: Changes Over Grades Seven to Twelve and Policy Implications," *Child Development*, 52, 538–44.

15. *Gillick vs West Norfolk and Wisbech Area Health* (1986) AC 112.

16. Ibid., 188–9.

17. Freeman, M. (2005) "Rethinking *Gillick*," *The International Journal of Children's Rights*, 13, 201–217.

18. Note that for Buchanan and Brock, this variable standard of competence does not just stand for children but for adults as well. Buchanan, A. & Brock, D. (1989) *Deciding for Others*, 238.

19. Ibid.

20. Ibid.

21. Ibid.

22. Harrison, C., et al. (1997) "Bioethics for Clinicians: Involving Children in Medical Decisions," 826.

23. Buchanan, A. & Brock, D. (1989) *Deciding for Others*, 241.

24. Delemarre-van de Waal, H. A. & Cohen-Kettenis, P. T. (2006) "Clinical Management of Gender Identity Disorder in Adolescents: A Protocol on

Psychological and Paediatric Endocrinology Aspects," *European Journal of Endocrinology*, 155, 135–137.

25. Hewitt, J. K., Campbel, P., Kasiannan, P., Grover, S. R., Newman, L. K. & Warne, G. L. (2012) "Hormone Treatment of Gender Identity Disorder in a Cohort of Children and Adolescents," *The Medical Journal of Australia*, 196(9), 578–581.

26. Strickland, S., The Hon Justice (2014) "To Treat or Not to Treat, Legal Responses to Transgender Young People," 5.

27. Hewitt, J. K., et al. (2012) "Hormone Treatment of Gender Identity Disorder in a Cohort of Children and Adolescents," 578–581.

28. Previously called Gender Identity Disorder but now referred to as Gender Dysphoria following criticism that the term disorder was stigmatizing. Updated in the 2013 American Psychiatric Association's Diagnostic and Statistical Manual of Mental Disorders (the DSM) American Psychiatric Association, DSM-5 fact sheets, *Gender Dysphoria,* http://www.psychiatry.org/dsm5 (accessed May 1, 2014).

29. Korte, A., Goecker, D., Krude, H., Lehmkul, U., Gruters-Kieslich, A. & Beier, K. M. (2008) "Gender Identity Disorders in Childhood and Adolescence: Currently Debated Concepts and Treatment Strategies," *Deutsches Arzteblatt International*, 105(48), 834.

30. Wallbank, R. (2007) "*Re: Kevin* in Perspective," *Deakin Law Review*, 22; Beh, G. H. & Diamond, M. (2005) "Ethical Concerns related to Treating Gender Nonconformity in Childhood and Adolescence: Lessons from the Family Court of Australia," *Journal of Law-Medicine*, 15, 2.

31. It should be noted that the definition of Gender Identity Disorder as a psychiatric condition previously had consequences for how these types of cases were dealt with in Australia. Applications for hormone-blocking treatment had to be made to the Family Court of Australia as it is considered that parents cannot consent to these types of procedures. In the case of *Re: Bernadette* (2010) FamCA 94, it was argued that transsexualism in children was a natural variant of human sexuality and, as such, does not fall within the meaning of a special medical procedure.

32. Cohen-Kettenis, P. T., Delemarre-van de Waal, H. A. & Gooren, L. J. G. (2008) "The Treatment of Adolescent Transsexuals," *Journal of Sex* Medicine, 5,1892–1897.

33. Royal College of Psychiatrists (1998) "Gender Identity Disorders in Children and Adolescents, Guidance for Management," *Council Report CR63*.

34. Korte, A., et al. (2008) "Gender Identity Disorders in Childhood and Adolescence," 835.

35. Heylens, G., De Cuypere, G., Zucker, K. J., Schelfaut, C., Elaut, E., Vanden Bossche, H., De Baere, E. and T'Sjoen, G. (2012) "Gender Identity Disorder in Twins: A Review of the Case Report Literature," *Journal of Sex Medicine*, 9, 751–757; de Vries, A., Noens, I. & Cohen-Kettenis, P. (2010) "Autism Spectrum Disorders in Gender Dysphoric Children and Adolescents," *Journal of Autism Development Disorders*, 40, 930–936.

36. Korte, A., et al. (2008) "Gender Identity Disorders in Childhood and Adolescence," 835; Kipnis, K. & Diamond, M. (1998) "Pediatric Ethics and the Surgical Assignment of Sex," *Journal of Clinical Ethics*, 9, 398–410.

37. Korte, A., et al. (2008) "Gender Identity Disorders in Childhood and Adolescence," 834; Cohen-Kettenis, P. T., Owen, A., Kaijser, V. E., Bradley, S. J. & Zucker, K. J. (2003) "Demographic Characteristics, Social Competence and Behavioural Problems in Children with Gender Identity Disorder: A Cross-national, Cross-clinic Comparative Analysis," *Journal of Abnormal Child Psychology*, 31, 41–53; Wallien, M. S., Swaab, H. & Cohen-Kettenis, P. T. (2007) "Psychiatric Comorbidity Among Children with Gender Identity Disorder," *Journal of the American Academy of Child Adolescent Psychiatry*, 46, 1307–1314.

38. Cohen-Kettenis, P. T., et al. (2008) "The Treatment of Adolescent Transsexuals," 1892–1897.

39. Ibid.

40. Ibid., 1897.

41. Money, J. & Ehrhardt, A. (1972) *Man and Woman, Boy and Girl*, Baltimore: John Hopkins University Press.

42. Money, J., Hampson, J. G. & Hampson, J. L. (1955), "An Examination of Some Basic Sexual Concepts: The Evidence of Human Hermaphroditism," *Bulletin of the Johns Hopkins Hospital*, 97, 301–319; Money, J., Hampson, J. G. & Hampson, J. L. (1955) "Hermaphroditism: Recommendations Concerning Assignment of Sex, Change of Sex and Psychological Management," *Bulletin of the Johns Hopkins Hospital*, 97, 284–300; Money, J. (1975) "Ablatio Penis: Normal Male Infant Sex-reassignment as a Girl," *Archives of Sexual Behavior*, 4, 65–71.

43. Kipnis, K. & Diamond, M. (1998) "Pediatric Ethics and the Surgical Assignment of Sex," *Journal of Clinical Ethics*, 9(4), 398–410.

44. Ibid.

45. Drummond, K. D., Bradley, S. J., Peterson-Badali, M. & Zucker, K. J. (2008) "A Follow- up Study of Girls with Gender Identity Disorder," *Developmental Psychology*, 44, 34–45; Green, R., Roberts, C. W., Williams, K., Goodman, M. & Mixon, A. (1987) "Specific Cross-gender Behaviour in Boyhood and Later Homosexual Orientation," *British Journal of Psychiatry*, 151, 84–88; Zucker, K. J. (2005) "Gender Identity Disorders in Children and Adolescents," *Annual Review of Clinical Psychology*, 1, 467–492.

46. Cohen-Kettenis, P. T., et al. (2008) "The Treatment of Adolescent Transsexuals: Changing Insights," 1892.

47. Daily Mail (2012) "Teenager Who Became Youngest Person to Have Sex Change Clinches Semi-final Spot in Miss England Contest," published May 8, 2012, available at: http://www.dailymail.co.uk/news/article-2140775/Jackie-Green-Youngest-person-sex-change-reaches-Miss-England-semi-finals.html.

48. Henriette, A., Delemarre-van de Waal, H. A. & Cohen-Kettenis, P. T. (2006) "Clinical Management of Gender Identity Disorder in Adolescents: A Protocol on Psychological and Paediatric Endocrinology Aspects," *European Journal of Endocrinology*, 155, 131–137.

49. Cohen-Kettenis, P. T. & van Goozen, S. H. (1997) "Sex Reassignment of Adolescent Transsexuals: A Follow up Study," *Journal of the American Academy of Child and Adolescent Psychiatry*, 36, 263–271.
50. Kuiper, B. & Cohen-Kettenis, P. (1988) "Sex Reassignment Surgery: A Study of 141 Dutch Transsexuals," *Archives of Sexual Behaviour*, 17, 439–457; Smith, Y. L., can Goozen, S. H., Kuiper, A. J. & Cohen-Kettenis, P. T. (2005) "Sex Reassignment: Outcomes and Predictors of Treatment for Adolescent and Adult Transsexuals," *Psychological Medicine*, 35, 89–99.
51. Delemarre-van de Waal, H. A. & Cohen-Kettenis, P. T. (2006) "Clinical Management of Gender Identity Disorder in Adolescents: A Protocol on Psychological and Paediatric Endocrinology Aspects," 135–137.
52. Ibid.
53. Cohen-Kettenis, P. T., et al. (2008) "The Treatment of Adolescent Transsexuals: Changing Insights," , 1894.
54. GIRES (2007) "Transphobic Bullying in Schools," available at http://www.gires.org.uk/medpros.php.
55. GIRES (2005) *National School Climate Survey Sheds New Light on Experiences of Lesbian, Gay, Bisexual and Transgender (LGBT) Students*, available at http://glsen.org/cgi-bin/iowa/all/library/record/1927.htm.
56. Hall, H. R. (2006) "Teach to Reach: Addressing Lesbian, Gay, Bisexual and Transgender Youth Issues in the Classroom," *New Educator*, 2, 149–157.
57. Cohen-Kettenis, P. T., et al. (2008) "The Treatment of Adolescent Transsexuals: Changing Insights," 1896.
58. Ibid.; Ray, N. (2006) *Lesbian, Gay, Bisexual and Transgendered Youth: An Epidemic of Homelessness*, New York: National Gay and Lesbian Task Force Institute and the National Coalition for the Homeless, 62; Di Ceglie, D., Freedman, D., McPherson, S., et al (2002) "Children and Adolescents Referred to a Specialist Gender Identity Development Service: Clinical Features and Demographic Characteristics," *International Journal of Transgenderism*, 6; Whittle, S., Turner, L., & Al-Alami, M. (2007) "Engendered Penalties: Transgender and Transsexual People's Experiences of Inequality and Discrimination," *The Equalities Review*, available at http://www.pfc.org.uk/pdf/EngenderedPenalties.pdf.
59. Cohen-Kettenis, P. T. & van Goozen, S. H. (1997) "Sex Reassignment of Adolescent Transsexuals: A Follow up Study."
60. Ibid., 1896.
61. Delemarre-van de Waal, H. A. & Cohen-Kettenis, P. T. (2006) "Clinical Management of Gender Identity Disorder in Adolescents," 135–137.
62. Ross, M. W. & Need, J. A. (1999) "Effects of Adequacy of Gender Reassignment Surgery on Psychological Adjustment: A Follow up of Fourteen Male to Female Patients," *Archives of Sexual Behaviour*, 18, 145–153; Cohen-Kettenis, P. T. & Gooren, L. J. (1999) "Transsexualism: A Review of Etiology, Diagnosis and Treatment," *Journal of Psychosomatic Research*, 46, 315–333.

63. Lindemalm, G., Korlin, D. & Uddenberg, N. (1987) "Prognostic Factors vs Outcome in Male-to-female Transsexualism. A Follow up Study of 13 Cases," *Acta Psychiatrica Scandinavica*, 75, 268–274.
64. Giordano, S. (2008) "Lives in a Chiaroscuro: Should We Suspend the Puberty of Children with Gender Identity Disorder?," *Journal of Medical Ethics*, 34(8), 580–584.
65. Ibid., 582.
66. For Giordano's original argument on this point, see his rebuttal on Giordano, S. (2008) "Lives in a Chiaroscuro," 582.
67. Delemarre-van de Waal, H. A. & Cohen-Kettenis, P. T. (2006) "Clinical Management of Gender Identity Disorder in Adolescents," 135–137.
68. Korte, A., et al. (2008) "Gender Identity Disorders in Childhood and Adolescence," 838–839.
69. Giordano, S. (2008) "Lives in a Chiaroscuro," 582.
70. Cohen-Kettenis, P. T., et al. (2008) "The Treatment of Adolescent Transsexuals: Changing Insights," 1897.
71. Delemarre-van de Waal, H. A. & Cohen-Kettenis, P. T. (2006) "Clinical Management of Gender Identity Disorder in Adolescents," 135–137.
72. Ibid.
73. Giordano, S. (2008) "Lives in a Chiaroscuro," 582.
74. *Re: Alex* (2004) FamCa 297.
75. Ibid., 345–346.
76. Ibid., 340–345.
77. Ibid.
78. Giordano, S. (2008) "Lives in a Chiaroscuro."
79. Buchanan & Brock, 251
80. Cohen-Kettenis, P. T., et al. (2008) "The Treatment of Adolescent Transsexuals: Changing Insights," 1896.
81. Korte, A., et al (2008) "Gender Identity Disorders in Childhood and Adolescence," 834.
82. Ibid., 839.
83. Ibid.
84. Ibid., 839.
85. Delemarre-van de Waal, H. A. & Cohen-Kettenis, P. T. (2006) "Clinical Management of Gender Identity Disorder in Adolescents," 135–137.
86. Royal College of Psychiatrists (1998) "Gender Identity Disorders in children and Adolescents, Guidance for Management."
87. Wren, B. (2000) "Early Physical Intervention for Young People with a Typical Gender Identity Development," *Clinical Child Psychology and Psychiatry*, 5, 220–231.
88. Cohen-Kettenis, P. T., et al. (2008) "The Treatment of Adolescent Transsexuals: Changing Insights," 1894.
89. There may be a situation with the cultural fallout where not having gone through the practice of genital cutting would impact on the individual's acceptance in society and their ability to enjoy the good life. However, this

assessment of harm would have to be fairly high to justify her undertaking this.

90. O'Neill, O. (2003) "Some Limits of Informed Consent," *Journal of Medical Ethics*, 29(1), 4–7.
91. Raz, J. (1984) "Legal Rights," *Oxford Journal of Legal Studies*, 4(1), 200
92. Law Reform Commission of New South Wales (2004) "Minor's Consent to Medical Treatment," *Issues Paper*, 24, 4.
93. Strickland, S., The Hon Justice (2014) "To Treat or Not to Treat, Legal Responses to Transgender Young People," 39.
94. *Re: Jamie* [2013] FamCAFC 110 at [67].
95. *Re: Jamie* [2013] FamCAFC 110 at [134]; *Re: Spencer* [2014] FamCA 310 at [45].
96. Re: Shane (Gender Dysphoria) [2013] FamCA 864; Re: Sarah [2014] FamCA 208; Re: Spencer [2014] FamCA 310.

Chapter 9

1. This chapter was first published as an article in the *Critical Review of Social and Political Philosophy*. Thanks to the editors for allowing the reprint and expansion of this article here. For the original, see Cowden, M. (2012) "What's Love Got to do with it? Why a Child Does Not Have a Right to be Loved," *Critical Review of Social and Political Philosophy*, 15(3), 325–345.
2. Foster, H. & Freed, D. (1972) "A Bill of Rights for Children," *Family Law Quarterly*, 6, 347.
3. For detailed analysis of these domestic documents, see Veerman, P. E. (1992) *The Rights of the Child and the Changing Image of Childhood*. Martinius Nijhoff: Dordrecht.
4. Exceptions include Liao, M. (2006) "The Right of Children to be Loved," *Journal of Political Philosophy*, 4, 420–440; MacCormick, N. (1976) "Children's Rights: A Test Case for Theories of Right," *Archiv fur Recht-und Sozialphilosophie*, LXII, 305–316, reprinted in MacCormick, N. (1982) *Legal Rights and Social Democracy*, Oxford: Clarendon Press and Archard, D. (2004) *Children, Rights, and Childhood*, 2nd Edition, London: Routledge.
5. Liao, M. (2006) "The Right of Children to be Loved"
6. Ibid., 422
7. Griffin, J. (2008) *On Human Rights*, Oxford: Oxford University Press.
8. Liao, M. (2006) "The Right of Children to be Loved," 422
9. Ibid., 423
10. Ibid.
11. Emde, R. (1992) "Individual Meaning and Increased Complexity: Contributions of Sigmund Freud and Rene Spitz to Developmental Psychology," *Developmental Psychology*, 22(3), 347–359.
12. Ainsworth, M. (1962) "The Effects of Maternal Deprivation: A Review of Findings and Controversy in the Context of Research Strategy" in *Deprivation of Maternal Care: A Reassessment of Its Effects, Public Health Papers*, Geneva:

World Health Organization, 97–165; Rutter, M. (1981) *Maternal Depriva-tion Reassessed*, 2nd Edition, Hammondsworth: Penguin; Yarrow, L. (1961) "Maternal Deprivation: Toward an Empirical and Conceptual Re-evaluation," *Psychological Bulletin*, 6, 459–490.

13. Ainsworth, M. (1962) "The Effects of Maternal Deprivation," 99.
14. Rutter, M. (1972) "Maternal Deprivation Reconsidered," *Journal of Psychoso-matic Research*, 16, 241–250.
15. Ibid.
16. Spitz, R. & Wolf, K. (1946) "Anaclitic Depression—an Inquiry into the Genesis of Psychiatric Conditions in Early Childhood," *Psychoanalytic Study of the Child*, 2, 313.
17. Rutter, M. (1972) "Maternal Deprivation Reconsidered," 242.
18. Spitz, R. (1945) "Hospitalism: An Inquiry into the Genesis of Psychiatric Conditions in Early Childhood," *Psychoanalytic Study of the Child*, 1, 70.
19. Ibid..
20. Rutter, M. (1972) "Maternal Deprivation Reconsidered," 244.
21. Spitz, R. (1945) "Hospitalism," 63.
22. Ainsworth, M. (1962) "The Effects of Maternal Deprivation."
23. Dodsworth, R. O. & Harlow, M. K. (1965) "Total Social Isolation in Monkeys." *Proceedings of the National Academy of Sciences*, 54, 90–96.
24. Ibid., 90.
25. Ibid.
26. Liao, M. (2006) "The Right of Children to be Loved," 423.
27. Champoux, C., Schanberg, K. & Suami, S. J. (1989) "Hormonal Effects of Early Rearing Conditions in the Infant Rhesus Monkey," *American Journal of Primatology*, 19, 111–117; Wang, S., Bartolome, V. & Schanberg, S. M. (1996). "Neonatal Deprivation of Maternal Touch May Suppress Ornithine Decarboxylase Via Down Regulation of Proto-oncogenes C-Myc and Max," *Journal of Neuroscience*, 16, 836–842.
28. Scafidi, F. A., Field, T. M., Schanberg, S. M., Bauer, C. R., Tucci, K., Roberts, J., Morrow, C. & Kuhn, C. M (1990) "Massage Stimulates Growth in Preterm Infants: A Replication," *Infant Behavior and Development*, 13, 167–188.
29. Hodges, J. & Tizzard, B. (1989) "Social and Family Relationships of Ex-institutional Adolescents," *Journal of Child Psychology and Psychiatry*, 1, 77–97.
30. Kahler, S. R. & Freeman, B. J (1994) "Analysis of Environmental Deprivation: Cognitive and Social Development in Romanian Orphans," *Journal of Child Psychology and Psychiatry*, 4, 769–781.
31. Champoux, Coe, Schanberg, Kuhn & Suami (1989); Higley, Suomi & Linnoila, 1991; Higley, J. D., Suomi, S. J. & Linnoila, M. (1991) "CSF Monoamine Metabolite Concentrations Vary According to Age, Rearing and Sex, and are Influences by the Stressor of Social Separation in Rhesus Monkeys," *Psychopharmacology*, 103, 551–556; Coplan, J. D., Trost, R. C., Owens, M. J., Cooper, T. B., Gorman, J. M., Nemeroff, C. B. & Rosenblum, L. A (1988) "Cerebrospinal Fluid Concentrations of Somatostatin and Biogenicamines

in Grown Primates Reared by Mothers Exposed to Manipulated Foraging Conditions," *Archives in General Psychiatry*, 55, 473–477.

32. Prior, V. & Glaser, D. (2006) "Understanding Attachment and Attachment Disorders: theory, Evidence and Practice," *Child and Adolescent Mental Health*, RCPRTU. London: Jessica Kingsley.

33. Rutter, M. (1972) "Maternal Deprivation Reconsidered," 18.

34. Hohfeld, W. (1964) *Fundamental Legal Conceptions as Applied in Judicial Reasoning*, New Haven, CT: Yale University Press.

35. Liao, M. (2006) "The Right of Children to be Loved," 422–423.

36. ibid., 427.

37. MacCormick, N. (1976) "Children's Rights: A Test Case for Theories of Right," 305–316, reprinted in MacCormick, N. (1982) *Legal Rights and Social Democracy*, Oxford: Clarendon Press.

38. Liao, M. (2006) "The Right of Children to be Loved," 426

39. Ibid., 429

40. Waldron, J. (1988) "When Justice Replaces Affection: The Need for Rights," *Harvard Journal of Law and Public Policy*, 11, 629.

41. Feinberg, J. (1970) "The Nature and Value of Rights," *Journal of Value Inquiry*, 4, 252.

42. Ibid., 252.

43. Liao, M. (2006) "The Right of Children to be Loved," 439.

Chapter 10

1. King, M. (1994) "Children's Rights as Communication: Reflections on Autopoietic Theory and the United Nations Convention," *The Modern Law Review* 57(3), 385.

2. Brennan, S. and Noggle, R. (1997) "The Moral Status of Children: Children's Rights, Parent's Rights and Family Justice," *Social Theory and Practice* 23(1), 3–4.

3. Ibid., 6.

4. Ibid., 7.

5. Lau, J. C. (2012) "Two Arguments for Child Enfranchisement," *Political Studies* 60(4), 860–876.

6. Feinberg, J. (1980) "The Child's Right to an Open Future," *Freedom & Fulfillment: Philosophical Essays*, Princeton: Princeton University Press.

7. Mills, C. (2003) "The Child's Right to an Open Future," *Journal of Social Philosophy* 34(4) 499–509.

8. O'Neill, O. (2003) "Some Limits of Informed Consent," *Journal of Medical Ethics* 29(1), 4–7.

9. Taylor, C. (1992) "Atomism" in Avineri, A. and de Shalit, A. (eds), *Communitarianism and Individualism*, Oxford: Oxford University Press, 29–50.

10. Minow, M. (1986) "Rights for the Next Generation: A Feminist Approach to Children's Rights," *Harvard Women's Law Journal* 9(1), 1–24.

11. Wenar, L. (2005) "The Nature of Rights," *Philosophy and Public Affairs* 33(3), 223–252.

12. Brennan, S. and Noggle, R. (1997) "The Moral Status of Children:," 144.

13. See "André Agassi Profile," available at: http://edition.cnn.com/CNN/ Programs/people/shows/agassi/profile.html and Agassi, A. (2009) *Open: An Autobiography*, New York: Random House.

14. Law Reform Committee (2012) "Inquiry into Access by Donor-Conceived People to Information about Donors," *Parliamentary Paper*, 120, session 2010–2012, xvii.

15. Doctors for the Family (2012) *Submission to Senate Inquiry re Marriage Equality Amendment Bill 2010*, available at: http://www.aph.gov.au/Parliamentary_ Business/Committees/Senate/Legal_and_Constitutional_Affairs/Completed_ inquiries/2010-13/marriageequality2012/submissions

16. A good example of this argument was made by Joe Hockey MP on the ABC television program *Q&A*, May 14, 2012. See http://www.youtube.com/watch? v=TuIbEJz23uY

17. Vanfraussen, K., Ponjaert-Kristoffersen, I. and Brewaeys A (2001) "An Attempt to Reconstruct Children's Donor Concept: A Comparison Between Children's and Lesbian Parents' Attitudes Towards Donor Anonymity," *Human Reproduction* 16, 2019–2025.

18. Bikrland, T. (2011) *An Introduction to the Policy Process: Theories, Concepts and Models of Public Policy Making*, New York: Armonk.

19. Elliott, E. (2011) "Alcohol Use in Pregnancy in Remote Australia: the Liliwan Project," presented at the *11th National Rural Health Conference*, available at: http://www.healthinfonet.ecu.edu.au/key-resources/programs-projects?pid=878.

20. Australian Bureau of Statistics (2015) *Apparent Consumption of Alcohol, Australia, 2013–14*, available at: http://www.abs.gov.au/ausstats/abs@.nsf/mf/ 4307.0.55.001/.

21. Stewart, J. (2014) "Alcohol Research Groups Oppose Northern Territory Proposal to Criminalise Drinking While Pregnant," *ABC News* Online, available at: http://www.abc.net.au/news/2014-03-15/research-groups-oppose-nt-prosecuting-pregnant-women-drinking/5322814.

22. Savulescu, J. and de Crespigny (2014) "Should it be a Crime to Harm an Unborn Child?," *The Conversation*, available at: http://theconversation.com/ should-it-be-a-crime-to-harm-an-unborn-child-24407.

References

List of Legislation

Assisted Reproductive Technology Act 2007 (NSW) (Australia).
Assisted Reproductive Treatment Act 2008 (Vic) (Australia).
Embryo Research Amendment Act 2006 (Cth) (Australia)
Human Reproductive Technology Act Directions 2004 (WA) (Australia).
National Health and Medical Research Act 1992 (Cth) (Australia).
Prohibition of Human Cloning for Reproduction and the Regulation of Human

International Documents

African Charter on the Rights and Welfare of the Child 1990 (African Union).
Declaration of the Rights of the Child 1959 (United Nations).
Declaration of the Rights of the Child 1989 (Israel)
Declaration of the Rights of Mozambican Children 1979 (Mozambique)
Geneva Declaration of the Rights of the Child 1924 (League of Nations).
The Charter of the Rights of the Arab Child (League of Arab States).
The Children's Charter 1950 (Japan).

Cases

Amaca Pty ltd v Ellis; The State of South Australia v Ellis; Millennium Inorganic Chemicals Limited v Ellis (2010) HCA 5.
Gillick vs West Norfolk and Wisbech Area Health (1986) AC 112.
Re: Alex (2004) FamCA 297.
Re: Bernadette (2010) FamCA 94.
Re: Jamie (Special Medical Procedure) (2011) FamCA 248.
Re: Jamie (2013) FamCAFC 110.
Re: Sam & Terry (Gender Dysphoria) (2013) FamCA 563.
Re: Sarah (2014) FamCA 208.
Re: Shane (Gender Dysphoria) (2013) FamCA 864;
Re: Spencer (2014) FamCA 310.

Bibliography

Ainsworth, M. (1962) "The Effects of Maternal Deprivation: A Review of Findings and Controversy in the Context of Research Strategy," in *Deprivation of Maternal*

Care: A Reassessment of its Effects, Public Health Papers, Geneva: World Health Organization, 97–165.

American Psychiatric Association's Diagnostic and Statistical Manual of Mental Disorders (the DSM) (2014) American Psychiatric Association, DSM-5 Fact Sheets, *Gender Dysphoria,* available at http://www.psychiatry.org/dsm5 (accessed 1 May 2014).

Anda, R. F., Felitti, V. J., Bremner, J. D., Walker, J. D., Whitfield, Perry B. D., Dube, R. & Giles, W. H. (2005) "The Enduring Effects of Abuse and Related Adverse Experiences in Childhood," *European Archives of Psychiatry and Clinical Neuroscience,* 256(3), 174–186.

Andrews, A. B. & Kaufman, N. H. (1999) *Implementing the UN Convention on the Rights of the Child: A Standard of Living Adequate for Development,* Westport: Praeger Publishers.

Annas, C. (1995) "Irreversible Error: The Power and Prejudice of Female Genital Mutilation," *Journal of Contemporary Health Law and Policy,* 12, 325–354.

Albrecht, G. L. & Devlieger, P. L. (1999) "The Disability Paradox: High Quality of Life Against all Odds," *Social Science & Medicine,* 48(8), 977–988.

Alison, J., Jenks, C. & Prout, A. (1998) *Theorizing Childhood,* Cambridge: Polity Press.

Alston, P. (1994) "The Best Interests Principle: Towards a Reconciliation of Culture and Human Rights," *International Journal of Law, Policy and the Family,* 8(1), 1–25.

Appelbaum, P. S., Lidz, C. W. & Meisel, A. (1987) "Informed Consent: Legal Theory and Clinical Practice," *Systems and Psychosocial Advances Research Center Publications and Presentation,* paper 119.

Archard, D. (2003) *Children, Family and the State,* Aldershot: Ashgate Publishing Limited.

Archard, D. (2004) *Children, Rights, and Childhood,* 2nd Edition, London: Routledge.

Archard, D. (2007) "The Wrong of Rape," *The Philosophical Quarterly,* 57, 371–393.

Ariès, P. (1962) *L'Enfant et la vie familial sous l'anien régime,* Paris, Libraire Plon, 1960. Translated from the French by Robert Baldick as *Centuries of Childhood,* London: Jonathan Cape.

Arneson, R. J. & Shapiro, I. (1996) "Democratic Autonomy and Religious Freedom: A Critique of *Wisconsin v. Yoder,*" in Shapiro, I. & Hardin, R. (eds), *Political Order,* Nomos XXXVIII, New York: New York University Press, 365–411.

Baran, A. & Panor, R. (2003) *Lethal Secrets. The Psychology of Donor Insemination Problems and Solutions,* 2nd Edition, New York: Amistad.

Beauchamp, T. & Childress, J. (2001) *Principles of Biomedical Ethics,* Oxford: Oxford University Press.

Beck, S. & Guthrie, C. (2011) "Almost Thinking Counterfactually: Children's Understanding of Close Counterfactuals," *Child Development,* 82(4), 1189–1198.

Beh, G. H. & Diamond, M. (2005) "Ethical Concerns related to Treating Gender Nonconformity in Childhood and Adolescence: Lessons from the Family Court of Australia," *Journal of Law-Medicine,* 15, 2.

Bellis, M. A., Hughes, K., Hughes, S. & Ashton, J. R. (2005) "Measuring Paternal Discrepancy and its Public Health Consequences," *Journal of Epidemiology and Community Health*, 59, 749–754.

Bikrland, T. (2011) *An Introduction to the Policy Process: Theories, Concepts and Models of Public Policy Making*, New York: Armonk.

Blair, M. (2002) "The Impact of Family Paradigms, Domestic Constitutions and International Conventions on Disclosure of an Adopted Person's Identities and Heritage: A Comparative Examination," *Michigan Journal of International Law*, 22, 587.

Blood, J., Pitt, P. & Parker, H. W. G. (1998) "Parents' Decision to Inform Children of Their Donor: Sperm Conception and the Impact of a Register Which Legislated to Enable Identification of Donors," unpublished paper, *Royal Women's Hospital and the University of Melbourne*.

Boorse, C. (1977) "Health as a Theoretical Concept," *Philosophy of Science*, 44, 542–573.

Bouchard, T. J., Lykken, D. T., McGue, M., Segal, N. L. & Tellegen, A. (1990) "Sources of Human Psychological Differences: The Minnesota Study of Twins Reared Apart," *Science*, 250, 223–228.

Bouchard, T. J. & McGue, M. (2003) "Genetic and Environmental Influences on Human Psychological Differences," *Journal of Neurobiology*, 54, 4–45.

Braham, M. & Steffen, F. (2008) *Power and Freedom: Conceptual, Formal and Applied Dimensions*, New York: Springer.

Brennan, S. & Noggle, R. (1997) "The Moral Status of Children: Children's Rights, Parent's Rights and Family Justice," *Social Theory and Practice*, 23(1) 1–26.

Brennan, S. (2002) "Children's Choices or Children's Interests: Which do their Rights Protect?," in Archard, D. & MacLeod, C. (eds), *The Moral and Political Status of Children, The Moral and Political Status of Children*, Oxford: Oxford University Press, 53–69.

Brewaeys, A. (1996) "Donor Insemination and Child Development," *Journal of Psychology, Obs. Gynae*, 17, 1–13.

Brighouse, H. (2002) "What Rights (If Any) Do Children Have?," in Archard, D. & MacLeod, C. (eds), *The Moral and Political Status of Children*, Oxford: Oxford University Press, 31–52.

Brink, D. (2001) "Impartiality and Associative Duties," *Utilitas*, 13, 152–172.

Brock, D. (2002) "Human Cloning and Our Sense of Self," *Science*, 296(5566), 314–314.

Brodzinsky, D. M., Lang, R. & Smith, D. W. (1995) "Parenting Adopted Children," in Bornstein, M. H. (ed.), *Handbook of Parenting*, 3, New Jersey: Status and Social Conditions of Parenting, Mahwah, 209–232.

Brodzinsky, D. M., Schechter, M. D. & Henig, R. M. (1992) *Being Adopted: The Lifelong Search for Self*, New York: Doubleday.

Buchanan, A. & Brock, D. (1989) *Deciding for Others: The Ethics of Surrogate Decision Making*, Cambridge: Cambridge University Press.

Campbell, T. (1992) "The Rights of the Minor: As Person, As Child, As Juvenile, As Future Adult," *International Journal of Law and the Family*, 6, 1–23.

Cassidy, C. (2007) *Thinking Children*, London: Continuum International Publishing Group.

Champoux, C., Schanberg, K. & Suami, S. J. (1989) "Hormonal Effects of Early Rearing Conditions in the Infant Rhesus Monkey," *American Journal of Primatology*, 19, 111–117.

Cohen, H. (1980) *Equal Rights for Children*, Totowa, NJ: Rowman and Littlefield.

Cohen-Kettenis, P. T., Delemarre-van de Waal, H. A. & Gooren, L. J. G. (2008) "The Treatment of Adolescent Transsexuals," *Journal of Sex* Medicine, 5, 1892–1897.

Cohen-Kettenis, P. T. & Gooren, L. J. (1999) "Transsexualism: A Review of Etiology, Diagnosis and Treatment," *Journal of Psychosomatic Research*, 46, 315–333.

Cohen-Kettenis, P. T. & van Goozen, S. H. (1997) "Sex Reassignment of Adolescent Transsexuals: A Follow up Study," *Journal of the American Academy of Child and Adolescent Psychiatry*, 36, 263–271.

Cohen-Kettenis, P. T., Owen, A., Kaijser, V. E., Bradley, S. J. & Zucker, K, J, (2003) "Demographic Characteristics, Social Competence and Behavioural Problems in Children with Gender Identity Disorder: A Cross-national, Cross-clinic Comparative Analysis," *Journal of Abnormal Child Psychology*, 31, 41–53.

Commonwealth of Australia. (2011) "Donor Conception Practices in Australia," *Inquiry into Donor Conception Practices in Australia*, Senate Standing Committee on Legal and Constitutional Affairs, available at http://www.aph.gov.au/Parliamentary_Business/Committees/Senate/Legal_and_Constitutional_Affairs/Completed_inquiries/2010-13/donorconception/report/index

Compas, B. E., Connor-Smith, J. K., Saltzman, H., Thomsen, A. H. & Wadsworth, M. E. (2001) "Coping With Stress During Childhood and Adolescence: Problems, Progress and Potential in Theory and Research," *Psychological Bulletin*, 127(1), 87–12.

Coplan, J. D., Trost, R. C., Owens, M. J., Cooper, T. B., Gorman, J. M., Nemeroff, C. B. & Rosenblum, L. A. (1988) "Cerebrospinal Fluid Concentrations of Somatostatin and Biogenic Amines in Grown Primates Reared by Mothers Exposed to Manipulated Foraging Conditions," *Archives in General Psychiatry*, 55, 473–477.

Cowden, M. (2012) "No Harm, no Foul: A Child's Right to Know their Genetic Parents," *International Journal of Law, Policy and the Family*, 26(1), 102–126.

Cowden, M. (2012) "What's Love Got to do With it? Why a Child Does Not Have a Right to be Loved," *Critical Review of Social and Political Philosophy*, 15(3), 325–345.

Crouch, R. (1997) "Letting the Deaf Be Deaf: Reconsidering the Use of Cochlear Implants in Prelingually Deaf Children," *The Hasting Centre Report*, 27(4), 14–21.

Cunningham, H. (1998) "Review Essay: Histories of Childhood," *The American Historical Review*, 103(4). 1195–1208.

Daniels, N. (1985) *Just Health Care*, Cambridge: Cambridge University Press.

Daniels, K. & Lalos, O. (1997) "The Swedish Insemination Act and the Availability of Donors," *Human Reproduction*, 7, 1871–1874.

Daniels, K. & Taylor, K. (1993) "Secrecy & Openness in Donor Insemination," *Political & Life Sciences*, 12, 155.

Darwall, S. L. (1977) "Two Kinds of Respect," *Ethics*, 88, 36–49.

Davidson, D. (1980) *Essays on Actions and Events*, Oxford: Oxford University Press.

Davies, D. (1997) "Genetic Dilemmas and the Child's Right to an Open Future," *The Hastings Center Report*, 27(2), 7–15.

Davis, D. (1997) "What's Wrong with Cloning," *Jurimetrics*, 18(83), 83–90.

Delemarre-van de Waal, H. A. & Cohen-Kettenis, P. T. (2006) "Clinical Management of Gender Identity Disorder in Adolescents: A Protocol on Psychological and Paediatric Endocrinology Aspects," *European Journal of Endocrinology*, 1, 155, 135–137.

Dembour, M. (2010) "What are Human Rights? Four Schools of Thought," *Human Rights Quarterly*, 32, 1–20.

Dennison, M. (2008) "Revealing Your Sources: The Case for Non-Anonymous Gamete Donation," *Journal of Law and Health*, 1–27.

Dewar, J. (1989) "Fathers in Law? The Case of AID," in Lee, R. & Morgan, D. (eds), *Birthrights: Law and Ethics at the Beginnings of Life*, London: Routledge, 115–131.

Di Ceglie, D., Freedman, D., McPherson, S. & Richardson, P. (2002) "Children and Adolescents Referred to a Specialist Gender Identity Development Service: Clinical Features and Demographic Characteristics," *International Journal of Transgenderism*, 6, 1.

Dodsworth, R. O. & Harlow, M. K. (1965) "Total Social Isolation in Monkeys," *Proceedings of the National Academy of Sciences*, 54, 90–96.

Dolncik, E. (1993) "Deafness as Culture," *The Atlantic Monthly*, September, 37–52.

Dowding, K. (2006) "Can Capabilities Reconcile Freedom and Equality?' *The Journal of Political Philosophy*, 14, 323–336.

Dowding, K. & van Hees, M. (2003) "The Construction of Rights," *American Political Science Review*, 97(2), 281–293.

Dowding, K. & van Hees, M. (2008) "Freedom, Coercion and Ability," in Braham, M. & Steffen, F. (eds.), *Power, Freedom and Voting*, New York: Springer, pp. 303–304

Drummond, K. D., Bradley, S. J., Peterson-Badali, M. & Zucker, K. J. (2008) "A Follow- up Study of Girls with Gender Identity Disorder," *Developmental Psychology*, 44, 34–45.

Dworkin, R. (1986) *Law's Empire*, Cambridge, MA: Harvard University Press.

Eekelaar, J. (1986) "The Emergence of Children's Rights," *Oxford Journal of Legal Studies*, 6(2), 170.

Eekelaar, J. (2006) *Family Law and Personal Life*, Oxford: Oxford University Press.

Edwards, S. A. (2004) "Disability, identity and the 'expressivist objection'," *Journal of Medical Ethics*, 30, 418–420.

Elliott, E. (2011) "Alcohol Use in Pregnancy in Remote Australia: The Liliwan Project," presented at the *11th National Rural Health Conference*, available at http://www.healthinfonet.ecu.edu.au/key-resources/programs-projects?pid= 878.

Emde, R. (1992) "Individual Meaning and Increased Complexity: Contributions of Sigmund Freud and Rene Spitz to Developmental Psychology," *Developmental Psychology*, 22(3), 347–359.

Ethical Guidelines on the use of Assisted Reproductive Technology in Clinical Practice and Research. (2004) available at www.nhmrc.gov.au/_files_nhmrc/file/publications/synopses/e78.pdf.

Faden, R. R., Beauchamp, T. L. & King, N. M. (1986) *A History and Theory of Informed Consent*, New York: Oxford University Press

Farson, R. (1978) *Birthrights*, Harmondsworth: Penguin.

Federle, K. H. (1994) "Rights Flow Downhill," *International Journal of Children's Rights*, 2, 343–368.

Feinberg, J. (1970) "The Nature and Value of Rights," *Journal of Value Inquiry*, 4, 243–257.

Feinberg, J. (1980) "The Child's Right to an Open Future," *Freedom & Fulfillment: Philosophical Essays*, Princeton: Princeton University Press, 76–97

Feinberg, J. (1985) *Harm to Others: The Moral Limits of the Criminal Law*, Oxford: Oxford University Press, 145–146

Feinberg, J. (1986) "Wrongful Life and Counterfactual Element in Harming," *Social Philosophy and Policy*, 4, 145–178.

Firth, L. (2001) "Gamete Donation and Anonymity: The Ethical and Legal Debate," *Human Reproduction*, 16, 818–824.

Fortin, J. (2005) *Children's Rights and the Developing Law*, 2nd Edition, Cambridge: Cambridge University Press.

Foster, H. and Freed, D. (1972) "A Bill of Rights for Children," *Family Law Quarterly*, 6, 343–376.

Fraga, M., Ballestar, E., Paz, M., Ropero, S., Setien, F., Ballestar, M., Heine-Suner, D., Cigudosa, J. C., Uroste, M., Benitez, J., Boix-Chornet, M., Sanchez-Aguilera, A., Ling, C., Carlsson, E., Poulsen, P., Vaag, A., Stephen, Z., Spector, T. D., Wu, Y. Z., Plass, C. & Esteller, M. (2005) "Epigenetic Differences Arise During the Lifetime of Monozygotic Twins," *Proceedings of the National Academy of Sciences of the United States of America*, 102(30), 10604–10609.

Franklin, B. (2004) *New Handbook of Children's Rights*, Oxford: Routledge.

Freeman, M. (1997) *The Moral Status of Children: Essays on the Rights of the Child*, The Netherlands: Martinus Nijhoff Publishers, 91.

Freeman, M. (2005) "Rethinking *Gillick*," *The International Journal of Children's Rights*, 13, 201–217.

Fried, B. (2012) "What Does Matter? The Case for Killing the Trolley Problem (Or Letting it Die)," *The Philosophical Quarterly*, 62(248), 505–529.

Gardner, J. & Shute, S. (2000) "The Wrongness of Rape," in Horder, J. (ed.), *Oxford Essays in Jurisprudence*, Fourth Series, Oxford: Oxford University Press, 193–217.

Geers, A. E., Nicholas, J. G. & Sedey, A. L. (2003) "Language Skills of Children with Early Cochlear Implantation," *Ear & Hearing*, 24(1), 465–585.

Goldstein, J., Freud, A. & Solnit, A. J. (1979) *Beyond the Best Interests of the Child*, New York: The Free Press.

Golombok, S., Brewaeys, A., Cook, R., Giavazzi, M. T., Guerra, D., Manovani, A., van Hall, E., Crosignani, P. G. & Dexeus, S. (1996) "The European Study of Assisted Reproduction Families: Family Functioning and Child Development," *Human Reproduction*, 11, 2324–2331.

Golombok, S., Brewaeys, A., Giavazzi, M., Guerra, D., MacCullum, F. & Rusi, J. (2002) "The European Study of Assisted Reproduction Families; the transition to Adolescence," *Human Reproduction*, 17, 830–840.

Golombok, S., Lycett, E., MacCallum, F., Jadva, V., Murray, C. & Rust, J. (2004) "Parenting Infants Conceived by Gamete Donation," *Journal of Family Psychology*, 18, 448.

Golombok, S., Maccallum, F., Goodman, E. & Rutter, M. (2002) "Families with Children Conceived by Donor Insemination: A Follow up at Age 12," *Child Development*, 73, 952–958.

Golombok, S., Murray, C., Brisden, P. & Abdalla, H. (1999) "Social vs Biological Parenting: Family Functioning and the Socio-Emotional Development of Children Conceived by Egg or Sperm Donation," *Journal of Child Psychology Psychiatry*, 40, 519–527.

Gottlieb, C., Othorn, L. & Lindblad, F. (2000) "Disclosure of Donor Insemination to the Child: The Impact of Swedish Legislation on Couples' Attitudes," *Human Reproduction*, 15, 2052–2056.

Green, R., Roberts, C. W., Williams, K., Goodman, M. & Mixon, A. (1987) "Specific Cross-gender Behaviour in Boyhood and Later Homosexual Orientation," *British Journal of Psychiatry*, 151, 84–88.

Griffin, J. (2002) "Do Children have Rights?," in Archard, D. & MacLeod, C. (eds), *The Moral and Political Status of Children*, Oxford: Oxford University Press, 19–30.

Griffin, J. (2008) *On Human Rights*, Oxford: Oxford University Press.

Grisso, T. & Appelbaum, P. (1998) *Assessing Competence to Consent to Treatment: A Guide for Physicians and Other Health Professionals*, New York: Oxford University Press.

Groce, N. E. (1985) *Everyone Here Spoke Sign Language: Hereditary Deafness on Martha's Vineyard*, Cambridge: Harvard University Press.

Hafen, B. (1976) "Children's Liberation and the New Egalitarianism: Some Reservations About Abandoning Youth to Their Rights," *Brigham Young University Law Review*, 605–658.

Hall, H. R. (2006) "Teach to Reach: Addressing Lesbian, Gay, Bisexual and Transgender Youth Issues in the Classroom," *New Educator*, 2, 149–157.

Hammarberg, T. (1990) "The UN Convention on the Rights of the Child and How to Make It Work," *Human Rights Quarterly*, 12, 97–105.

Hart, H. L. A. (1955) "Are There Any Natural Rights?," *Philosophical Review*, 64, 175–191.

Hart, H. L. A. (1982) *Essays on Bentham: Studies in Jurisprudence and Political Theory*, Oxford: Clarendon Press.

Harrison, C., Kenny, N. P., Sidarous, M. & Rowell, M. (1997) "Bioethics for Clinicians: Involving Children in Medical Decisions," *Canadian Medical Association*, 156(6) 825 – 828

Heylens, G., De Cuypere, G., Zucker, K. J., Schelfaut C, Elaut E, Vanden Bossche H, De Baere, E. and T'Sjoen, G. (2012) "Gender Identity Disorder in Twins: A Review of the Case Report Literature," *Journal of Sexual Medicine*, 9, 751–757.

Heywood, C. (2001) *A History of Childhood*, Cambridge: Polity Press.

Hewitt, J. K., Campbell, P., Kasiannan, P., Grover, S. R., Newman, L. K. & Warne, G. L. (2012) "Hormone Treatment of Gender Identity Disorder in a Cohort of Children and Adolescents," *The Medical Journal of Australia*, 196(9), 578–581.

Himes, J. R. (1995) *Implementing the Convention on the Rights of the Child: Resource Mobilization in Low-Income Countries*, The Netherlands: Kluwer Law International.

Hobbes, T. (2004) *De Cive, 1642*, Whitefish: Kessinger Publishing.

Hodges, J. & Tizzard, B. (1989) "Social and Family Relationships of Ex-institutional Adolescents," *Journal of Child Psychology and Psychiatry*, 1, 77–97.

Hohfeld, W. (1913) "Some Fundamental Legal Conceptions as Applied in Judicial Reasoning," *Yale Law Journal*, 23, 16–59.

Holmes, S. & Sunstein, C. R. (1999) *The Cost of Rights*, New York: W. W. Norton.

Holt, J. (1975) *Escape from Childhood*, Harmondsworth: Penguin.

Johnson, L. & Kane, H. (2007) "Regulation of Donor Conception and the 'time to tell' Campaign," *Journal of Law and Medicine*, 15(1), 117–127.

Kahler, S. R. & Freeman, B. J. (1994) "Analysis of Environmental Deprivation: Cognitive and Social Development in Romanian Orphans," *Journal of Child Psychology and Psychiatry*, 4, 769–781.

Kim, S. Y. H. (2010) *Evaluation of Capacity to Consent to Treatment and Research*, Oxford: Oxford University Press.

King, M. (1994) "Children's Rights as Communication: Reflections on Autopoietic Theory and the United Nations Convention," *The Modern Law Review*, 57(3), 385–401.

King, N. M. P. & Cross, A. W. (1989) "Children as Decision Makers: Guidelines for Pediatricians," *Journal of Paediatrics*, 115, 10–16.

King, P. (1998) "Thomas Hobbes's Children," in Turner, S. M. and Matthews, G. B. (eds), *The Philosopher's Child: Critical Essays in the Western Tradition*, Rochester: University of Rochester Press, 67–84.

Kipnis, K. & Diamond, M. (1998) "Pediatric Ethics and the Surgical Assignment of Sex," *Journal of Clinical Ethics*, 9(4), 398–410.

Kirkman, M. (2003) "Parents' Contributions to the Narrative Identity of Offspring of Donor-assisted Conception," *Social Science and Medicine*, 57, 2229–2242.

Klock, S. C. & Maier, D. (1991) "Psychological Factors Related to Donor Insemination," *Fertility Sterility*, 56, 489–495.

Koocher, G. P. & DeMaso. (1990) "Children's Competence to Consent to Medical Procedures," *Pediatrician*, 17, 68–73.

Korte, A., Goecker, D., Krude, H., Lehmkul, U., Gruters-Kieslich, A. & Beier, K. M. (2008) "Gender Identity Disorders in Childhood and Adolescence: Currently Debated Concepts and Treatment Strategies," *Deutsches Arzteblatt International*, 105(48), 834–841.

Kramer, M., Simmonds, N. & Steiner, H. (1998) *A Debate Over Rights: Philosophical Enquiries*, Oxford: Oxford University Press.

Krueger-Jago, M. J. & Hanna, F. J. (1997) "Why Adoptees Search: An Existential Treatment Perspective," *Journal of Counselling & Development*, 75, 195–202.

Kuiper, B. & Cohen-Kettenis, P. (1988) "Sex Reassignment Surgery: A Study of 141 Dutch Transsexuals," *Archives of Sexual Behaviour*, 17, 439–457.

Lamport, A. (1988) "The Genetics of Secrecy in Adoption, Artificial Insemination, and in Vitro Fertilization," *American Journal of Law and Medicine*, 14, 109–124.

Lane, H. & Grodin, M. (1997) "Ethical Issues in Cochlear Implant Surgery: An Exploration into Disease, Disability, and the Best Interests of the Child," *Kennedy Institute of Ethics Journal*, 7, 231–251.

Lansdown, G. (2005) "The Evolving Capacities of the Child," *UNICEF Innocenti Research Centre*, Florence, 1–82.

Lasker, J. N. & Borg, S. (1989) *In Search of Parenthood: Coping with Infertility and High Tech Conception*, Sydney: Pandora.

Lau, J. C. (2012) "Two Arguments for Child Enfranchisement," *Political Studies*, 60(4), 860–876.

Law Reform Committee. (2012) "Inquiry into Access by Donor-Conceived People to Information about Donors," *Parliamentary Paper*, 120, session 2010–2012, xvii.

Lewis, C. (1981) "How Adolescents Approach Decisions: Changes Over Grades Seven to Twelve and Policy Implications," *Child Development*, 52, 538–544.

Lewis, D. (1976) "The Paradoxes of Time Travel," *American Philosophical Quarterly*, 13, 145–152.

Lewis, D. (1987) *Philosophical Papers*, Oxford: Oxford University Press.

Lewis, D. (1996) "Elusive knowledge," *Australasian Journal of Philosophy*, 74, 549.

Lewis, M. A. & Lewis, C. E. (1990) "Consequences of Empowering Children to Care for Themselves," *Pediatrician*, 17, 63–67.

Liao, M. (2006) "The Right of Children to be Loved," *Journal of Political Philosophy*, 4, 420–440.

Lindemalm, G., Korlin, D. & Uddenberg, N. (1987) "Prognostic Factors vs Outcome in Male-to-female Transsexualism. A Follow up Study of 13 Cases," *Acta Psychiatrica Scandinavica*, 75, 268–274.

Lopez-Guerra, C. (2010) "The Enfranchisement Lottery," *Politics, Philosophy and Economics*, 10 (2) 1–23..

Lupien, S. J., McEwen, B. S., Gunnar, M. R. & Heim, C. (2009) "Effects of Stress Throughout the Lifespan on the Brain, Behavior and Cognition," *Nature: Neuroscience Reviews*, 10, 434–445.

Lyons, D. (1970) "The Correlativity of Rights and Duties," *Nous*, 4(1), 45–55.

Lysaught, M, T. (2004) "Respect: Or, How Respect for Persons Became Respect for Autonomy," *Journal of Medicine and Philosophy*, 29, 665–680.

MacCormick, N. (1976) "Children's Rights: A Test Case for Theories of Right," *Archiv fur Recht-und Sozialphilosophie*, LXII, 305–316, reprinted in MacCormick, N. (1982) *Legal Rights and Social Democracy*, Oxford: Clarendon Press.

MacCormick, N. (1997) "Rights in Legislation," in Hacker, P. M. S. & Raz, J. (eds), *Law, Morality and Society: Essays in Honour of H. L. A Hart*, Oxford: Oxford University Press, 189–209.

Macklin, R. (1999) *Against Relativism: Cultural Diversity and the Search for Ethical Universals*, Oxford: Oxford University Press,

Manuel, C., Chevret, M. & Cyzba, J. (1980) "Handling of Secrecy by AID Couples," in David, G. & Price, W. (eds), *Human Artificial Insemination and Semen Preservation*, New York: Plenum Press.

Martin. (1983) "Human Brain Evolution in an Ecological Context," *52nd James Arthur Lecture*, New York: American Museum of Natural History.

Matthews, G. R. (1989) "Children's Conceptions of Illness and Death," in Kopelman, L. M. & Moskop, J. C. (eds), *Children and Health Care: Moral and Social Issues*, Holland: Kluwer Academic Publishers, 133–146.

McDowell, J. (2011) *Perception as a Capacity for Knowledge*, Milwaukee: Marquette University Press.

McEwan, J. E. (2003) "Genetic Information, Ethics, and Information Relating to Biological Parenthood," *Encyclopedia of Ethical, Legal and Policy Issues in Biotechnology*, 356–363.

McGee, G., Brakman, S. V. & Gurmankin, A. D. (2001) "Gamete Donation and Anonymity: Disclosure to Children Conceived with Donor Gametes Should Not be Optional," *Human Reproduction*, 16, 2033–2038.

McWhinnie, A. M. (1995) "A Study of Parenting of IVF and DI Children," *Medical Law*, 14, 501–508.

Merricks, W. (2011) "Paying Gamete and Embryo Donors: What are the Right Principles?," *BioNews*, 591, available at http://www.bionews.org.uk/page_86196. asp

Mill, J. S. (1985) *On Liberty (1859)*, London: Penguin.

Mills, C. (2003) "The Child's Right to an Open Future," *Journal of Social Philosophy*, 34(4), 499–509.

Minow, M. (1986) "Rights for the Next Generation: A Feminist Approach to Children's Rights," *Harvard Women's Law Journal*, 9(1), 1–24.

Money, J. (1975) "Ablatio Penis: Normal Male Infant Sex-reassignment as a Girl," *Archives of Sexual Behavior*, 4, 65–71.

Money, J. & Ehrhardt, A. (1972) *Man and Woman, Boy and Girl*, Baltimore: John Hopkins University Press.

Money, J., Hampson, J. G. & Hampson, J. L. (1955) "An Examination of Some Basic Sexual Concepts: The Evidence of Human Hermaphroditism," *Bulletin of the Johns Hopkins Hospital*, 97, 301–319.

Money, J., Hampson, J. G. & Hampson, J. L. (1955) "Hermaphroditism: Recommendations Concerning Assignment of sex Change of Sex and Psychological Management," *Bulletin of the Johns Hopkins Hospital*, 97, 284–300.

Moorhead, C. (1997) "All the World's Children," *Index on Censorship*, 26, 151–160.

Morriss, P. (2002) *Power: A Philosophical Analysis*, 2nd Edition, Manchester: Manchester University Press.

Morrow, V. (1999) "'We are people too': Children's and Young People's Perspectives on Children's Right and Decision Making in England," *The International Journal of Children's Rights*, 7, 149–170.

Newman, J. L., Roberts, L. R. & Syre, C. R. (1993) "Concepts of Family Among Children and Adolescents: Effect of Cognitive Level, Gender and Family Structure," *Development Psychology*, 29, 952–962.

New South Wales Law Reform Commission. (1986) *Artificial Conception: Human Artificial Insemination*, Report 49, Sydney: New South Wales Law Reform Commission.

Nussbaum, M. (1997) "Capabilities and Human Rights," *Fordham Law Review*, 273–300.

O'Donovan, K. (1989) "What Shall We Tell The Children?," in Lee, R. & Morgan, D. (eds), *Birthrights: Law and Ethics at the Beginnings of Life*, London: Routledge, 96–114.

Official Committee Hansard, Senate, Legal and Constitutional Affairs References Committee, Reference: *Donor conception in Australia*, available at http://www.aph.gov.au/hansard

O'Neill, O. (2003) "Some Limits of Informed Consent," *Journal of Medical Ethics*, 29(1), 4–7.

Parfit, D. (1984) *Reasons and Persons*, Oxford: Oxford University Press.

Parker, S. (1994) "The Best Interests of the Child – Principles and Problems," *International Journal of Law, Policy and the Family*, 8(1) 26–41.

Palmer, T. C. (1992) "How Much Power Should a Child Wield Anyway?," *Boston Globe*, August 16th.

Peacocke, C. (1999) *Being Known*, Oxford: Oxford University Press.

Pennings, G. (2007) "The Double Track Policy for Donor Anonymity," *Human Reproduction*, 12(12), 2839–2844.

Pollock, L. (1983) *Forgotten Children: Parent-child Relations from 1500–1900*, Cambridge: Cambridge University Press.

Prout, A. (2005) *The Future of Childhood: Towards the Interdisciplinary Study of Children*, London: Routledge Palmer.

Ray, N. (2006) *Lesbian, Gay, Bisexual and Transgendered Youth: An Epidemic of Homelessness*, New York: National Gay and Lesbian Task Force Institute and the National Coalition for the Homeless.

Raz, J. (1982) "On the Nature of Rights," *Mind*, XCIII, 192–214.

Raz, J. (1984) "Legal Rights," *Oxford Journal of Legal Studies*, 4(1), 1–21.

Raz, J. (1986) *The Morality of Freedom*, Oxford: Clarendon Press.

Reproductive Technology Accreditation Committee. (2010) *Code of Practice for Assisted Reproductive Technology Units*, Fertility Society of Australia, available at www.fertilitysociety.com.au/home/about/

Rodham, H. (1973) "Children Under the Law," *Harvard Educational Review*, 43(4), 487–517.

Ross, M. W. & Need, J. A. (1989) "Effects of Adequacy of Gender Reassignment Surgery on Psychological Adjustment: A Follow up of Fourteen Male to Female Patients," *Archives of Sexual Behaviour*, 18, 145–153.

Rothman, B. K. (1989) *Recreating Motherhood: Ideology and Technology in a Patriarchal Society*, New York: Norton.

Rousseau, J. (2013) *Emile (1911)*, USA: Dover Publications Inc.

Royal College of Psychiatrists. (1998) "Gender Identity Disorders in Children and Adolescents, Guidance for Management," *Council Report CR63*.

Prior, V. & Glaser, D. (2006) "Understanding Attachment and Attachment Disorders: Theory, Evidence and Practice," in *Child and Adolescent Mental Health*, RCPRTU. London: Jessica Kingsley.

Sants, H. J. (1964) "Genealogical Bewilderment in Children with Substitute Parents," *British Journal of Medical Psychology*, 37, 133–141.

Satz, A. B. (2006) "A Jurisprudence of Dysfunction: On the Role of 'Normal Species Functioning," in Disability Analysis," *Yale Journal of Health Policy, Law and Ethics*, 221–269.

Savulescu, J. & Bostrum, N. (eds) (2009) *Human Enhancement*, Oxford: Oxford University Press.

Scafidi, F. A., Field, T. M., Schanberg, S. M., Bauer, C. R., Tucci, K., Roberts, J., Morrow, C. & Kuhn, C. M. (1990) "Massage Stimulates Growth in Preterm Infants: A Replication," *Infant Behavior and Development*, 13, 167–188.

Schane, S. A. (1986) "The Corporation is a Person: The Language of a Legal Fiction," *Tulane Law Review*, 61, 563.

Schapiro, T. (1999) "What is a Child?," *Ethics*, 109(4), 715–738.

Scheib, J. E., Riordan, M. & Rubiri, S. (2003) "Choosing Identity – Release Sperm Donors: The Parents Perspective 13–18 Years Later," *Human Reproduction*, 18, 1115–1127.

Schellenberg, S. (2007) "Action and Self-Location in Perception," *Mind*, 116, 622–623.

Schneller, E. A. (2005) "The Rights of Donor Inseminated Children to Know Their Genetic Origins in Australia," *Australian Journal of Family Law*, 19, 222–244.

Schull, W. J. (1958) "Empirical Risks in Consanguineous Marriages: Sex Ration Malformation and Viability," *American Journal of Human Genetics*, 10, 294–343.

Scully, J. L., Banks, S. & Shakespeare, T. (2006) "Chance, Choice and Control: Law Debate on Prenatal Social Sex Selection," *Social Science & Medicine*, 63(1), 21–31.

Shapiro, I. & Kymlicka, W. (2006) *Ethnicity and Group Rights*, New York: New York University Press.

Shaw, A. (1973) "Dilemmas of 'informed consent,' in Children," *The New England Journal of Medicine*, 289(17), 885–890.

Shenfield, F. (1994) "Ethics and Society: Filiation in Assisted Reproduction: Potential Conflicts and Legal Implications," *Human Reproduction*, 12, 1348–1354.

Shiffrin, S. V. (1999) "Wrongful Life, Procreative Responsibility, and the Significance of Harm," *Legal Theory*, 5, 117–148.

Singer, P. (1974) "All Animals are Equal," *Philosophical Exchange*, Brockport, New York: The Center for Philosophical Exchange, 103–116.

Singer, P. (1975) *Animal Liberation*, London: Random House.

Smith, A. B. (2002) "Interpreting and Supporting Participation Rights: Contributions from Sociocultural Theory," *The International Journal of Children's Rights*, 10, 73–88.

Smith, Y. L., can Goozen, S. H., Kuiper, A. J. & Cohen-Kettenis, P. T. (2005) "Sex Reassignment: Outcomes and Predictors of Treatment for Adolescent and Adult Transsexuals," *Psychological Medicine*, 35, 89–99.

Sparrow, R. (2005) "Defending Deaf Culture: The Case of Cochlear Implants," *Journal of Political Philosophy*, 13(2), 135–152.

Spitz, R. (1945) "Hospitalism: An Inquiry into the Genesis of Psychiatric Conditions in Early Childhood," *Psychoanalytic Study of the Child*, 1, 53–74.

Spitz, R. & Wolf, K. (1946) "Anaclitic Depression – an Inquiry into the Genesis of Psychiatric Conditions in Early Childhood," *Psychoanalytic Study of the Child*, 2, 313–342.

Steiner, H. (1998) "Working Rights," in Kramer, M., Simmonds, N. & Steiner, H. (eds), *A Debate Over Rights: Philosophical Enquiries*, Oxford: Oxford University Press, 237–302.

Stewart, J. (2014) "Alcohol Research Groups Oppose Northern Territory Proposal to Criminalise Drinking While Pregnant," *ABC News* Online, available at http://www.abc.net.au/news/2014-03-15/research-groups-oppose-nt-prosecuting-pregnant-women-drinking/5322814

Strickland, S., the Hon Justice. (2014) "To Treat or Not to Treat, Legal Responses to Transgender Young People," *Association of Family and Conciliation Courts, 51st Annual Conference*, Toronto: Canada, 1–81.

Strong, C. (2003) "Two Many Twins, Triplets, Quadruplets, and So On: A Call for New Priorities," *The Journal of Law, Medicine and Ethics*, 31(2), 272–282.

Svirsky, M., Teoh, S. & Neuburger, H. (2004) "Development of Language and Speech Perception in Congenitally, Profoundly Deaf Children as a Function of Age at Cochlear Implantation," *Audiology & Neurotology*, 9, 224–233.

Szoke, H. (2003) "Australia – A Federated Structure of Statutory Regulation of ART," in Gunning, J. & Szoke, H. (eds), *The Regulation of Assisted Reproductive Technology*, Aldershot: Ashgate Publishing Limited, 75–94.

Tang, K. (2003) "Implementing the United Nations Convention on the Rights of the Child: The Canadian Experience," *International Social Work*, 46(3), 277–288.

Taylor, C. (1985) "Atomism," in his *Philosophy and the Human Sciences: Philosophical Paper 2*, Cambridge: Cambridge University Press, 187–210.

Teitelbaum, L. E. (1998) "Children's Rights and the Problem of Equal Respect," *Hofstra Law Review*, 27, 799.

Tobin, J. & Alston, P. (2005) "Laying the Foundations for Children's Rights," *Innocenti Insight Series* 05/19, available at http://www.unicef-irc.org/publications/pdf/ii_layingthefoundations.pdf.

Tomblin, J. B., Spencer, L., Flock, S., Tyler, R. & Gantz, B. (1999) "A Comparison of Language Achievement in Children With Cochlear Implants and Children Using Hearing Aids," *Journal of Speech, Language, and Hearing Research*, 42, 497–511.

Triseliotis, J. (1988) "Identity and Genealogy," in Bruce, N., Mitchell, A. & Priestly, K. (eds), *Truth and the Child: A Contribution to the Debate on the Warnock Report*, Family Care: Edinburgh.

Turkmendag, I., Dingwall, R. & Murphy, T. (2008) "The Removal of Donor Anonymity in the UK: The Silencing of Claims by Would-be-Parents," *International Journal of Law, Policy and the Family*, 22(3) 283–310.

Turner, A. J. & Coyle, A. (2002) "What Does it Mean to be a Donor Offspring? The Identity Experience of Adults Conceived by Donor Insemination and the Implications for Counseling and Therapy," *Human Reproduction*, 15, 2041–2051.

Turner, S. M. & Matthews, G. B. (eds) (1998) *The Philosopher's Child: Critical Essays in the Western Tradition*, Rochester: University of Rochester Press.

UN Committee on the Rights of the Children, *General comment No. 14 (2013) on the right of the child to have his or her best interest taken as a primary consideration (art. 3, para 1)*, adopted 62nd session, January 14–February 1, 2013.

Vanfraussen, K., Ponjaert-Kristoffersen, I. & Brewaeys, A. (2000) "An Attempt to Reconstruct Children's Donor Concept: A Comparison Between Children's and Lesbian Parents' Attitudes Towards Donor Anonymity," *Human Reproduction*, 16, 2019–2025.

Veerman, P. E. (1992). *The Rights of the Child and the Changing Image of Childhood*, Martinius Nijhoff: Dordrecht.

de Vries, A., Noens, I. & Cohen-Kettenis, P. T. (2010) "Autism Spectrum Disorders in Gender Dysphoric Children and Adolescents," *Journal of Autism Development Disorder*, 40, 930–936.

Wald, M. (1979) "Children's Rights: A Framework for Analysis," *U. C. D. Law Review* 12, 255–282.

Waldron, J. (1988) "When Justice Replaces Affection: The Need for Rights," *Harvard Journal of Law and Public Policy*, 11, 625–648.

Wallbank, R. (2007) "*Re: Kevin* in Perspective," *Deakin Law Review*, 22, 9(2), 461–502.

Wallien, M. S., Swaab, H. & Cohen-Kettenis, P. T. (2007) "Psychiatric Comorbidity Among Children with Gender Identity Disorder," *Journal of the American Academy of Child Adolescent Psychiatry*, 46, 1307–1314.

Walter, C. (2013) *Last Ape Standing: The Seven-Million-Year Story of How and Why We Survived*, Bloomsbury: Sydney.

Weithorn, L. A. & Campbell, S. B. (1982) "The Competency of Children and Adolescents to make Informed Treatment Decisions," *Child Development*, 53, 1589–1598.

Wenar, L. (2005) "The Nature of Rights," *Philosophy and Public Affairs*, 33(3), 223–252.

Wellman, C. (1985) *A Theory of Rights*, New Jersey: Rowman & Allanheld.

Wellman, C. (2002) "The Proliferation of Rights: Moral Progress or Empty Rhetoric?," in Gearon, L. (ed.), *Human Rights and Religion: A Reader*, Brighton: Sussex Academic Press, 368–389.

Whitehurst, G. & Lonigan, C. (1998) "Child Development and Emergent Literacy," *Child Development*, 69(3), 848–872.

Whittle, S., Turner, L., & Al-Alami, M. (2007) "Engendered Penalties: Transgender and Transsexual People's Experiences of Inequality and Discrimination," *The Equalities Review*, available at http:////www.pfc.org.uk/pdf/EngenderedPenalties.pdf

Wilfred, J. & Finegold, M. D. (1964) *Artificial Insemination*, Springfield IL: Charles C Thomas Publisher.

Wren, B. (2000) "Early Physical Intervention for Young People with a Typical Gender Identity Development," *Clinical Child Psychology and Psychiatry*, 5, 220–231.

Wong, A. H. C., Gottesman, I. & Petronis, A. (2005) "Phenotypic Differences in Genetically Identical Organisms: The Epigenetic Perspective," *Human Molecular Genetics*, 14(1), 11–18.

Yarrow, L. (1961) "Maternal Deprivation: Toward an Empirical and Conceptual Re-evaluation," *Psychological Bulletin*, 6, 459–490.

Yoos, H. L. (1994) "Children's Illness Concepts: Old and New Paradigms," *Paediatric Nursing*, 20, 134–145.

Zucker, K. J. (2005) "Gender Identity Disorders in Children and Adolescents," *Annual Review of Clinical Psychology*, 1, 467–492.

Index

CPSIA information can be obtained
at www.ICGtesting.com
Printed in the USA
LVOW04*2117231215

467649LV00011B/96/P